Law and Market Economy
Reinterpreting the Values of Law a

In this book, Malloy presents a fundamen... ...aditional law and economics based on an ethic of so... ...ponsibility and its relationship to creativity, entrepreneurism, and wealth formation. He examines the meaning and structure of the market exchange process, and demonstrates that wealth-promoting exchanges are sustainable only in so far as they are embedded within dynamic and multivalued communities. He uses numerous examples in reinterpreting classic problems related to rational choice, the Coase Theorem, public choice, efficient breach, social contract theory, and wealth maximization, among others.

Advance praise for *Law and Market Economy*

"Malloy develops a semiotic interpretation of work in law and economics that links exchange and creativity to ethical values. The result is a powerful new perspective on law and markets that brings to mind work from Hayek to Hurst. This book is an exceptionally important contribution to contemporary scholarship on the nature of law."

John Brigham, Professor of Political Science, University of Massachusetts
Board of Trustees, The Law & Society Association

"In bringing the language and concerns of ethics, moral theory, and social responsibility back into the discipline of market theory and law, this book is timely and significant, and should be read by anyone who cares about more just and inclusive alternatives to present forms of social organization."

Sharon Hom, Professor of Law, City University of New York

"Providing the reader with a rich menu of humanistic values, economic analysis, and interpretation theory, this work will enliven debate and open new avenues of inquiry in an academic field on the verge of becoming arid by its current confining focus."

Denis Brion, Professor of Law, Washington and Lee University

Law and Market Economy

Reinterpreting the Values of Law and Economics

Robin Paul Malloy

Professor of Law and Economics
Syracuse University, New York

PUBLISHED BY THE PRESS SYNDICATE OF THE UNIVERSITY OF CAMBRIDGE
The Pitt Building, Trumpington Street, Cambridge, United Kingdom

CAMBRIDGE UNIVERSITY PRESS
The Edinburgh Building, Cambridge CB2 2RU, UK   www.cup.cam.ac.uk
40 West 20th Street, New York, NY 10011–4211, USA   www.cup.org
10 Stamford Road, Oakleigh, Melbourne 3166, Australia
Ruiz de Alarcón 13, 28014 Madrid, Spain

First published 2000

Printed in the United Kingdom at the University Press, Cambridge

Typeface Plantin 10/12pt   *System* 3B2   [CE]

A catalogue record for this book is available from the British Library

ISBN 0 521 78214 7 hardback
ISBN 0 521 78731 9 paperback

For Margaret
"As Time Goes By"

Contents

Preface   *page* ix

1 Introduction   1

2 A general framework   23

3 Law and market economy: further clarification   57

4 Wealth as a process of discovery: wealth, discovery, and
   imaginative choice   78

5 Social organization and the discovery process   106

6 Implications of law and market economy   136

7 Conclusion   166

Index   176

Preface

In writing this book I see my primary audience as made up of people interested in legal theory, law and society, jurisprudence, applied semiotics, law and interpretation, and in market theory as more generally understood. I suspect that traditional practitioners of law and economics will find much here that is challenging, unfamiliar, and disquieting. I hope, however, that some of them will see this work as an exciting, new, and complementary addition to our search for a better understanding of the relationship between law and market theory.

In undertaking this project, I have benefited greatly from the research support of the Oxford Centre for the Environment, Ethics, and Society ("OCEES") at Mansfield College, Oxford University, where I served as a 1997 Sun Life Visiting Research Fellow, as well as from the Syracuse University College of Law. I also benefited from the feedback, discussion, and support of participants in a number of workshops, seminars, and conferences including: the 1997 Trinity Term Seminar Series of OCEES; the Tenth Round Table on Law and Semiotics sponsored by the University of Massachusetts at Amherst and the Pennsylvania State University; the Eighth Annual Canadian Law and Economics Association meeting (particularly participants in the working papers session on "Frontiers in Law and Economics"); the faculty workshop series at the University of Georgia, College of Law; the Twelfth Round Table on Law and Semiotics held at the Pennsylvania State University; the 1998 meeting of Law and Society (particularly participants in the working papers session on "Interpretation Theory and the Market"); the Tenth Annual Meeting of the Canadian Law and Economics Association; and the 1998 Annual Meeting of the Semiotic Society of America.

I extend special thanks to Peter Bell, Alan Childress, Maurie Cohen, Antonia Layard, and Bhaskar Vira for taking time to discuss some of my ideas for the book, and to Denis Brion, Maggie Chon, Kenneth Dau-Schmidt, Jerry Evensky, and Roberta Kevelson, for reviewing and commenting on various drafts. I thank Neil Summerton and Anne Maclachlan for their help and assistance while I was at Oxford, and

Stacy Crynock for assistance with footnote form. I acknowledge my indebtedness to Robert Moffat and Winston Nagan for introducing me to legal theory, and to Margaret for her support during the duration of my research and writing for this book. I also thank my editor at Cambridge University Press, Finola O'Sullivan, for her patience and guidance during the process of publication, and my copy editor, Katy Cooper, for her helpful assistance in reviewing the final manuscript.

Finally, I should say that I personally benefited from twelve years of ongoing support from Roberta "Bobbie" Kevelson who first turned my attention and then my mind to a consideration of the work of Charles Sanders Peirce. Over those years she constantly pushed me to think about law and about economics in a new and intellectually exciting way. She had a profound influence on the development of my work over those years. In November of 1998 Bobbie departed from this world. Her passing is a great loss to me for if I had never met Bobbie this book would never have been written and I would not be the person that I am today. Thank you, Bobbie.

1   Introduction

> *An open society, in which an open legal system usually predominates, rests not on the assumption that the world is fully created once and for all, but rather on the belief in the possibility of real change in the world, that is, on the conviction that the universe becomes and not that it is, that something really new may be created, and that this real novelty is not manifest in the actual order of things but is present in the evolving concepts of signs which stand for a reinterpretation of values and meanings of relationships between things.*
>
> Roberta Kevelson, *The Law as a System of Signs*[1]

The relationship between law and market theory is one that invokes a variety of opinions. To the traditional law and economics scholar the relationship is positive, efficient, and wealth maximizing. It is a relationship that inherently promotes autonomy, prosperity, and social justice. To others, the relationship may seem exploitative, chaotic, and oppressive. It is a relationship that fosters self-interested behavior and institutions of greed and profit. To me, however, the matter seems more complicated. The relationship between law and market theory is dynamic. It is at one and the same time determinate and yet indeterminate; self-interested and yet community situated. It is not merely an object of investigation or simply a set of institutions. It is a relationship grounded in the human practice of exchange and it therefore involves a continuous process of meaning and value formation.

In this book I explore these meanings and values in a way that goes beyond the boundaries of traditional law and economics. I examine issues related to racial discrimination, surrogate motherhood, prostitution, mortgage markets, environmental protection, international trade, and new technologies, among others. In each of these situations I look closely at the way in which exchange takes place as a dynamic process. I explore the networks and patterns of exchange by placing the individual back into a community context linked to experience, and I suggest that

---

[1] Roberta Kevelson, *The Law as a System of Signs* 35 (1988) (emphasis in original).

wealth-promoting exchanges are sustainable only in so far as they are embedded within dynamic and multivalued communities. In doing this I introduce the idea of "law and market economy" as a new way of understanding the relationship between law and market theory.

The object of this new approach is different than that of traditional law and economics. Law and market economy uses a form of semiotic interpretation theory to uncover the dynamic process of creativity and sustainable wealth formation, whereas traditional law and economics concerns itself with static analysis and the calculation of contextualized notions of efficiency. The difference between these approaches is important because it influences the nature of our existence as human beings. As such, the difference presents both a challenge and an opportunity to traditional law and economics. It challenges some basic assumptions of an economic analysis of law while creating an opportunity for an expanded jurisprudence of social exchange.

At the outset, since I am crossing three interdisciplinary boundaries (law, economics, and semiotics), it may be helpful for me to frame the three most significant conceptual challenges raised in this work. First, semiotic interpretation theory allows me to question the conventional thinking that positions the primary tension in law and market theory as one between efficiency, and the related concepts of social responsibility, justice, and fairness.[2] In contrast to this view, I suggest that the real conflict is one between *efficiency and creativity*. This paradigm shift breaks rank with the conventional debates in law and economics and in legal theory, but the application of semiotic interpretation theory to the market exchange process reveals that such a shift is fundamental to an understanding of wealth formation.

My conclusion on this point is based on an appreciation of the distinction between efficiency and creativity. Efficiency, the traditional and predominant concern of the law and economics movement,[3] is grounded, as an interpretive matter, in a contextual framework of habit,

[2] For an example of standard considerations, *see, e.g.*, Cass R. Sunstein, *Free Markets and Social Justice* (1999); Herbert Hovenkamp, "Positivism in Law and Economics," 78 Cal. L. Rev. 815, 815–852 (1990) (in particular at 835–851); Richard A. Posner, *Economic Analysis of Law* 16–18, 23–28 (4th ed., 1992); Robin Paul Malloy, "Invisible Hand or Sleight of Hand? Adam Smith, Richard Posner and the Philosophy of Law and Economics," 36 U. Kan. L. Rev. 210, 210–274; Robin Paul Malloy and Richard A. Posner, "Debate: Is Law and Economics Moral?" 24 Val. U. L. Rev. 147, 147–184 (1990); Robin Paul Malloy, "Equating Human Rights and Property Rights – The Need for Moral Judgment in an Economic Analysis of Law and Social Policy," 47 Ohio St. L. J. 163, 163–177 (1986). For some alternative perspectives *see Law and Economics: New and Critical Perspectives* (Robin Paul Malloy and Christopher K. Braun, eds., 1995).

[3] *See, e.g.*, Posner, *Economic Analysis*, at 1–29; David Barnes and Lynn Stout, *Law and Economics* (1992); Robert Cooter and Thomas Ulen, *Law and Economics* (2nd ed., 1997); Mark Seidenfeld, *Microeconomic Predicates to Law and Economics* (1996).

convention, and continuity. It involves a determinate process of calculation identifiable within a static and closed environment.[4] It is reactive
and grounded in the status quo because it is concerned with making the
most of our current understanding of market opportunities. In simple
terms, it focuses on how we cut the pie rather than how we increase the
size of the pie or make an entirely new pie, or perhaps even bake a cake.
Creativity on the other hand, is grounded in an environment of potentiality, of discontinuity, and indeterminacy.[5] From a semiotic perspective,
it involves a dynamic process of discovery, which is enhanced by an
ethical environment of social responsibility. It is by definition proactive
and continually evolving.

The distinction between efficiency and creativity, as outlined above,
leads me to my second fundamental challenge to traditional law and
economics. Using semiotic method, I argue that a primary engine of
wealth formation and social prosperity is creativity and, thus, efficiency
analysis should not be given primacy in the study of law and market
theory. Instead of focusing so much attention on efficiency, we should
examine more carefully the process of creativity as related to market
exchange and the networks and patterns of interaction in society.
Efficiency analysis has a role to play in market theory but it is incapable
of adequately addressing creativity because creativity is indeterminate.
To understand creativity as a habit-breaking and convention-challenging
concept, one must look to the types of legal, ethical and value laden
environments most likely to promote creativity through extended and
unconventional patterns of thought and interaction. One must identify
the types of communities which, by ethics and social values, tend to
foster diversity, experimentation, and unconventional networks and
patterns of exchange. In other words, creativity must be examined
indirectly by reference to the context in which convention-breaking
ideas and relationships are encouraged and facilitated. Consequently,
social values and ethical norms are central to an understanding of
market theory because they relate to the potential for creativity and
wealth formation. This position runs counter to the conventional
"wisdom" of traditional law and economics.

My third fundamental challenge to traditional law and economics
involves an understanding of the process of market choice. I suggest that
market choice is not the rational, objective, and scientific product of
cost and benefit analysis, but rather the consequence of an *interpretation*

---

[4] *See* Israel M. Kirzner, *The Meaning of Market Process* 1–54 (1992).
[5] Kirzner, *Meaning*; Roberta Kevelson, *Peirce's Esthetics of Freedom: Possibility, Complexity, and Emergent Value* 1–47 (1993); John K. Sheriff, *Peirce's Guess at the Riddle: Grounds for Human Significance* xiii–xxi, 9–16, 31–49 (1994).

of such incentives and disincentives. This means that market choice, in a system of iterative exchange, is grounded in the process of interpretation and is, therefore, informed by reference to our experiences as participants in dynamic networks and patterns of social intercourse. This distinction is important because the process of interpretation is community based, and because it indicates that even though exchange takes place as a continuous part of a dynamic system, our understanding of the exchange process is shaped by the interpretive "lens" or "screen" through which we view it. Furthermore, this lens or screen, as an indexical reference in semiotics, is grounded in a system of values informed by experience rather than by purely objective and rational choice. In this sense it is, in some respects, subjective and arational, and undercuts the centrality of two key assumptions in traditional law and economics – objectivity and rationality.

Similarly, the interpretation of cost and benefit relationships undercuts the commitment of traditional law and economics to the primacy of methodological individualism because the process of interpretation involves a reference to the community(ies) in which people are positioned. This means that the process of interpretation is always one that displays a certain degree of independence, of inexactness or variance, as no two individuals have exactly the same experiences or point of reference. It is not, however, entirely indeterminate because communities are bound together by conventions that "mark" the limits of authoritative interpretive variance. Consequently, a principal concern of law and market economy is not simply price coordination, nor the question of how to distribute goods and resources efficiently. Rather, it is the mediation of conflicting meanings and values in the exchange process itself. In particular, there is a concern for facilitating an authoritative frame of reference that is capable of addressing both determinate (habit/convention-based) and indeterminate (creativity-based) modes of interpretive logic while promoting: extensive exchange networks; patterns of sustainable wealth formation; and the mediation of value differences between competing interpretive communities. In this regard, law and market economy explores a "world' beyond the boundary lines of traditional law and economics.

In going beyond the boundaries of traditional law and economics I am mapping out a new way of thinking about the relationship between law and market theory. I am arguing that there is a need to expand the nature of market inquiry and I assert that the authoritative positioning of an interpretive screen or indexical reference is significant because it has implications for the patterns and networks of exchange and for the process of wealth formation. I call my method of understanding law and market theory, "law and market economy." My approach is different, although not unfamiliar, from that of traditional law and economics and it reflects a concern for an important aspect of market theory that is not properly addressed in the current law and economics literature. The focus of traditional law and economics, as I see it, is on the use of economic analysis, as a science of choice, to bring more certainty, objectivity, and impartiality to law. It positions most disagreements over law and social policy as disagreements of fact in which a positive and scientific method of economic analysis can be used to resolve differences.

Law and market economy, in comparison, seeks to understand and to influence, the meanings and consequences of legal economic relationships within a dynamic and complex system of exchange. It is an interpretive approach that positions the market as a place of meaning and value formation and which identifies a wealth-based ethic of social responsibility. It is an approach that investigates different questions than law and economics. It does not seek so much to determine the outcome of transactions as to understand the *meaning* of exchange. It studies problems in a market context and reasons about the relational meaning, value and consequences of particular actions, inactions, or ideas. The law and market economy approach questions the ability of economics to bring certainty, objectivity, or impartiality to law and public policy. More particularly, it focuses attention on disputes in law and social policy that are fundamentally grounded in disagreement as to underlying values rather than to perceptible objects or facts. It seeks, therefore, to focus attention on the *exchange process* – on the networks and patterns of social interaction – rather than on cost and benefit analysis, and it integrates concerns for efficiency while addressing the indeterminate nature of change. In so doing it suggests that a variety of ethical and multidimensional factors are logically consistent with a concern for wealth maximization and social prosperity.

My conception of law and market economy emerges from the application of interpretation theory to the process of exchange. The method of interpretation that I use is grounded in semiotic theory, that is a branch of philosophy concerned with grammar, logic, and rhetoric.[6] My

---

[6] My approach to interpretation theory is grounded in the semiotic theory of Charles Sanders Peirce. *See The Essential Peirce*, vol. 1 (Nathan Houser and Christian Kloesel, eds., 1992); *The Essential Peirce*, vol. 2 (edited by the Peirce Edition Project, 1998). *See generally*, Roberta Kevelson, *Peirce, Science, Signs* (1996); Kevelson, *Peirce and Freedom*, at 17; Roberta Kevelson, *Charles S. Peirce's Method of Methods* (1987); Kevelson, *Law*; Winfried Noth, *Handbook of Semiotics* 39–47 (1995); Sheriff, *Peirce*; James Jacob Liszka, *A General Introduction to the Semeiotic of Charles Sanders Peirce* (1996); Vincent M. Colapietro, *Peirce's Approach to the Self: A Semiotic Perspective on Human Subjectivity*

use of semiotic theory, as will be explained and applied in this book, involves the investigation of the meaning and value relationships of social/market exchange. As such, my approach might be thought of as "a semiotic of law and market theory," or as "interpretive law and economics," but whatever it is called, the basic point of my inquiry relates to the way in which our networks and patterns of exchange, in fact, create value and meaning. Consequently, the concerns of law and market economy are not merely the economic analysis of legal rules, but rather the market context in which social exchange takes place; takes place as a *process* made coherent and understandable by reference to law.

Law and market economy involves more than an inquiry into efficiency as the source of wealth maximization because it focuses on the social, political, and cultural context in which exchange takes place, and on the way in which our characterization and understanding of the exchange process itself affects wealth creation and social prosperity. Therefore, law and market economy involves the examination and exploration of pressing social problems within an integrative market context – within a reciprocal and multidimensional exchange process, rather than by reference to a particular or specific economic criterion such as efficiency.

Some of my colleagues in law and economics have asked, "But why call this approach 'law and market economy'? What is the difference – don't we all do law and market economy?" To them I suggest that we do *not* all do law and market economy. The concerns of law and market economy, as expressed above, are different in nature and scope from those of traditional law and economics. The law and economics movement, a movement I have been a part of for all of my seventeen years as an academic, is not focused on the meaning and substantive implications of market economy as a system of social exchange. It is not focused on the process of social exchange as a system of continuous substitution and permutation. It is not focused on the cultural, historical, and contextualized nature of exchange nor on the meanings and values generated by such interaction. The law and economics movement is centered around concerns for economic calculation and particularized conceptions of efficiency.[7]

(1989); Karl-Otto Apel, *Charles S. Peirce: From Pragmatism to Pragmaticism* (1995); *Philosophical Writings of Peirce* (Justus Buchler, ed., 1955); Christopher Hookway, *Peirce* (1992); *Reasoning and the Logic of Things: Charles Sanders Peirce* (Kenneth Laine Ketner ed., 1992); Floyd Merrell, *Peirce, Signs, and Meaning* (1997); for additional references *see* below, Chap. 2, n. 3.

[7] *See* Robin Paul Malloy, *Law and Economics: A Comparative Approach to Theory and Practice* 1–93 (1990); Posner, *Economic Analysis*; Cooter and Ulen, *Law and Economics*; Barnes and Stout, *Law and Economics*; Seidenfeld, *Law and Economics* (in particular at 49–60); "Symposium on Efficiency as a Legal Concern," 8 Hofstra L. Rev. 485 (1980); Malloy and Posner, "Debate."

The law and economics movement has always identified itself, its associations, its journals, and law school courses as "law and economics," not as law and market economy. This is not mere coincidence, it is "significant" (meaning that it has consequence in the way we perceive the field) because law and economics has sought to avoid an express concern for the normative and philosophical issues and implications of social organization and exchange within a market context. It has intentionally narrowed the definition and scope of inquiry so as to preclude broader considerations of market economy and to distinguish itself from the rich, but less "scientific," tradition of political economy.[8] This positioning of the law and economics movement, as a positive inquiry into matters of efficiency in law, has mirrored the positioning of economics with respect to its relationship to the other social sciences.[9]

Law and economics, in its reference to economics, has likewise sought recognition for being a more concrete, more scientific, approach to law. Its positive structure of inquiry and argument is meant to radiate a sense of objectivity, a feeling of existential separation between a rule of law and the mere normative squabbles of philosophers, political scientists, sociologists, and other "less insightful" participants in social discourse. As a result of this positioning, the law and economics movement has traditionally frowned upon, outright ignored, or declared beyond its boundaries, normative approaches to the questions of fairness, justice, diversity, and inclusion.[10] It has similarly been unreceptive to problems of interpretation, historical inequality, and cultural and situational difference. This positioning is unfortunate because market theory should contribute to such discussions. As a result of its positioning, the discourse of efficiency, provided by traditional law and economics, is simply unpersuasive to many people when it comes to a wide range of

---

[8] *See, e.g.*, *Beyond Economic Man: Feminist Theory and Economics* (Marianne A. Ferber and Julie A. Nelson, eds., 1993) (discussing the narrowness of the field); Donald N. McCloskey, *The Rhetoric of Economics* (1985); Donald N. McCloskey, *If You're so Smart: The Narrative of Economic Expertise* (1990) (McCloskey challenges the "science" in economics).

[9] On positive economics *see* Milton Friedman, *Essays in Positive Economics* (1953); Hovenkamp, "Positivism." *See also*, McCloskey, *Rhetoric*; McCloskey, *If You're So Smart*; Donald N. McCloskey, *Knowledge and Persuasion in Economics* (1994); Thorstein Veblen, *The Place of Science in Modern Civilization and Other Essays* 1–179 (1961); Friedrich A. Hayek, *The Counter-Revolution of Science: Studies on the Abuse of Reason* (1979, 1st ed. 1952).

[10] *See* Malloy and Posner, "Debate"; Malloy, *Law and Economics*; Robin Paul Malloy, "A New Law and Economics" in Malloy and Braun (eds.), *Law and Economics*; Richard B. McKenzie and Gordon Tullock, *The New World of Economics: Explorations into the Human Experience* 6 (1975); David W. Barnes, "Economics 2001: A Carpenter's Odyssey," 42 Syracuse L. Rev. 197, 197–208 (1991). *See contra* Joseph A. Schumpeter, *Capitalism, Socialism and Democracy* 190–191 (1950); Hovenkamp, "Positivism."

particular social policy matters, including issues concerning such things as family values, personal relationships, and social justice. Not surprisingly, this lack of persuasiveness seems most acute when economic analysis is applied to those areas of life where underlying value differences, between interpretive communities, are likely to be at their greatest.

Even law and economic authorities of the stature of Judge Richard Posner and Judge Guido Calabresi recognize that, in practice, we cannot simply apply law and economic analysis as a sufficient theory of law or adjudication – we need something more.[11] The question this raises is do we need something outside of law and market theory or do we need to move forward by embracing a broader and more inclusive vision of the relationship between law and market economy. This in turn raises yet another question: if we seek to extend the boundaries of law and market theory, can we do so while retaining the core focus of our discipline? I think that we can, provided we believe that a central tenet of law and market inquiry is the promotion of a theory of sustainable wealth formation leading to a form of social organization capable of enjoying both freedom and prosperity.

In speculating as to a theory of law and market economy, therefore, I seek to investigate the possibility of advancing a new jurisprudence of exchange while retaining a commitment to this central tenet. I use semiotic interpretation theory to extend and reconceptualize the relationship between law and market theory – not to reject it. My inquiry, therefore, synthesizes market theory with an expanded, relational, and multidisciplinary approach to legal reasoning in a market context of social exchange. This synthesis enables us better to understand the role of law and of market theory in the promotion of creativity and sustainable wealth formation.

Several shortcomings in traditional law and economics have led me to contemplate the need for a broader approach to law and market theory. I believe, for example, that one such shortcoming of traditional law and economics has been that it borrows too heavily from positive economics without acknowledging that the tools and methods of economics are directed at a different "end" than that of law. A central focus of the economist, it must be remembered, is on the construction of a model of human behavior capable of providing predictive information with

[11] *See* Richard A. Posner, *The Problems of Jurisprudence* 454–469 (1990); Posner, *Economic Analysis*, at 27. Also, Judge Calabresi made this point clear in his comments at the Eighth Annual Canadian Law and Economics Association (CLEA) conference held on September 27, 1996 at the University of Toronto – in his John M. Olin Lecture in Law and Economics entitled "What Economic Analysis of Law Must Address Next: Some Thoughts on Theory."

respect to a limited field of activities within clearly defined constraints. The assumptions of the economist embody certain subjective choices concerning what gets measured and valued and what is ignored or excluded.[12] This naturally results in conclusions that reflect these assumptions and constraints. Nevertheless, the economics profession can assert a particular level of accomplishment in predicting at least some outcomes with respect to choices and trade-offs confronting society. As an example, consider what economists can tell us about the market for gasoline. If there is a shortage of gasoline, prices will rise and people will tend to reduce consumption. Conversely, if the supply of gasoline increases, prices will go down and people will increase consumption. This simple exchange relationship is useful to know and it provides insightful implications for a variety of public policy concerns. At the same time, it tells us little about the extent or fairness of the distribution of gasoline in either situation, and it provides little, if any, insight respecting the interpretive values at work in competing exchange communities.

The role of the lawyer is different than that of the economist. The lawyer is not simply interested in constructing a predictive model. The legal profession is challenged to go beyond prediction because the discourse of law is one of persuasion and of mediation between conflicting interpretive viewpoints and value frameworks. Law, for instance, must deal with the claims of distributive inequality and of the unfairness of a price-based allocation system when disgruntled consumers, in our example of the market for gasoline, raise them. Law, must, in other words, mediate between competing claims when market processes fail to produce results acceptable to all of the parties involved. Law, therefore, directs its attention to influencing the normative *ground* upon which social organization rests.[13] This means that law must influence beliefs about underlying relationships in the meaning and value-formation process of social interaction and exchange. Consequently, the real mission of the lawyer is different than that of the economist.

An economist may find it sufficient to conclude that given such-and-such constraints in the US economy African-American men will

---

[12] Malloy, *Law and Economics*, 2–13; Malloy, "New Law and Economics," at 1–30; *see* Robin Paul Malloy, "Toward a New Discourse of Law and Economics," 42 Syracuse L. Rev. 27 (1991); Robin Paul Malloy, "Letters From the Longhouse: Law, Economics and Native American Values," Wisc. L. Rev. 1569 (1992); Malloy and Posner, "Debate."

[13] The *ground* serves as the *basis* upon which a sign can represent its object in some regard or respect. *See* Liszka, *Introduction to Peirce*; Sheriff, *Peirce*, at 49. To Peirce the ground was a *belief* about underlying relationships that allows us to make conclusions or references from signs. Hookway, *Peirce*, at 124. There are three types of grounds: the *icon*, the *index*, and the *symbol*. *Id.*, at 124–144.

experience lower levels of employment and lower wages than other Americans. Similarly, the economist does her job when she constructs a model allowing us accurately to predict lower levels of home ownership, higher rates of infant mortality, and higher levels of police brutality for some groups in our society relative to others. The economist, in other words, uses market mechanisms to mediate our understanding of social "facts" within a conventionalized and authoritative frame of interpretive reference – a frame of reference grounded in the values and assumptions of the "science" of positive economics. Such predictions, consistent with her model, therefore, are generally all that is expected from the economist, but the lawyer and the legal system must deal, openly and expressly, with the normative questions of meanings and values, including those of fairness and justice, associated with the construction of such models and their predictions.

In order to persuade and to mediate between competing claims, the law must influence opinions, beliefs, and values – it must shape and influence behavior. Law must be concerned with the *meanings* of economic assumptions and predictions, and with the exercise of market choice which always involves a process of interpretation – of selecting between the meanings and values of "A" or "B," for example, and their various relationships. This requires the identification of an interpretive frame of reference capable of both signaling and influencing the networks and patterns of social exchange. The lawyer cannot simply approach the relationship between law and market theory by purporting to use a method of inquiry that is objective and amoral. This may discharge the social obligation of the economist who seeks only to provide theoretical answers for a theoretically constructed world grounded in one interpretive set of values, but it is an insufficient response from the lawyer who must mediate real-world conflicts between people with different experiences, different values, and alternative frames of reference. The lawyer must act pragmatically to solve problems as they arise and to mediate the tension between real people situated in conflicting interpretive communities. This means that the lawyer must strive for an understanding of the meaning and value-formation process of social/market exchange – including its many subjective and value-laden elements.

A second shortcoming of traditional law and economics has been its general acceptance of an artificial dichotomy between wealth maximization and an ethic of fairness and social responsibility. It has viewed concerns for efficiency, which it associates with rational choice based on human reason standing above and apart from society and nature, as the key to wealth maximization and the goal of social organization. It has

positioned this view as being in opposition to concerns for social ethics
and values that it associates with more normative considerations that are
difficult or impossible to quantify. This difficulty seemingly renders
normative considerations uninformative to the traditional legal economist concerned with questions of efficiency and wealth maximization.
Judge Richard Posner, for instance, has expressed this view and has
indicated that he finds little value in moral discourse.[14] As a result, it has
become a central premise of traditional law and economics that an ethic
of social responsibility is either inconsistent with a concern for efficiency,
and thus contrary to a goal of wealth maximization, or that efficiency
and wealth maximization are in themselves a suitable ethic for social
organization. This conception is incorrect and I believe that it arises
from the inability of traditional law and economics to identify a wealth-
based justification, or ground, for an ethic of fairness and social
responsibility independent of a forced and uneasy argument that efficiency is, in itself, such an ethic. This misconception is rooted in the use
of static equilibrium-based models of economic analysis, which are
incapable of dealing with the process of creative discovery, and it can be
overcome by thinking in terms of markets as dynamic and creative
exchange processes.

Semiotic theory can help us overcome this theoretical problem by
providing an interpretive frame of reference capable of revealing that the
real tension or conflict between law and market theory is one of
efficiency and creativity, rather than one of efficiency and fairness or an
ethic of social responsibility. Semiotic theory indicates that an ethic of
social responsibility really comes into play, not as the logical counterpart
to efficiency, but as a normative means of promoting a receptive
environment for the wealth-producing process of creative discovery.
Traditional law and economics, using static equilibrium analysis, fails to
account for the process of creative discovery because it focuses on
convention and habit and fails to incorporate indeterminacy. This is
problematic since indeterminacy is essential to understanding market
theory and the role of creativity in promoting sustainable wealth formation. Semiotic theory accounts for both convention/habit and indeterminacy and, thus, allows us to identify these different modes of logic
within market theory and between competing interpretive communities.
Therefore, we can enrich our approach to law and market theory by
seeking to understand the logical relationship between creativity and
efficiency, and by promoting a wealth-facilitating ethic of social responsibility.

[14] *See* Malloy and Posner, "Debate."

A third shortcoming of traditional law and economics has been its failure to appreciate the significance of interpretation theory in understanding the market exchange process. The importance of interpretation theory became clear to me as a result of spending three consecutive summers in China working with Chinese legal experts on issues of law and market economy.[15] In that setting I learned to think of markets and of market relationships from an entirely new frame of reference. I also learned to appreciate the interpretive context of market choice.

The importance of context on the choice process revealed itself most clearly when I conducted a simple exercise concerning the concept of the prisoners' dilemma – a concept well known to those of us engaged in the study of law and market theory. In introducing this concept to Chinese legal scholars, lawyers, and officials I selected six teams composed of two people each as "players." Using the classic scenario, I informed all players that they had just committed a serious criminal offense, such as a robbery. I told them they and their partner had both been arrested and that the police would deal with each of them individually. Then I separated the teams and isolated each player from the other member of his or her team.

A "pay-off" matrix was presented to each player in which they were given incentives to work with the police in an attempt to set up an easy conviction against the other player on the same team. In order to make the incentive structure more realistic I offered real cash payments of different amounts set to correspond with the consequences of each choice. The matrix presented the highest cost/penalty (extensive jail time) for the situation in which one team member "snitched" on the other while the other player remained silent. The silent partner in this situation received the maximum penalty. The best pay-off (no jail time and largest cash payment) was given to the snitch, provided the other team player opted to remain silent. In the situation where both parties decided to cooperate with the police, each received jail time but with a greatly reduced sentence. In the event that each player independently opted to remain silent – refused to cooperate with the police – both players would walk free without doing any jail time. In this classic arrangement, self-interest is supposed to lead each player to snitch on the other so that we end up with a less than optimal strategy being selected. Clearly both players are best off when they each remain silent, but the incentive structure of the game motivates the rational self-interested player to cooperate with the police. This is because neither

[15] *See generally*, Sharon Hom and Robin Paul Malloy, "China's Market Economy: A Semiosis of Cross Boundary Discourse Between Law and Economics and Feminist Jurisprudence," 45 Syracuse L. Rev. 815, 815–851 (1994).

player wants to be left "holding the bag," so to speak, in the event that the other player uses a cooperation strategy in order to pin the crime on his or her accomplice.

In all six teams, each composed of players who did not know each other prior to attending this training program, every single player opted to remain silent. Thus, not one of the twelve players was convicted and no one acted in the way that traditional law and economic approaches would predict. When we took class time to discuss the outcome I explained how the pay-off matrix was supposed to encourage them to snitch on each other. Participants in the exercise responded that they understood the costs and the incentives presented by the matrix. They said that they understood that the incentive structure encouraged them to cooperate with the police but none of them gave credence to the incentives. They interpreted the incentive structure from within a community understanding in which no one in China trusts the police. Any incentive structure offered by the police would, therefore, not be expected to be honored. The best course of action when dealing with the police, I was told, was to say nothing.

This meant that each of my players had contextualized the game with a certain interpretive overlay that I had not anticipated even when there were, in fact, no police involved. It was, after all, only a game in which the actual rewards were cash payments to be made by me. Their choice-making process, however, was shaped by their own cultural experience and they did not abstract themselves from their interpretive framework for the purposes of my exercise. This result is both interesting and troubling because it means that the market incentive structure, while understood, was simply ignored and the price signals being sent out were irrelevant to the culturally based responses to the choices/opportunities being presented. Their exercise of choice was, thus, an interpretive process influenced by a cultural and community experience in which one's understanding of various social relationships controlled the calculus of cost and benefit incentives for any given course of action.

In another example of the importance of interpretive context, I had the opportunity to work with one of the lead drafters of a proposed property code for Shanghai. The proposed code was short and simplistic by American legal standards. The draft proposal was less than one page long and it consisted of very simple statements about the right to sell and to buy an ownership interest in real property. It also indicated that the ownership interest would be something less than a fee ownership as the fee was to be held by the State or a State-related entity for the benefit of the people. There was also a provision requiring timely use and development of property so as to prevent mere speculation. As I looked over the proposal I quizzed my Chinese counterpart. I asked, "How do we know that the seller actually owns the property interest to be sold without provisions in place for a good system of recording or registration; and what if the seller sells the same property interest to you at 11:00 after having already sold it to me at 10:00?" The point of my inquiry was to show how real estate markets depend on more than property law definitions. They require a complex legal infrastructure including recording and registration laws, surveying standards, credit systems, and mortgage and foreclosure laws, among others.

To these and other basic questions my Chinese friend suggested that he had not fully considered all of these potential problems. Furthermore, he wondered why I was so quick to run through a long catalog of negative scenarios regarding transactional relationships in the new Chinese marketplace. He wondered why a seller would not own the property interest he was purporting to sell, and why he might sell a single property more than once. I explained to him that in America the court dockets and law books were full of such cases. He responded by suggesting that the market economy in China would not be the same as in America. History, culture, and the way in which people do business would make it different. The long and the short of it is that the networks and patterns of exchange in China are historically different than those in America and this difference has a substantive influence on the newly emerging marketplace. In particular, he pointed out that in the early stages of this market participants would be generally well known by "proper governmental authorities." Additionally, participants in the emerging market would likely have important personal relationships that would make it "unwise" to behave in the manner I had been suggesting with some of my inquiries. Prior experience and relationships between people would continue to give meaning and value to the exchange process in China, and this alternative frame of reference would make the Chinese market economy different from that of the United States. Once again, therefore, the interpretive framework of social interaction provided a referential filter or signaling mechanism for market exchange. Stated more generally, market signals seemingly have different meanings and values as one moves between alternatively positioned individuals and groups. The exercise of choice involves an interpretive process and therefore market exchange is at least partially subjective rather than objective.

During my three summers of work I had many opportunities, beyond the two examples mentioned above, to observe the Chinese and the way in which they always evaluated the prescriptions of economic analysis against other cultural, political, and historical objectives and conditions.

Their process of "borrowing" economic ideas from the West was a "filtering" process wherein new ideas were always referenced against multiple interpretive frameworks. This reflective process of interpretation resulted in a synthesis leading to the emergence of what they referred to as a *Chinese approach* to the particular problem or matter at hand. The Chinese spoke of this in terms of a "market economy with Chinese characteristics." They wanted to borrow from the West but understood that politics, culture, and other factors would contextualize the borrowing process. In essence, new market ideas were filtered through a lens of "habit-taking" convention and resulted in a new value, a new meaning, of "market" that was neither completely Western nor completely Chinese. "Habit-taking," as such, involves a natural tendency to conventualize that which emerges from choice and spontaneity. In this context I mean to suggest that the Chinese process of borrowing occurred with reference to a set of beliefs or a semiotic *ground* that filtered their interpretations. The new meanings were, therefore, anchored in a reference to other beliefs, and the development of new habits or modes of relating were thus shaped by considerations of continuity in the presence of change.

This interpretive process of borrowing that I observed in China is not just a process peculiar to Chinese thinking, nor is it simply related to the peculiar dynamics of an emerging economy. The same process takes place on a continuous basis, for example, right here in the United States. When we read, for instance, of a new law and economics insight arguing for the advancement of such-and-such a law or change in social policy we immediately begin to reflect on it or subject the idea to a preestablished and conventionalized code of value and meaning. We ask, with reference to a particular set of criteria is the analysis valid; do the conclusions make sense; is the result fair; how will the political environment respond to such a proposal; how does such a view correspond to my own views, values, and beliefs? All of these points of inquiry are referential considerations that play a central role in understanding the social/market exchange process. In order to influence and mediate this referential process of market interpretation, law and market theory needs to develop a method of interpretation, and this method must be capable of going beyond the predictive confines of positive economics. There is, in other words, a need to investigate the market as a meaning and value-formation process and to seek an understanding of how alternative networks and patterns of exchange have interpretive and substantive consequences for communities. Semiotic theory, as developed in this book, can help us achieve this goal through the approach of law and market economy.

In this book, therefore, I use semiotic interpretation theory as a philosophical system of inquiry to broaden our approach to law and market theory. Semiotics informs us that market choice is an interpretive process and that it is, therefore, relational and grounded in experience. Furthermore, by reference to semiotics, we can go beyond the communicative insights of McCloskey's work on rhetoric and beyond the pioneering efforts of Julie Nelson and Marianne Ferber in their work on a discourse of feminist economics. McCloskey's work focuses on the traditional structure of rhetoric and uses its methodology to critique economics.[16] His essential theme is both descriptive and normative in that he declares economics to be engaged in a standard form of rhetorical argument and he asserts that this is, in fact, as it should be. His work on rhetoric positions economics as a discourse within a community of scholars where rhetorical devices are used to persuade. He is skeptical of the claim of economics to predictive power, and asserts that the entire enterprise would be more fruitful, more persuasive, if it willingly acknowledged its rhetorical structure and openly worked to persuade by reference to a broader and more inclusive set of assumptions. Similarly, Ferber and Nelson, as economists, borrow from feminist theory to critique traditional approaches to economics.[17] The points they raise, as economists, are all relevant to law and market theory. Like McCloskey, they seek a broader and more inclusive framework for economic analysis – a framework that includes feminist values and perspectives in its interpretive approach to market arrangements.

My own views, influenced by semiotics, are very much sympathetic to these perspectives, but unlike McCloskey, Ferber, and Nelson I assert that the networks and patterns of exchange, including those of rhetoric and discourse, have substantive influences on creativity and on the process of sustainable wealth formation. This goes beyond simply arguing about how to make economics a more persuasive discourse, and suggests the need for a broader and more inclusive method of inquiry than either classical rhetoric or feminist theory. It also goes beyond the idea of law and economics as objects of study because it understands the exchange relationship as a complex system of signs. In this context, therefore, we need to be concerned with interpretation theory because it is fundamental to our study of market choice and because the nature of

---

[16] McCloskey, *Rhetoric*; McCloskey, *If You're So Smart*; Robin Paul Malloy, "Legal Economic Discourse: A Review of *If You're So Smart: The Narrative of Economic Expertise* by Donald McCloskey," 42 J. Legal Educ. 324 (1992); Donald N. McCloskey, "The Lawyerly Rhetoric of Coase's 'The Nature of the Firm,'" 18 J. Corp. L. 425 (1993); McCloskey, *Knowledge*.

[17] *See* Ferber and Nelson, *Feminist Economics*.

the interpretive point of reference itself is significant in its influence on the wealth-formation process.

In developing my argument I use the terms *extensive* and *restrictive* in connection with the social/market exchange process. I use this terminology as a way of reflecting a more accurate image of the market exchange process than that which is typically presented in such dualistic terminology as "free" or "open" versus "closed" or "controlled" economies. I do not think that the language of such a polar positioning helps us to understand the exchange process. The exchange process is a continuum and it is therefore more accurate to speak in terms of extensive/restrictive relationships rather than in terms of free or controlled relationships. My focus, within an *extensive* market exchange context, can, therefore, be understood as an inquiry into the exchange process of market economy, an exchange process of substitution and permutation involving ideas, meanings, and values as well as goods, services, and natural resources. It, thus, goes beyond the more narrow concerns of traditional law and economics by subjecting law and market theory to interpretive evaluation. In this regard, I use semiotic method, as an interpretive theory, to clarify the meaning of wealth, wealth maximization, and social prosperity.

I also use semiotics to examine the consequences of employing particular economic concepts and assumptions. For instance, the traditional assumption that there is no declining marginal utility to money raises a variety of implications. To the extent that every dollar is of equal value it means that someone like Bill Gates values his next dollar as much as his first dollar even though he is a billionaire. This assumption is then coupled with a further assumption in positive economics that says we cannot make interpersonal utility comparisons. In such a setting, we cannot assume that more social value or utility is generated by taxing away a portion of Bill Gates' next marginal dollar and using it to provide a subsistence diet to a poor and homeless child. In traditional positive economics nothing meaningful can be said about the comparison between how Bill Gates and such a child value the exchange. Since we assume an inability to make interpersonal utility comparisons, we assume that we cannot say that the child values that marginal dollar more than Bill does. The assumption of no declining marginal utility of money and of an inability to make interpersonal utility comparisons means that wealth transfers cannot be easily justified as socially efficient or desirable.

These assumptions also imply that wealth transfers from rich people to poor people are harmful because they remove resources from highly productive people and place them in the hands of less productive people. In positive economics such transfers can only be justified in one of two ways. First, rich people can be motivated to provide a social safety net for the poor as a way of seeking to reduce the possibility of crime and destructive social unrest that will be directed at the rich if the situation of the poor becomes desperate. If people are hungry, homeless, and desperate they are more likely to commit crimes against the property and person of those people that have wealth. In order to reduce the prospect of such unpleasantness the rich may well find it in their own interest to provide some minimal provisions for the poor. Secondly, to the extent that the rich feel charitable they will be moved to provide for the less fortunate among them. Both of these views, of course, mean that the poor are merely part of the utility function of people with wealth. The poor have no independent claim or justifiable expectation for social provision, but like common household pets must rely upon the expression of someone else's preferences for their care and survival.

When understood in this way, traditional approaches to law and economics imply that some people exist simply to be the mere instruments of someone else's ends or desires. It also implies that the poor are somehow less human, have less meaning and value, precisely because they fail to offer anything of substantial productive value to commercial society. These economic assumptions reveal a community value system that is very different from one that respects human dignity and the meaningful contribution to exchange made by each and every person. These assumptions position poor people as instrumental means for use in the pursuit of economically efficient ends rather than seeing market mechanisms as the means for human expression and creativity. Furthermore, by denying the poor an authoritative role in the market exchange process these assumptions reveal a preference for a restrictive exchange environment, and I will suggest that a restrictive exchange environment hinders creative discovery, and thus puts sustainable wealth formation at risk.

We can go even further with this analysis. To say, for instance, that money has no declining marginal utility is to say that money stands as a symbolic sign or representation of all values. Unlike other goods and services, money is assumed to be unique. Money is understood as a proxy or a representative token for all other goods and services, and it is assumed that one can never grow tired of its ability to deliver whatever one desires. This is the only meaningful way of understanding such an assumption. The problem is that we know money functions as a semiotic sign of value and as such it can only represent value in some respects, not in all respects. Money cannot express or interpret all social values and, therefore, it cannot be a universal medium for perfect exchange and substitution. For example, money cannot meaningfully capture important environmental values, the value of child bearing and child rearing, nor can it capture social values such as love, affection, and respect. Yet, we know these values are important to many communities. In as much as money cannot logically stand as a perfect representative placeholder or symbol for all values, it seems inappropriate to put so much certainty into the assumption of its lack of declining marginal utility. At some point its inability perfectly to substitute for other values must give rise to a declining marginal utility. A failure to recognize a declining marginal utility, however, privileges the value of those things that are more easily quantifiable while conventionalizing the habit of assuming the superiority of highly monetized relationships.

More can also be said about the assumption of an inability to make interpersonal utility comparisons. This assumption is problematic because it seems to rely upon the further assumption that preferences are individually and monologically informed. From an interpretive point of view, we know that preferences are not formed in isolation but emerge from within interpretive communities. Preferences, like interpretive references, involve a dialogic relationship between the individual and the community. This is understandable in the same way that Adam Smith explained that individuals acted within communities and under the watchful guise of an impartial spectator. Individuals do not form conceptions of right and wrong in isolation, deprived of all society, any more than they can determine beauty in the absence of social influence, participation, and convention. To the contrary, preferences and interpretive references are informed by the experiences of individuals within community. It should, therefore, be possible to say something meaningful about a comparison between interpersonal utility functions or preferences. Market theory should not, in other words, find it impossible to say something meaningful with regard to a comparison between the value of a marginal dollar going either to Bill Gates or to a starving child.

To presume an inability to compare interpersonal utility functions is as problematic as to presume that any one individual's interpretation of a social text is as equal or as good as any other interpretation. People do not live in isolated and detached worlds, and words and semiotic signs cannot simply mean anything a person wants them to mean. This is because interpretive references, like personal preferences, are socially contextualized. Words or signs may be capable of several plausible interpretations but this does not mean that they are capable of having every possible meaning. Interpretive communities have, in other words, some say over the authoritative value of individual acts of interpretation.

Similarly, individual preferences are not fully autonomous since they too are informed and given interpretive meaning within a particularized social context. Society, as an impartial spectator, can rightfully, therefore, express a comparative judgment with respect to the privileging of competing interpersonal utilities or preferences in the same way that it can express judgment on personal expressions of social meaning. Consequently, it is not at all clear that we should be governed by a determinate assumption that deprives us of the ability to make such interpersonal evaluations.

These examples are merely introductory illustrations of the type of analysis provided in the rest of this book. In the chapters that follow I go beyond these introductory matters and explain the terms and concepts of semiotic method with particular reference to Peirce's triadic theory of signs. I also provide examples of how semiotics informs a variety of issues in legal and market analysis. This includes discussion of an ethic of social responsibility, the problem of market ignorance, entrepreneurism, the Coase Theorem, public choice theory, social contract theory, market equilibration, the theory of efficient breach, and the process of creative discovery. Similarly, I make use of semiotic method to illustrate the interpretive relationship between dynamic exchange processes and a positive theory of law and economics.

In using semiotic method I am advancing an interpretive framework that facilitates an understanding of the consequences of legal reasoning in a market context. The objective of this approach, and of law and market economy more generally, is not merely to study the efficiency of law and legal institutions, but to explain how market theory can legitimately involve a variety of other considerations. This is important because advocates of market theory need a way of understanding and responding to critics who reject the importance of promoting sustainable wealth formation. These critics do not value the central significance of the market exchange process. They have a different perspective. Critical, gender, and race-based theories, for example, do not promote extensive market exchange networks nor do they value market theory as a meaningful reference point for legal and social progress. Advocates of critical theory generally position themselves as being against market relationships and they offer an explicit interpretive framework for advancing a view of markets as destructive, exploitative, and unnatural. In the absence of the development of an interpretive framework that can respond to such critical commentary, advocates of law and market theory have been rendered speechless on the important matters of market meanings and values. Unable to engage meaningfully in interpretive discourse, legal economists have conceded considerable social space and authoritative influence to critical theorists. I believe this concession is unnecessary and I will show how semiotic method can broaden the scope of market inquiry while preserving space for the relevance of traditional legal economic investigation. I will also show that multiple points of view and a concern for diversity are better facilitated without reference to the rhetorical strategies of critic theory.

In working through this process of semiotic interpretation, I will show that the traditional equilibrium-based models of law and economics provide a useful but incomplete explanation of wealth formation and of the market exchange process. I argue that sustainable wealth formation is best understood when we relate it both to equilibrium theory, or determinate analysis, *and* to the indeterminate or chaotic nature of discovery and creativity. In order to think of market theory in a way that embraces this more complete understanding of wealth formation, therefore, I suggest that we must reconsider some of the assumptions of traditional law and economics. This does not mean that traditional law and economic assumptions will be completely displaced. It does mean, however, that the method of understanding a dynamic exchange process is different than that used to address equilibrium analysis. Consequently, traditional assumptions must be properly positioned for use within a broader framework of social inquiry. Using semiotic theory, I show how both methods become integrated into a complex systems approach to law and market economy.

In developing my ideas, I proceed in several steps. First, in Chapter 2 I present a general framework for understanding the interpretive method of semiotics and its relationship to wealth creation, ethics, and the process of social exchange. This discussion serves as a basic outline for the rest of the book. Second, in Chapter 3 I expand on and clarify my conception of law and market economy. I do this by looking at the market in the context of community and by providing a more detailed discussion of the market as a semiotic system of signification. Third, in Chapter 4 I elaborate on wealth as a process of discovery and draw a distinction between "reactive" and "proactive" wealth maximization. This includes a discussion of wealth as it relates to creative discovery, investigation, and experimentation. Through a process of semiotic synthesis, or *semiosis*, these different modes of wealth are given meaning in the term "social prosperity." Fourth, in Chapter 5 I discuss the form of social organization that I believe is most likely to be conducive to the generation of proactive wealth. This involves the identification of an ethic of social responsibility suitable for advancing the process of creative discovery. Fifth, in Chapter 6 I address the implications of a shift to an expanded paradigm of law and market economy. Here my analysis suggests three things. First, the traditional pursuit of economic efficiency does not maximize sustainable wealth formation. Second, the nature and extent of the distribution of scarce resources and access to the exercise of political authority influences wealth formation. Third, alternative theories of legal discourse can be understood as normative rhetorical strategies competing for substantive influence over the networks and patterns of social/market exchange – that is, they compete for authoritative interpretive influence over the exercise of market choice and the process of meaning and value formation. As such, I suggest that the referential influence of any given rhetorical strategy is significant because some strategies are more likely than others to facilitate sustainable wealth formation.

In all of this, my overarching purpose is threefold. First, to offer a more general theoretical framework than that of traditional law and economics for investigating the relationship between law and market theory. Second, to demonstrate the relevance of semiotic interpretive method to law and market theory, and, third, to challenge a core assumption, or guiding principle, of traditional law and economics – the traditional view being that law should be efficient and focused on wealth maximization without concern for (other) moral, ethical, or social values. In contrast to this view, I argue that a general ethic of social responsibility is fundamental to the support of a creative environment capable of generating and maximizing sustainable wealth formation and social prosperity.

2   A general framework

In this book I develop a new jurisprudence of exchange based on an improved understanding of the relationship between law and market theory. I call this new jurisprudence "law and market economy." It is an approach that is based on the philosophical insights of semiotics, and in particular that school of semiotic theory grounded in the work of American philosopher and "pragmaticist" Charles Sanders Peirce.[1] At first mention, many legal academics display a sense of puzzlement when they hear the term "semiotics." The term strikes them as exotic and out of place. In reality, however, semiotics is a long-recognized branch of philosophy and C.S. Peirce is one of its most important figures. He was a founding figure in what came to be known as American Pragmatism. Furthermore, I am certainly not the first to relate Peirce or semiotics to law. In fact, my reference to semiotics expands on the approving references to Peirce made by Judge Richard Posner in his book, *The Problems of Jurisprudence,*[2] and on a corpus of work on *legal semiotics* produced by such scholars as Roberta Kevelson[3] (the leading voice of the "Penn State Semiotic Circle" or Penn State "School of Semiotics"),

---

[1] *See The Essential Peirce,* Vol. 1 (Nathan Houser and Christian Kloesel, eds., 1992); *The Essential Peirce,* Vol. 2 (edited by the Peirce Edition Project, 1998). *See also,* Winfried Noth, *Handbook of Semiotics,* 39 (1995), ("America's greatest philosopher"); also, sources in Chap. 1, above, nn. 1, 5, 6.

[2] *See* Richard A. Posner, *The Problems of Jurisprudence* 454–469 (1990).

[3] My work is influenced, in part, by Kevelson's work on the interpretation of Peirce. A sample of Kevelson's work includes: Roberta Kevelson, *The Law as a System of Signs* (1988); Roberta Kevelson, *Peirce's Esthetics of Freedom: Possibility, Complexity, and Emergent Value* (1993); Roberta Kevelson, *Peirce, Science, Signs* (1996); Roberta Kevelson, *Peirce's Method of Methods* (1987); *Codes and Customs* (Roberta Kevelson, ed., 1994); *Flux, Complexity, and Illusion* (Roberta Kevelson, ed., 1993); *Law and the Conflict of Ideologies* (Roberta Kevelson, ed., 1996); *Conscience, Consensus, and Crossroads in the Law* (Roberta Kevelson, ed., 1995); *Peirce and Law: Issues in Pragmatism, Legal Realism, and Semiotics* (Roberta Kevelson, ed., 1991); *The Eyes of Justice* (Roberta Kevelson, ed., 1994); *Law and Semiotics,* vol. 3 (Roberta Kevelson, ed., 1989); Roberta Kevelson, *Property as Rhetoric in Law,* 4 Cardozo Stud. L. and Lit. 189–206 (1992); Roberta Kevelson, "Transfer, Transaction, Asymmetry: Junctures Between Law and Economics From the Fish-Eye Lens of Semiotics," 42 Syracuse L. Rev. 7 (1991).

Peter Goodrich,[4] and Bernard Jackson.[5] These scholars have recently been joined by a new group of people who are interested in the application of semiotic theory to law, including Duncan Kennedy,[6] Jack Balkin,[7] Jeremy Paul,[8] John Brigham,[9] and Vivian Grosswald Curran.[10] In addition, a number of legal scholars frequently participate in the annual Round Table on Law and Semiotics sponsored by or held in conjunction with the Pennsylvania State University and the University of Massachusetts at Amherst. Others participate, on a regular basis, in organizations such as the International Society for the Semiotics of Law, the Semiotic Society of America, and the Law and Society Association, which recognizes semiotics as one of its designated areas of membership interest.

With respect to the more particular enterprise of applying legal semiotics to an understanding of law and market theory, my own efforts have corresponded to similar interests and scholarly work done by Denis Brion[11]

---

[4] *See, e.g.*, Peter Goodrich, *Reading The Law: A Critical Introduction to Legal Method and Techniques* (1986); Peter Goodrich, *Oedipus Lex: Psychoanalysis, History, Law* (1995); Peter Goodrich, *Languages of Law: From Logics of Memory to Nomadic Masks* (1990); Peter Goodrich, " 'The Unconscious is a Jurist': Psychoanalysis and Law in the Work of Pierre Legendre," 20 Legal Stud. Forum 195 (1996).

[5] Jackson applies the Greimassian School of Semiotics (rather than Peirce) to his work in law. *See, e.g.*, Bernard S. Jackson, *Semiotics and Legal Theory* (1995); Bernard S. Jackson, *Law, Fact and Narrative Coherence* (1988); Bernard S. Jackson, *Making Sense in Law: Linguistic Psychological and Semiotic Perspectives* (1995).

[6] *See, e.g.*, Duncan Kennedy, "A Semiotic of Legal Argument," 42 Syracuse L. Rev. 75 (1991).

[7] *See, e.g.*, Jack M. Balkin, "The Promise of Legal Semiotics," 69 Tex. L. Rev. 1831 (1991).

[8] *See, e.g.*, Jeremy Paul, "The Politics of Legal Semiotics," 69 Tex. L. Rev. 1179 (1991).

[9] *See generally*, John Brigham, *The Constitution of Interests: Beyond the Politics of Rights* (1996); John Brigham, *The Cult of The Court* (1991); John Brigham, *Constitutional Language* (1978).

[10] *See, e.g.*, Vivian Grosswald Curran, "The Legalization of Racism in a Constitutional State: Democracy's Suicide in Vichy France," 50 Hastings L.J. 1 (1998); Vivian Grosswald Curran, "Cultural Immersion, Difference and Categories in US Comparative Law," 46 Am. J. Comparative L. 43 (1998).

[11] Denis Brion, "The Shopping Mall: Signs of Power" in *Law and Semiotics*, vol. 1, 65 (Roberta Kevelson, ed., 1989); Denis Brion, "An Essay on LULU, NIMBY, and the Problem of Distributive Justice," B.C. Envtl. Aff. L. Rev. 437 (1988); Denis Brion, "What is a Hay Baler? The Semiotic Answer from Contract Law" in *Law and Semiotics*, vol. 2, 61 (Roberta Kevelson, ed., 1989); Denis Brion, "Making the Appalachian World: The Judicial Conception of Land" in *Law and Semiotics*, vol. 3, 73 (Roberta Kevelson, ed.); Denis Brion, "Rhetoric and the Law of Enterprise," 42 Syracuse L. Rev. 117 (1991); Denis Brion, "The Meaning of the City: Urban Redevelopment and the Loss of Community," 25 Ind. L. Rev. 685 (1992); Denis Brion, "Performing the Constitution," 49 Wash. & Lee L. Rev. 293 (1992); Denis Brion, "The Hidden Persistence of Witchcraft," 4 Law & Critique 227 (1993); Denis Brion, "Richard Posner's 'Sex and Reason': Meaning and the Ghost in the Machine" in *Eyes of Justice* (Roberta Kevelson, ed., 1994); Denis Brion, "The Chaotic Indeterminacy of Tort Law: Between Formalism and Nihilism" in *Radical Philosophy of Law* (D. Caudill and

and Pertti Ahonen.[12] Professor Brion has used semiotic methods to explore meanings and values in property and contract law as well as to investigate both legal and economic theory. Professor Ahonen, a leading Scandinavian scholar in the field of public administration and management, has used semiotic theory to investigate administrative, economic, and financial issues within the context of Finland and Europe. My own work has also involved the application of semiotic theory to a variety of legal and economic considerations.[13] It is only recently, however, that I

S. Gold eds., 1995); Denis Brion, "Making Differences and Making all the Difference: Community and the Dilemma of Difference" in *Conscience, Consensus and Crossroads in Law* (Roberta Kevelson, ed., 1995); Denis Brion, "The Paradox of Principles and the Critique of Pragmatism" in *Law and the Conflict of Ideologies* (Roberta Kevelson, ed., 1996); Denis Brion, "The Semiotics of Constitutional Meaning" in *Semiotics* (C.W. Spinks and John Deely, eds., 1995); Denis Brion, "The Ritual of the Judicial Opinion" in *Law and Ritual* (J. Knaack and R. Lindgreen, eds., 1997); Denis Brion, "Naming and Forgetting" in *Semiotics* 1996 (J. Deely et al., eds., 1997) at 219–228; Denis J. Brion, "The Pragmatic Genesis of Constitutional Meaning," 10 International J. for the Semiotics of L. 159 (1997); Denis J. Brion, "Utilitarian Reasoning in Judicial Decisionmaking," 23 Legal Stud. Forum 93 (1999).

[12] *Tracing the Semiotic Boundaries of Politics* (Pertti Ahonen, ed., 1993); *Political Economy of Finnish Public Administration* (Pertti Ahonen, ed., 1994); Pertti Ahonen, "Regulating, Deregulating and Reregulating Universities: Law and Economics of Institutional and Contractual Design" in *Law and Economics: New and Critical Perspectives* (Robin Paul Malloy and Christopher K. Braun, eds., 1995) at 127–152; Pertti Ahonen, "The Meaning of Money: Comparing a Peircean and Saussurean Perspective" in *Law and Semiotics*, vol. 3 (Kevelson, ed.), at 13–30; Pertti Ahonen, "Pragmatic Aspects of the Political Economy of Law: With Applications to Environmental Policies" in *Law and the Human Sciences* (Kevelson, ed., 1992).

[13] Robin Paul Malloy, *Law and Economics: A Comparative Approach to Theory and Practice* (1990); Malloy and Braun, *Law and Economics*; Robin Paul Malloy, *Planning for Serfdom: Legal Economic Discourse and Downtown Development* (1991); *Adam Smith and the Philosophy of Law and Economics* (Robin Paul Malloy and; Jerry Evensky, eds., 1995); Robin Paul Malloy, "Toward a New Discourse of Law and Economics," 42 Syracuse L. Rev. 27 (1991); Sharon Hom and Robin Paul Malloy, "China's Market Economy: A Semiosis of Cross Boundary Discourse between Law and Economics and Feminist Jurisprudence," 45 Syracuse L. Rev. 815 (1994); Robin Paul Malloy, "Letters from the Longhouse: Law, Economics and Native American Values," Wisc. L. Rev. 1569 (1992); Robin Paul Malloy, "A New Law and Economics" in *Codes and Customs* (Kevelson, ed.); Robin Paul Malloy, "Of Icons, Metaphors, and Private Property – The Recognition of 'Welfare' Claims in the Philosophy of Adam Smith" in *Law and Semiotics*, vol. 3 (Kevelson, ed.); Robin Paul Malloy, "Adam Smith's Conception of Individual Liberty" in *Law and Enlightenment in Britain* 82 (T. Campbell and N. MacCormick, eds., 1990); Robin Paul Malloy, "A Classical Liberal Critique of Takings Law" in *Taking Property and Just Compensation: Law and Economics Perspectives of the Takings Issue* (N. Mercuro, ed., 1992); Robin Paul Malloy, "Freedom from Authority – Discovering 'The Discovery of Freedom' by Rose Wilder Lane" in *Action and Agency* 211 (R. Kevelson, ed., 1991); Robin Paul Malloy, "A Law and Economics Perspective on Politically Correct Thinking" in *Flux, Complexity and Illusion* 299 (R. Kevelson, ed., 1993); Robin Paul Malloy, "Legal Economic Discourse: A Review of *If You're So Smart: The Narrative of Economic Expertise* by Donald McCloskey," 42 J. Legal Educ. 324 (1992); Robin Paul Malloy, "Planning for Serfdom – An Introduction to a New Theory of Law and Economics," 25 Ind. L. Rev. 621 (1991); Robin Paul

developed a deeper and clearer understanding of how I might use semiotic method to advance my work on law and market theory. This book emerged from a concentrated effort to extend and further develop ideas present in my prior work. Collectively, Professors Brion and Ahonen and I have been interested in legal semiotics because of the potential that it holds for further illuminating connections between law and market theory, and because of its ability to facilitate interdisciplinary inquiry.

Semiotic method helps us to reflect on the social and cultural consequences of invoking and validating economic assumptions in law and social institutions. In this regard it helps focus attention on not only what might be efficient, but on what the social significance might be of declaring an efficiency criterion to be of primary significance in determining social policy. Thus, we want to ask what it means, in terms of social relationships, to say as Richard Posner has said: that the presence of Jews or blacks in a neighborhood can be analyzed in economic terms like the presence of a common law nuisance;[14] or that the market for baby adoptions would be more efficient if babies went to the highest bidder rather than being placed with families through adoption agencies;[15] or that rape can be understood as an act that circumvents the market for voluntary sexual exchange.[16] In each of these examples Posner uses a form of interpretive or semiotic substitution to equate people with commodities traded in the commercial marketplace. We believe that these shifts in analysis raise important questions about the nature of social meaning and that they have implications for cultural norms as well as for the process of exchange. Consequently, it is important to examine how community meanings and values change

Malloy, "Planning for Serfdom – An Epilogue on Law, Economics and Values," 25 Ind. L. Rev. 825 (1991); Robin Paul Malloy, "If Pigs Could Fly Where Would They Go? A Reply to Professor Posin," 38 Wayne L. Rev. 83 (1991); Robin Paul Malloy, "A Sign of the Times – Law and Semiotics," 65 Tulane L. Rev. 211 (1990); Robin Paul Malloy and Richard A. Posner, "Debate: Is Law and Economics Moral?" 24 Val. U. L. Rev. 147 (1990); Robin Paul Malloy, "Market Philosophy in the Legal Tension Between Children's Autonomy and Parental Authority," 21 Ind. L. Rev. 889 (1988); Robin Paul Malloy, "Invisible Hand or Sleight of Hand? Adam Smith, Richard Posner and the Philosophy of Law and Economics," 36 U. Kan. L. Rev. 210 (1988); Robin Paul Malloy, "The Political Economy of Co-Financing America's Urban Renaissance," 40 Vand. L. Rev. 67 (1987); Robin Paul Malloy, "Equating Human Rights and Property Rights – The Need for Moral Judgment in an Economic Analysis of Law and Social Policy," 47 Ohio St. L. J. 163 (1986); Robin Paul Malloy, "Law and Market Economy: The Triadic Linking of Law, Economics and Semiotics," 12 International J. for the Semiotics of Law 285–307 (1999).

[14] *See* Richard A. Posner, *The Economics of Justice* 84–85 (1983).
[15] *See, e.g.*, Elisabeth M. Landes and Richard A. Posner, "The Economics of the Baby Shortage," 7 J. Legal Stud. 323 (1978).
[16] *See, e.g.*, Richard A. Posner, *Sex and Reason* (1992).

when legal analysis takes on the interpretive lens of efficiency as borrowed from positive economics.

Similarly, we believe that it is important to apply the same semiotic method of analysis when comparing efficiency analysis to that of alternative approaches such as ones grounded in critical theory. When critical theorists offer a radical critique of current market exchange networks they frequently do so with reference to an interpretive framework that rejects the ideas of objectivity, neutrality, rationality, equality, reciprocity, and self-interest.[17] In a semiotic approach to law and market theory it is important to consider the significance of such an interpretive shift. As a rhetorical strategy for reforming the patterns and networks of exchange, critical theory presents an alternative system for allocating scarce resources and access to political authority. It does this by grounding the critical frame of reference in values that support subjectivity, instinct, inequality, exclusion, and group identification. Ultimately, it is important to understand not only how such a transformation changes meanings and values, but to consider the implications it raises with respect to an ethic of social responsibility and a process of creative discovery.

In this regard, Peirce's semiotic method enhances our ability to understand the complex and dynamic relationship between law and market theory because of its conceptual compatibility with market process theory in general, and with the theories of F.A. Hayek[18] and Israel Kirzner in particular.[19] This connection is made express in Bobbie Kevelson's work because she argues that Hayek's theories of freedom, spontaneous social order and general rules are all derivable from, and consistent with, a Peircean logic and ground. Similarly, a review of Kirzner's work on the dynamic and indeterminate nature of market process theory shows that it corresponds to the same type of logical inquiry as reflected in the semiotic tension between habit/continuity and change/indeterminacy.[20] In each approach, concern is centered on the idea of spontaneous social order emerging out of systems of dynamic and complex change. Peircean semiotics, therefore, provides a theory of interpretation that is consistent with the market exchange process, and understandable in terms of market theory. This observation is important because it indicates the potential for using Peirce's theory

---

[17] *See generally,* sources below, in Chap. 6, n. 17.

[18] *See, e.g.,* Kevelson, *Peirce's Method* at 81, 93–94; Kevelson, *Law,* at 181–192, 266–269, 178–179, 255; Kevelson, *Peirce and Freedom,* at 118–120, 123–127, 205–210; Kevelson, *Peirce and Science,* at 36, 45, 93–110.

[19] *See* Israel M. Kirzner, *The Meaning of Market Process* (1992); Israel M. Kirzner, *Discovery and the Capitalist Process* (1985).

[20] *See* Kirzner, *Meaning* (in particular at 1–54); Kirzner, *Capitalist Process.*

in law and market economy, and because it shows that interpretation theory does not need to be associated with non-market oriented approaches to law.

In as much as Peircean semiotics corresponds with the market theory of people such as Hayek and Kirzner it is, Kevelson argues, antithetical to much of the legal interpretation theory produced and relied upon by people engaged in various forms of "critical" theory.[21] Kevelson emphasizes this distinction, for instance, when she says that the interpretive approaches of critical theory, in seeking to undercut liberal theories of law, "are not only fallacious but are malicious."[22] Consequently, one of the most significant characteristics of Kevelson's work, and of her influence upon those of us involved in the "Penn State School," is the way in which Peirce's philosophy of signs is interpreted as market compatible and extensive. Kevelson shows us that interpretation theory is not the exclusive domain of critics. Peirce's triadic theory of signs provides a method for understanding market theory and for identifying weakness in the positions both of traditional legal economists and critics.

Consistent with Kevelson's market-centered interpretation of Peirce's work, one finds that Peirce is rarely, if ever, cited by critical theorists even though his work is central to the subject matter of linguistics and interpretation theory, and his work is or should be known to most of them.[23] The recognition of this point is important because it is central to the conception of law and market economy as an extension of, rather than rejection of, market theory. Consequently, Peirce's theory of semiotics is ideal for grounding an interpretive theory for law and market economy, and it is a Peircean *influence* that guides my analysis in this book. This does not mean that I am asserting what Peirce said directly or what he would have said about the ideas of law and market theory that I raise and discuss. It means that my method of inquiry is influenced by Peirce's work and it is this influence that guides my application of semiotic method to the issues raised by the approach of law and market economy.

While semiotic method has a history of complexity and a peculiar terminology, a basic understanding is all that is needed to grasp and

---

[21] Kevelson, *Peirce and Science*, at 29–70; Kevelson, *Peirce and Freedom*, at 87–109. "Some Crits are evolved Legal Realists, while others are Utopians with a markedly anti-Peircean agenda." *Id.* at 88.

[22] Kevelson, *Peirce and Science*, at 48. "This malevolence is nothing other than a masked greed in the name of social morality." *Id.*

[23] *See* Robert W. Benson, "Peirce and Critical Legal Studies" in *Peirce and Law* (Kevelson, ed.), at 15–28.

begin working with its implications for law and market economy. In an attempt to facilitate an easy understanding I have tried to keep my semiotic analysis and terminology narrowly directed and relatively unencumbered so that the value of its implications does not get lost in the complexity of its finer details. The introduction provided in this Chapter is expanded upon throughout the rest of the book. I believe that those people already conversant with semiotics and with Peirce will readily see the application of his method in this work. I have, therefore, structured my discussion and my footnote references primarily for those people who will want to explore this field in more detail. I believe that little or nothing is lost by this approach while much is gained. In establishing a general framework for analysis, therefore, I will first present a basic introduction to semiotics and then outline my argument for understanding its application to the relationship between law and market economy. This basic introduction to semiotics and the ideas presented in this section are further explained and illustrated in the remaining parts of the book.

A basic introduction to semiotics

Semiotics is a long-recognized branch of philosophy that deals with the process of exchange. Semiotics, while literally the study of signs, provides a theoretical framework for investigating the process of "knowing," and the construction of meaning and value within a dialogic or relational system of exchange. It informs us about the substantive implications of the networks and patterns of exchange in which we participate and suggests that this participation shapes the experiential ground for meaning and value formation. It also addresses the role of theory as a mediating device for human understanding. As such, it provides a method of inquiry for the interpretation and analysis of the relationship between law and market theory.

Semiotic method can be applied to exchange systems in general and reveals that all such systems involve a continuous process of substitution and permutation. Since, in a semiotic sense, there are no perfect substitutes, all substitutions or exchanges generate the potentiality of new meaning and new value. As Kevelson explains it:

[t]he viewer and the viewed are a special interrelationship in this semiotics process, such that both relates of this union are mutually and reciprocally transformed and increased. The asymmetry of the process, in a Peircean sense, results in the fact that no reduplication ever takes place. Instead, what passes for repetition and which *permits* rhythms and measures to develop are approximate *duplications* only, i.e. are *verisimilitude representations* or interpretations such that

each representation is *more* than its referent: it is *more meaningful, more complex,* and literally *more valuable.*[24]

An exchange, therefore, does not merely substitute one value for another but rather transforms value by the extension of meaning between that which is exchanged. When law "borrows" from economics it engages in a process of substitution and permutation thereby creating new meanings and values. Semiotic theory is applicable to this borrowing process and to both law and economics independently, because each mode of inquiry represents a system of exchange. Both disciplines address the way in which people, their things, and actions are understood. Both systems give meaning, direction, and consequence to the process of social organization and each operates as a continuous process of substitution and permutation.

In economics, for example, inputs are exchanged for outputs, costs are exchanged for benefits, labor is exchanged for cash, cash is exchanged for goods and services, and so on and so on. Every exchange is a substitution and permutation telling us something about the meaning and value attached to the things exchanged and about the actors engaged in the process. Furthermore, every exchange expresses an imperfect substitution and thus gives rise to a new sign and a new meaning and value relationship.

Similarly, in law we are continually engaged in a process of substitution and permutation. The plaintiff's view of the case is substituted for that of the defendant, the jury determination is substituted for that of either party, and sometimes the judge's view is substituted for that of the jury notwithstanding the verdict. Likewise, when an appeal of a case is taken, the reviewing court substitutes its interpretation for that of the lower court. The process of dealing with precedent is also an exchange process where the facts of a current case are made to sit in reference to or in substitution of the facts from a similar case so that an earlier rule might be applied to the later dispute. Statutory interpretation involves a like process as rules or conventions of construction are applied to language in order to arrive at a meaning that is substituted for other interpretations of the words. The same substitution process is at work when a client settles a dispute for a cash payment, thus exchanging the cause of action for money or substituting a loss to person or property for a payment in cash.

Even the payment system itself is an exchange process. Consider that money in the "token" form of bills and coins is really a substitute or representation for an underlying value – the paper itself is not what is

---

[24] Kevelson, *Peirce and Freedom,* at 8; Kevelson, *Peirce's Method,* at 7.

highly valued but rather what the paper represents – money, as such, is an interpretation of value rather than the value itself.[25] By extension, the use of checks, credit cards, electronic fund transfers and the like are further exchanges and substitutions for the same idea. The variety of substitutes and the degree of their accessibility can tell us something about the community in which they operate. It can tell us about a community's technology and the distribution of authority to issue monetary directives, substitutions, and exchanges. It can also inform us about the fluidity of cash and credit, and, therefore, about loan security, access to credit histories, debt-collection processes, communications, information and currency controls, and public confidence. The more varied the types of money substitutes in a community, the more this can be a sign of a diverse and dynamic market exchange system as opposed to, say, a barter economy. Complex forms of money and exchange require a different legal, as well as technological, infrastructure relative to the needs of simple, barter, economies. In the approach of law and market economy the nature of these different relationships and patterns is important for understanding law in a market context. Furthermore, societies that deal only in simultaneous exchanges of real goods (barter), for example, reveal a different structure and pattern of interaction than that which is present in communities with highly abstract and contingent forms of exchange. Thus, the formal and informal rules of exchange not only govern the process of exchange, they give meaning and value to it.

Exchange systems, like those of both law and market economy, are relational in terms of the process of substitution and permutation. Law establishes relational positions for exchange including: plaintiff and defendant, owner and trespasser, landlord and tenant, mortgagor and mortgagee, and criminal and victim. In market economy we also deal with such relational positioning as in the examples of, producer and consumer, capitalist and laborer, and competitor and monopolist. In all such positioning, both legal and economic, there is social meaning and an expression of value. The relationship between ideas is part of the meaning. These relationships can reveal things about power and authority and imply elements of consent, access, and participation between members of the exchange community. The nature and content of what is exchanged, by whom, how, and in what relationship, is "significant" in a semiotic sense because it reveals something about the continuously reforming patterns and networks of social interaction, and of meanings and values within society. These networks and patterns are

[25] *See* Kevelson, *Peirce's Method*, at 83–95; *Money: A History* (Jonathan Williams, ed., 1997). For discussions of money and its meanings see George Simmel, *The Philosophy of Money* (1990); Ahonen, "The Meaning of Money."

also significant because they contribute to and inform the experiences of participants. The study of law and market economy, therefore, involves a consideration of the social meanings and values that emerge from the recognition of particular networks and patterns of exchange.

According to the Peircean semiotics that influences my work, social meaning in the exchange process emerges out of an original state of chaos or indeterminacy.[26] This is a state of pure chance and nothingness that becomes real with the emergence of a habit or formation of a pattern(s) of regularity.[27] The tendency toward habit and pattern formation is natural, according to Peirce, and, thus, potentiality always gives rise to an actuality.[28] Peirce's notion of the original state, and the tendency toward habit formation based on conventionalized patterns, is consistent with the idea of a "strange attractor" in chaos and complex systems theory,[29] and with the role Adam Smith ascribed to the Deity in his model of evolutionary transformation.[30] It is also compatible with F.A. Hayek's notion of spontaneous social order – an order that emerges out of an unplanned environment of dynamic interaction. One need not debate this understanding of the original position, however, in order to benefit from Peirce's insights on the transformation of value and meaning in the process of exchange.

Peirce's point is that signs are . . . anything we know or claim to know we know because it *is* a sign and interpretable. Persons, places, things, systems – are all signs. Peirce's argument is that signs interpret signs. It is only through the methods of semiotics – the method of methods – that we are able to account for the process whereby our system of signs interprets another system of signs and thus grows, and gives birth to new signs.[31]

Meaning, according to Peirce, arises from a continuous process of relational exchange operating within an environment of chance/indeterminacy and habit/continuity.[32] It is an evolutionary and dynamic process in which meanings and values continually evolve in a synthesis or semiosis of indeterminacy and continuity.[33] In market theory we can

[26] John K. Sheriff, *Peirce's Guess at the Riddle: Grounds for Human Significance* 8–16 (1994).
[27] *Id.; see also* Stuart Kauffman, *At Home in the Universe: The Search for the Laws of Self-Organization and Complexity* 277–279 (1995).
[28] *See* Sheriff, *Peirce*, at 9 ("The possibility evokes the actuality").
[29] *See* James Gleick, *Chaos: Making a New Science* 121–153 (1987) (discussing the case of strange attractors).
[30] *See* Jerry Evensky, "Setting the Scene: Adam Smith's Moral Philosophy" in Robin Paul Malloy and Jerry Evensky, *Adam Smith and the Philosophy of Law and Economics* 7–29 (R.P. Malloy and J. Evensky, eds., 1994); Gleick, *Chaos*, at 121–153.
[31] Kevelson, *Law*, at 239.
[32] Sheriff, *Peirce*, at 9–16; Kevelson, *Peirce and Freedom*, at 154.
[33] Sheriff, *Peirce*, at 8–59; Kevelson, "Rhetoric"; Kevelson, *Peirce and Freedom*, at 1–47.

see this connection when we think in terms of simple cost and benefit analysis. From the chaotic activities of numerous independent market actors emerges a set of patterns that formulate a habit and results in a temporary equilibrium.[34] The information provided by the equilibrium is useful and influential in thinking about extending the meaning/consequences of that relationship to the next exchange. Current prices influence, or inform, my thinking about alternative investment trade-offs and opportunity costs, for instance. At the same time, new information is constantly emerging in the marketplace and chance, surprise, and other factors all play a part in destabilizing the observed equilibrium. As a consequence, a new pattern emerges and a new equilibrium is located. This new equilibrium once again provides meaning for market actors and once again stands ready for revision in the dynamic interplay between conventionalized regularity and chaotic indeterminacy. The same process happens in law. The common law, for example, with its case-by-case analysis continually revises the meaning of legal rules. Continuity is preserved by reference to pre-cedent and legal doctrine, yet endlessly variable fact patterns give rise to constant extensions and revisions of meaning. Chance and indeter-minacy work toward diversity and freedom, while regularity and habit work toward continuity and convention. The synthesis of these states or modes of being results in the continuous creation and recreation of meanings and values in an infinite process of referential and substitu-tional exchange.

In Peirce's semiotics there are three modes of being which he identifies as universal categories of firstness, secondness, and thirdness.

Peirce developed a phenomenology based on only three universal categories called *firstness*, *secondness*, and *thirdness*. *Firstness* is the mode of being of that which is such as it is, positively and without reference to anything else. It is the category of unreflected feeling, mere potentiality, freedom, immediacy, of undifferentiated quality and independence. *Secondness* involves the relation of a first to a second. It is the category of comparison, facticity, action, reality, and experience in time and space. It meets us in such facts as another, relative, compulsive, effect, dependence, independence, negative, occurrence, reality, result. *Thirdness* brings a second in relation to a third. It is the category of mediation, habit, memory, continuity, synthesis, communication (semiosis), representation, and signs.[35]

[34] Sheriff, *Peirce*, at 9–59. *See* Gleick, *Chaos*, at 16–30, 56, 62–80, 113–118, 133–140, 304; Kauffman, *Universe*, at 3–56, 73–92, 188–189, 194–195; and it corresponds to Hayek's theory of spontaneous social order. Kevelson, *Law*, at 167–192. Friedrich A. Hayek, *Law, Legislation and Liberty: Rules and Order*, vol. 1, 35–54 (1973) (discussing spontaneous social order related to law and social cooperation); Malloy, *Serfdom*, at 1–60 (general rules and spontaneous social order with reference to Hayek).
[35] Noth, *Semiotics*, at 41.

All logical thought consists of these modes and thus all semiotics involves a triadic relationship between these modes.[36] The semiotic synthesis between firstness and secondness gives rise to a new meaning or value that stands in the position of a third.[37] This continuous synthesis is referred to as the process of *semiosis* and it is present in all systems of exchange.

Since every sign creates an interpretant which in turn is the representamen of a second sign, semiosis results in a series of successive interpretants *ad infinitum*. There is no "first" nor "last" sign in this process of unlimited semiosis . . . thinking always proceeds in the form of dialogue . . . every thought must adhere itself to some other . . . this endless series is essentially a *potential* one. Peirce's point is that any actual interpretant of a given sign *can* theoretically be interpreted in some further sign, and that in another without any necessary end being reached. The exigencies of practical life inevitably cut short such potentially endless development.[38]

Umberto Eco explains that Peirce's idea of unlimited semiosis does not mean that there are unlimited meanings to a text or a sign.[39] While there are multiple ways to interpret a sign it does not follow that a sign or a text can mean anything a reader wants it to mean. To a certain extent signs, like texts, are anchored in convention, and the community constrains the individual's ability to interpret meaning.

Importantly, depending upon the point of inquiry, the positional designation of firstness, secondness, and thirdness may change or shift.

[T]herefore a part of every thought continues in the succeeding thoughts. Every sign is interpreted by a subsequent sign or thought in which the-relation-of-the-sign-to-its-object becomes the object of the new sign. Not only does a sign refer to a subsequent thought-sign that interprets it, it also stands *for* some object through a previous thought-sign . . . Meaning, then, lies not in what is actually thought [immediately present], but in what this thought may be connected with in representation by subsequent thoughts; so that the meaning of a thought is

---

[36] *See also* Noth, *Semiotics*, at 39–47; Sheriff, *Peirce*, at 14 and 31–47; James Jacob Liszka, *A General Introduction to the Semeiotic of Charles Sanders Peirce* 18–52 (1996); *Reasoning and the Logic of Things: Charles Sanders Peirce* 68–102 (Kenneth Laine Ketner, ed., 1992); Christopher Hookway, *Peirce* 106–118, 121, 151, 166–180 (1992); *Philosophical Writings of Peirce* 75–93, 101–119 (Justus Buchler, ed., 1955); Karl-Otto Apel, *Charles S. Peirce: From Pragmatism to Pragmaticism* 23 (1995). This triadic relationship is a key distinguishing factor from Saussure. *See* Vincent M. Colapietro, *Peirce's Approach to the Self: A Semiotic Perspective on Human Subjectivity* 5 (1989); Sheriff, *Peirce*, at 41.

[37] *See* references above, n. 36; Sheriff, *Peirce*, at 33.

[38] Noth, *Semiotics*, at 43 (defining the idea of unlimited semiosis).

[39] *See* Umberto Eco, *The Limits of Interpretation* 57, 37–42, 27–32, 148–149 (1990). *See generally*, Umberto Eco, *A Theory of Semiotics* (1976); Umberto Eco, *Semiotics and the Philosophy of Language* (1984).

altogether something virtual. Meaning exists only as the dynamic relation of signs. To the degree that life has meaning, it is a train of thought.[40]

For an example of this idea consider my earlier references to the situation of the common law. In semiotic terms one may think of a given common law rule as a mode of firstness, to be referenced against a particular context, a mode of secondness, with the process of referencing giving rise to a new interpretive meaning or rule as a mode of thirdness. On the other hand, one may first choose to think in terms of a particular context or set of facts as a mode of firstness. This particular contextualized situation might be interpreted by reference to common law doctrines positioned, as such, in a mode of secondness. The referential process once again gives rise to a new interpretive meaning, a new expression of social and substitutional value, as a mode of thirdness. In either case, once this new meaning is derived, as a mode of thirdness, it immediately serves as a new mode of firstness for the next round of exchange.[41] This process continues in an ongoing synthesis or semiosis. The point is that the semiotic process is continuous and does not depend upon a particular set of first positions or preconditions. Instead, it works pragmatically to address the process of exchange itself. In the simplest of terms, this idea can be expressed with reference to the age-old question of the chicken and the egg. As such, one might understand this semiotic approach as not so much concerned with determining whether the chicken or the egg came first but rather with investigating the relationship between chickens and eggs in an ongoing process of dynamic change.

In this book I will use this semiotic approach to make three key points relevant to my conception of law and market economy. These points are highlighted below and elaborated upon in the remaining parts of the book.

First, the concept of semiotics, as a method of investigating relational exchange, will be used to explain the market process as a system of signification in which various approaches to market theory act as mediating constructs for interpretation. The market process, as such, acts to shape and is at the same time shaped by continually evolving meanings and values. This construct provides insight into the exchange process of law and market theory. By approaching a theory of market economy through semiotics, one can create a referential framework or lens capable of influencing interpretive meaning and substantive action. This approach can provide a choice or preference-shaping filter capable

---

[40] Sheriff, *Peirce*, at 37. *See generally, id.*, at 33–47. Eco provides a similar interpretation of Peirce. *See, e.g.*, Eco, *Limits of Interpretation*, at 60, 28–30.

[41] Sheriff, *Peirce*, at 37–47; Kevelson, *Law*, at 253.

of influencing the normative acceptance of particular wealth-based approaches to law and market theory. In other words, it can facilitate the synthesis process when new ideas are evaluated or borrowed for purposes of shaping and reshaping law and public policy. It also sheds light on the process of market choice since choice always involves an exercise in interpretation and this always includes a relational reference.

Second, the concepts of firstness, secondness, and thirdness can be used to distinguish two modes of wealth that I identify as *reactive* and *proactive* wealth. This deconstruction or subclassification of wealth is necessary to address the process of creative discovery and the role of indeterminacy in wealth formation.

Third, the concepts of firstness, secondness, and thirdness can be used to address the relationship between reactive wealth, understood by habit and convention and positioned as a mode of firstness (the general subject of the equilibrium models used in traditional law and economic analysis), and proactive wealth, a product of creativity and chance positioned as a mode of secondness (an idea further developed in this book). Their relationship, in the process of exchange, is understandable as a semiotic synthesis and points to a resulting measure of well-being or social prosperity that is identifiable as a mode of thirdness.

By reference to the interpretive insights of semiotics, I believe we can broaden our understanding of the relationship between law and market theory while promoting sustainable wealth formation based on an ethic of social responsibility grounded in a process of creative discovery. We can also uncover the substantive difference between the goals of law and market economy (extensive exchange participation and sustainable wealth formation), and those of traditional law and economics (efficiency and wealth maximization).

A brief overview of the general argument

Assuming that many of my readers will be unfamiliar with the application of semiotics to law and market theory, I provide a brief overview of my argument so as to set the stage for what is to be more fully explained in the remaining chapters of the book. I start by mapping out some of the assumptional shifts that distinguish a semiotic approach to law and market economy from that of traditional law and economics. Then I move on to present an outline of the major themes of the book. It must be remembered that these ideas will all be expanded upon later and are presented here in overview form so as to position the reader for a better understanding of what is to follow. In drawing distinctions between a law and market economy approach and that of law and economics, I am trying to develop a referential basis for clarifying the relationship of firstness, secondness, and thirdness in the market exchange process.

Law and market economy, with its focus on understanding law and legal relationships within a dynamic market context, differs from traditional law and economic analysis in several ways. Traditional law and economics, for example, examines the process of exchange and social organization from the theoretical perspective of wealth maximization and postulates the pursuit of efficient social arrangements. This view typically embraces a conception of economics as a science of choice under conditions of scarcity and uncertainty. It is a view that minimizes the relevance of normative, ethical, and moral meaning while positioning the individual as the focal point of all social order. It is grounded in a theory of rational and self-interested decision making and it addresses itself to the question of choice as confronted by isolated individuals struggling to survive on remote islands of personal autonomy. The choice process, in this context, is perceived as a rational exercise in calculating the costs and benefits of alternative courses of action or inaction. It is a choice process dominated by a concern for "static equilibriums" (continuities) where uncertainty and chance, as elements of indeterminacy, are considered to be aberrations and troublesome sources of distortion; they interfere with and diminish the predictive power of economics.

The study of rational choice may be misplaced, however, in terms of understanding the relationship between law and market theory. Nobel Prize-winning economist James Buchanan, for instance, argues that:

[t]he theory of choice must be removed from its position of eminence in the economist's thought processes. The theory of choice, of resource allocation, call it what you will, assumes no special role for the economist. . . . I want economist's to modify their thought processes to look at the same phenomena through "another window," to use Nietzsche's appropriate metaphor. I want them to concentrate on *exchange* rather than on *choice*.[42]

Buchanan's point is not generally appreciated in traditional approaches to law and economics. In traditional approaches law plays an instrumental role in facilitating a rational choice process and it is used to promote an amoral social calculus – amoral, that is, aside from its positivist commitment to advancing rational choice, efficiency, and wealth maximization. In other words, the borrowing of ideas from equilibrium models of economics has led traditional legal economists to follow a process of interpretive substitution that replaces normative

[42] *See* James M. Buchanan, *What should Economists Do?* 26 (1979); *see also id.*, 1–50.

concerns for creativity, fairness, and justice with the "positive" values of efficiency through rational choice.

Law and market economy, on the other hand, pays more attention to Buchanan's point and places eminence on the process of exchange and social organization rather than on the study of rational choice. Law and market economy examines an interactive process of discovery. This shift in focus establishes a new perspective from which to study the market exchange process. Instead of giving primary attention to points of equilibrium, it is concerned with the "spaces" between such points. In this paradigm, the market is a process of social exchange engaged in for the purpose of continually bringing about realignments in the value relationships, or *significances*, between individuals (together with the things that define them) and the communities in which they are positioned. The market, thus, serves as a semiotic system of significa-tion. It is a continually evolving *sign* that makes reference to a particular legal environment for its extensions of meaning.

The legal system is, in other words, a form of referential infrastructure for the extension of meaning and value in a process of social exchange.[43] The more advanced the legal system the greater its complexity and its potentiality for useful meaning and value formation. These extensions of meaning and value are of consequence because they have referential influence on the understandings and practices of human exchange. They have a dialogic impact on the way in which both the individual and the community are perceived and, consequently, upon how they are, in fact. Minor shifts in particular referential relationships can have dra-matic and substantive consequences for the way in which scarce resources and political authority are allocated. Differences in the ex-change process within the United States as compared to China reveal important distinctions with respect to social meanings and values. Furthermore, these distinctions are important not only for what they tell us about each society but also because the differences impact on the process of wealth formation.

Law and market economy involves a socially contextualized approach to market theory because it is grounded in the simple belief that markets involve exchange, and exchange implies interaction by and between people. It therefore centers attention on the social process of exchange rather than on the optimal or efficient exercise of purely rational choice. Exchange, in a market sense, does not take place on an isolated island of individual autonomy no matter how many choices a person must make under conditions of scarcity and uncertainty. Exchange only occurs

---

[43] *Id.*; Kevelson, "Rhetoric."

when there is a community of people involved, and law and market economy primarily concerns itself with the examination of the exchange process – with the study of the networks and patterns of exchange in society. As a consequence, law and market economy is about people interacting in and between interpretive communities – it is about individuals participating in reciprocal relationships, relationships that are not given and finite but which are continually evolving and trans-forming.

The idea of law and market economy as a place of meaning and value formation is a semiotic idea; a creation of the human imagination representing (referring to) the actual process of exchange in the real world.

Peirce insists that our ideas . . . in law must also be an evolving process which begins and concludes with reference to the experiential world, i.e. that world which we acknowledge as the basis for our ideas of the Real but which we can never know in entirety. The Real is always greater than our knowledge, our understanding. It is represented in sign-relations, and it is more approximate. In this respect every sign process must have as its object some aspect of a world which is not confined to ideational strata but which has a locative aspect, and is contingent upon something which exists.[44]

As a *sign system*, therefore, the market gives meaning and value to human action while making the exchange process comprehensible. As theoretical ideas market models, which we create for purposes of under-standing market theory, stand in referential relationship to that which they represent, namely the social/market exchange process of the real world. They give symbolic expression to the "real" that they are intended to describe. By this I mean that market models serve as ideational approximations of the real that we seek to understand. Through a continuous logic of investigation we put these models to the test and make revisions. By the nature of the limits to our human capacity, these models are always partial and incomplete, and this means there are "gaps" between what our models describe and the real world that we seek to comprehend. I refer to these gaps as constituting a "semiotic space," and it is this space that is important to the concept of creativity because this space represents potentiality in its relationship to habit and convention.

In a Peircean sense, our actual experience or emotive response to the real world of exchange is positioned as a mode of firstness. Our models and theories function as referential filters through which we attempt to make our experiences comprehensible, and in this role they are posi-tioned as a mode of secondness. Ultimately, our conclusions, responses,

[44] Kevelson, "Rhetoric," at 197.

and interpretations of our real-world experiences, as filtered through our referential guide posts, result in a Peircean mode of thirdness – that is, in a contingent, tentative, and fallible conclusion about the state of the real world in which we are situated. Stated differently, our ideas or models of the market are symbolic and representational. They are, in many ways, similar to a text and are, therefore, subject to interpretive influences and difficulties in the same manner as are other "texts." As representations of social/market exchange processes, market models as we know them, are signs projecting meanings and values with respect to exchange relationships in the real world to which they refer. Consequently, market theory, like all theory, stands in reference to, as an interpretive sign of, the real world but it is not, itself, real. "Ultimately we do not know this phenomenal world of which we are part. But we do know or are capable of knowing that which we construct as a means of knowing better and more fully the unknowable, ever changing circumstances of existence."[45] In this respect the market, as idea, stands as a referential mode of secondness. It helps us to interpret the real world that *is*, in all its evolving potentiality, which is positioned as a mode of firstness. The conclusions and meanings to be drawn from this relationship are, in the process of semiosis, a mode of thirdness.

As an illustration of this process consider a simple example. First, assume that we have collected basic data about the market for automobile sales. Our data indicates that product offerings are essentially the same across brands, prices for similar products by different manufactures are close to identical, and purchase or lease terms are virtually the same. This raw data makes up a Peircean mode of firstness – it is basic information about the nature of the thing or product itself. In the process of interpreting the data, so that we can draw a conclusion or response, we make a reference to an interpretive or indexical mediator that functions as a Peircean mode of secondness. The mediating point of interpretive reference is important because it shapes our economic and legal conclusion. For instance, if the data is reviewed through a "Chicago School" lens of neoclassical economics the conclusion may very well be that the data reveals the presence of a perfectly competitive market. In such a market no seller has the power to set terms but must, instead, take its terms from the marketplace, and as a consequence we would expect to find close similarity between product lines, prices, and sales terms. Such a competitive market makes the consumer the "king" or "queen" while the producer acts as servant. The conclusion, as to the meaning of the data, functions as a Peircean mode of thirdness and

---

[45] Kevelson, *Law*, at 269.

further informs our interpretation of the market as we use it to re-examine the data in light of our newly achieved understanding.

To understand this process better, imagine reviewing the data through an alternative frame of reference. From the point of view of some positions in critical theory, for example, one might conclude that the data reveals strong corporate power in a market where sellers band together to set terms of exchange in a way that leaves the consumer helpless. The signs of uniformity between products, prices, and terms, are interpreted as evidence of market power rather than as indications of market constraints. In other words rather than concluding that there is a competitive market, one might readily conclude just the opposite.

Interpretation of the data is important because our conclusions about the meaning of the exchange process will implicate particular responses. If we believe, for instance, the Chicago School interpretation we have no need for concern because we have a voluntary and consensual exchange process in which consumers are protected by competition. In such a setting, consumers receive exactly what they want. On the other hand, if we reach the opposite conclusion based upon the use of an alternative frame of reference, we may advocate a need for regulation to protect consumers and to break up the power of corporate dominance in the marketplace. Importantly, my point is that the facts themselves (the raw data) tell us little without the mediation of those facts through an interpretive frame of reference (a mode of secondness). The conclusions drawn from this mediation process function as a mode of thirdness and invoke a course of action or inaction. The point of this example is not to show the real world of exchange as unknowable or completely indeterminate. It is to illustrate that people positioned in alternative interpretive communities understand the world in different and sometimes conflicting ways. Therefore, we must be aware that the choice of mediating frame of reference influences the direction of law and social policy. Consequently, we must understand the role of interpretation method in law and market theory, and we must realize that alternative rhetorical strategies compete for authoritative influence over the interpretation process.

We can also gain an understanding of this semiotic process by making reference to a metaphor used by Adam Smith. Smith suggested that a market model is like the face of a clock and the nature of our investigation and inquiry is one of trying to imagine how it works – of imagining what mechanism lies hidden beneath the surface.[46] We can see the

---

[46] See Adam Smith, *The Theory of Moral Sentiments* 168 (E.G. West, ed., 1969). *See also* Adam Smith, *Essays on Philosphical Subjects* 33–105 (1980) (History of astronomy and our imagination).

exterior of the clock and recognize the social convention that substantiates the meaning of the position of the hands on its face. We do this in much the same way that we might understand a market model based on conventions concerning concepts of supply and demand. The clock, like our market model, is not, itself, the real to which it refers. The clock is not time but rather a comprehensible way of interpreting temporal relationships in the real world of our existence. The clock is a conventionalized designator of time. It is a mechanism for making time comprehensible and coherent and generally it makes implicit reference to other conventionalized markers of time such as days, weeks, months, seasons, and calendars, of which there are several in concurrent operation such as the Roman, Hebrew, and Chinese. The clock, in short, is an interpretation of time that has meaning to us but may have little or no meaning to people who do not share the same interpretive conventions. The position of the hands on a clock probably had little significance to native Americans when they encountered Europeans in the New World, for instance. This does not mean, however, that the idea of temporal reference is indeterminate; it merely means that the understanding of time may vary between interpretive communities. In this sense, the clock in Adam Smith's example and our theory of market exchange are significant because they both signify meanings that influence our behavior in the real world.

The market idea, as such, stands in a similar position to that of a clock and perhaps more aptly to that of a map and the territory, geopolitical space, to which the map makes reference. The map is useful and it is meaningful, but the map is not the territory.[47] The map is a representational text or sign and sometimes, depending upon scale, level of detail, and historical or environmental condition, the map may be misleading. It is also possible that such a map could be extremely accurate on all that it shows, but at the same time it may lack information that is relevant to a particular inquiry or investigation. Market theory is similar for it is merely a "map" or theoretical "text" of a human understanding of a complex social phenomenon. There are many influences and limitations to its construction and interpretation, but no matter how it is assembled it has consequence for all that use it.

Thinking about the interpretation and consequences of referring to particular maps of market exchange is the primary subject of law and market economy. It provides a way of understanding traditional law and economics while suggesting a method for enhancing our approach to law and market theory. It suggests that two mapping problems arise

---

[47] *See* S.I. Hayakawa and Alan R. Hayakawa, *Language in Thought and Action* 13–21 (5th ed., 1990).

from use of the static equilibrium approach of traditional law and economics. First, such a map presents a focusing problem in that it concerns itself with economics as a science of choice rather than with market theory as a process of dynamic relational exchange. Second, it presents a problem of scope because it fails to provide a theory of creative discovery. In recognizing these two shortcomings, law and market economy attempts to provide a better map of market theory with the hope of enhancing our overall understanding of law and market exchange.

Thinking of the market as a kind of map, or "textualized" idea, allows us more readily to appreciate its partiality – its incompleteness – and, therefore, the potential for divergence between the representational image of the market and the real dynamical world to which it refers. There is, in other words, a distance or "semiotic space" between the representational image of the market, the maps that we use, and the real dynamical world of social exchange. This space, or incongruence, represents the distance between social convention (habit and continuity), as expressed through the market sign or text, and the inherent indeterminacy of creative human interaction within an open-ended universe. It represents the distance between knowledge discovered, and knowledge of which we are currently ignorant.[48]

This distance or semiotic space provides an opportunity for social progress and wealth creation. It represents creative potential. To uncover or to discover elements of this space, however, one must be able to break through an artificially imposed barrier of social convention – to perceive the possibility of creating something new. One must be able to "go against the grain" and "think outside and through the box," so to speak, to challenge assumptional grounds that have become so conventionalized that they are accepted without question – without even being consciously visible. In this context, choice is a socially exercised interpretive expression of imaginative inquiry with the potentiality for creating new values, new meanings, new referential relationships, and new significations. *Imaginative choice*, in addition to rational choice, is essential to the creative process and the creative process is fundamental to the generation of wealth and the transformation of society.

By using semiotic theory to enhance our comprehension of the market we can bring to light the important role of values in the social exchange process. First, we can understand that the market itself is

---

[48] *See* Kirzner, *Meaning*, at 38–54. *See also* Kevelson, *Peirce and Freedom*, at 60–61; Friedrich A. Hayek, "The Use of Knowledge in Society," 35 Am. Econ. Rev. 519 (1945); Friedrich A. Hayek, "The Pretense of Knowledge," 79 Am. Econ. Rev. 3 (Nobel Memorial Lecture on December 11, 1974).

value laden. As a human idea, text, or map, it is subjectively constructed and given form, meaning, and consequence in relation to a particular set of values or ethical understandings. Second, some environments will be more conducive than others to the process of imaginative choice and creative discovery. Favorable environments will incubate a greater opportunity for wealth creation as a result of encouraging unconventional and imaginative actions that can lead to the uncovering of elements of the semiotic space between current conventionalized forms of knowledge, and that of extended human potentiality. In particular, the process of imaginative choice and creative discovery is influenced and nurtured by an environment of inclusion, diversity, experimentation, and investigation. It is an environment made possible by an ethic of social responsibility based on three general principles that I tentatively refer to as humility, diversity, and reciprocity. This favorable ethic of social responsibility is important and can be linked to the formation of wealth and social prosperity at both a macro level (national economies), and at a micro level (individual firms). Evidence in support of this linkage will be presented in Chapter 5. Consequently, a useful theory or map of market economy should include a basis for understanding the dynamic and ethical elements of the social/market exchange process. This means that we need to pay close attention to the way in which people interact and to how particular social arrangements might either favor or discourage creativity, discovery, and invention. As a practical matter, favorable environmental conditions may or may not be efficient. Democracy, for instance, is seldom considered to be efficient yet its participatory nature generally tends to facilitate more convention-breaking relationships and more extensive networks and patterns of exchange, all of which are important for creativity and the process of sustainable wealth formation. It is interesting to note, for example, that the United States, Canada, the countries of Western Europe, Japan, and Australia are among the richest countries in the world, and yet each employs a democratic form of political organization that might be thought of as inefficient. The key is, however, that these seemingly inefficient forms of political organization facilitate creativity by enhancing diverse participation in an extensive social/market exchange process.

In traditional law and economics, creativity is difficult to comprehend. The use of an equilibrium and wealth-maximization approach tends to promote communities of self-interested, cost and benefit calculating individuals. In such a society each individual is disconnected from every other and from a sense of a common good. It is a model of a society that promotes *things* as substitutes for the people and values that these things

represent. Actual values, in other words, are conflated into the interpretations or representations of these values. Price becomes a statement
of actual value rather than a contingent and contextualized interpretation of value, and the failure to distinguish these modes of logic results
in a limitation on our ability to appreciate the nature and possibility of
change.

An interpretive approach to law and market theory allows us to see
that wealth, in the method of traditional law and economics, is expressed
as the accumulation of "things" in quantifiable form. Wealth, as such,
must be systematically "unitized" for easy measure across all possible
goods and relationships. This is accomplished by use of a semiotic *token*
or *icon*.[49] The token, in this case, is generally a money or currency sign
which stands in for or represents that "thing" or "idea" that is said to be
measured by its image. In this way, all elements of social experience,
including personal relationships, the natural environment, and human
emotion, are translated into measurable and objectified units. In this
system of quantifiable substitution, those ideas and values that cannot
be readily monetized cannot be valued, and as a consequence they end
up as invisible and valueless in the exchange process.

The process of substitution, through quantification, results in the
reshaping and reprioritizing of social value and meaning because it
prioritizes the physically quantifiable over the imaginative, esthetic, and
intangible aspects of human existence. Through the use of monetary
tokens, all of human experience is made theoretically capable of mea-
surement and comparison, and money becomes the most important
signifier of individual and social value. As Schumacher cautions us:

In the marketplace, for practical reasons, innumerable qualitative distinctions
which are of vital importance for man and society are suppressed; they are not
allowed to surface . . . [In the market] everything is equated with everything
else. To equate things means to give them a price and then to make them
exchangeable . . . To press non-economic value into the framework of the
economic calculus, economists use the method of cost/benefit analysis . . . [I]t is
a procedure by which the higher is reduced to the level of the lower and the
priceless is given a price. It can therefore never serve to clarify the situation and
lead to an enlightened decision. All it can do is lead to self-deception or the
deception of others; for to undertake to measure the immeasurable is absurd
and constitutes but an elaborate method of moving from preconceived notions
to foregone conclusions; all one has to do to obtain the desired results is to
impute suitable values to the immeasurable costs and benefits. The logical
absurdity, however, is not the greatest fault of the undertaking: what is worse,

---

[49] Kevelson, *Peirce's Method*, at 13–15. A *token* is a mode of secondness. Noth, *Semiotics*,
at 44–45. *See also* Liszka, *Introduction to Peirce*, at 37–38; Hookway, *Peirce*, at 125–139;
Kevelson, "Rhetoric," at 193–194; Sheriff, *Peirce*, at 31–47; *Peirce – Writings* (Buchler,
ed.), at 98–119.

and destructive of civilization, is the pretense that everything has a price or, in other words, that money is the highest of all values.[50]

Such an approach fails, at one and the same time, to represent properly the real world to which it refers and to appreciate the dynamic and creative nature of wealth formation.

In contrast to the traditionalist view, the law and market economy approach presents a different understanding of society and of the measure of wealth and prosperity. Law and market economy seeks not to measure all social relationships in terms of monetary calculation but rather to understand the meanings and consequences of competing approaches to the networks and patterns of exchange. Law and market economy, as an interpretive approach, positions the individual as an ethical being connected to a community in which it is understood that positive social and economic progress depend upon cooperation and on the restraint of self-interest.[51] Meaning, as such, emerges from exchange that takes place within community.

This view focuses on wealth as a human activity or process and not simply as a quantifiable calculation. In this system, wealth is related to the process of discovery, of creativity, of imaginative choice and potentiality. Wealth is interpreted as emerging from human practices that lead to breaking through the semiotic spaces of conventionalized market thinking. Wealth comes from imagining a world that is round when the norm, the rationalized logic of the day, insists that it is flat. Consequently, in the approach of law and market economy, quantifiable wealth, the wealth of "things," becomes *symbolic*[52] and *indexical*.[53] Such a measure of wealth is symbolic because it reflects the product of social convention concerning that which we are taught to value, and it is

[50] *See* E.F. Schumacher, *Small is Beautiful: Economics as if People Mattered* 45–46 (1973).

[51] *See, e.g.*, Lawrence E. Mitchell, "Corporate Nature Versus Human Nature?" in *Law and Economics* (Malloy and Braun, eds.), at 361–386 (discussing the need for cooperative activity within the firm in order to enhance wealth); Amartya Sen, *On Ethics and Economics* (1987); Amitai Etzioni, *The Moral Dimension: Toward a New Economics* (1988); Francis Fukuyama, *Trust: The Social Virtues and the Creation of Prosperity* (1995); *Adam Smith* (Malloy and Evensky, eds.) (generally highlighting the ethical and cooperative aspects of Adam Smith's understanding of market relations).

[52] Symbol is a mode of thirdness. Noth, *Semiotics*, at 45. Liszka, *Introduction to Peirce*, at 39. *See also*, Hookway, *Peirce*, at 125–139 (further examples); Sheriff, *Peirce*, at 31–47; *Peirce – Writings* (Buchler, ed.), at 98–119.

[53] An index is a mode of secondness and performs a referencing function. Noth, *Semiotics*, at 44–45. Whereas a sign is an icon if it represents its object, a sign is an index if it indicates contiguity with its object. Liszka, *Introduction to Peirce*, at 38–9. Contiguity can be of three different sorts: (1) *deictic* (referential); (2) *causal* (existential); (3) *labeling*. *Id. See also*, Sheriff, *Peirce*, at 31–47; Hookway, *Peirce*, at 125–139; *Peirce – Writings* (Buchler, ed.), at 98–119.

indexical because it points to a measure of success grounded in a socially designated token form.

In other words physical or token measures of wealth are merely observable social "markers" that point to, or reference, an underlying set of social conventions and practices. They are like the faces on the clock in Adam Smith's metaphor. Traditional measures of wealth and wealth maximization result, therefore, in meanings and values that are merely crude and inaccurate proxies for measuring social prosperity because they are inherently linked to established codes of continuity, habit, and convention. They focus on and perpetuate the status quo. Their use results in too much attention being focused on quantifiable representations of prosperity within a given, reactive, universe of possibility. In contrast, law and market economy focuses attention on the process of exchange and the social conventions and practices that give rise to evolving values and referential relationships. This means that law and market economy focuses not so much on the accumulation of things, but on the conditions and circumstances that nurture human creativity in a prospective and open-ended universe of potentiality. Wealth comes not only from what is, but also from what could be.

In interpreting the traditional approach to law and economics, law is seemingly supposed to facilitate an efficient system of resource allocation for the purpose of maximizing wealth, in its tokenized form(s). This means that law should assist people in arranging their relationships by encouraging them to select the highest monetized option, or course of action, from the available choice alternatives. I refer to this approach as the quest for *reactive wealth maximization* because it seeks to maximize the value of relationships within a conventionalized framework of choice opportunities. It gives primacy to habit, convention, and determinate calculations of efficient outcomes.

In contrast to this view, law and market economy envisions sustainable wealth formation as emerging from the discovery of incongruence between the *representational appearance* of the market process as a conventionalized market model, and the real process of social exchange to which it refers. For this to occur, there must be a willingness and an ability to make an imaginative choice to challenge the status quo, to reinterpret the accepted norm and convention. Law and market economy must, therefore, address itself to *proactive wealth maximization* designed to maximize the potentiality for new value relationships within an indeterminate and dynamic framework where the subject/object of markets is constantly in flux. Both perspectives are important to a meaningful theory of wealth formation and social prosperity. Thus, we should attend to the proper study of both. To our current work in traditional law and economics we must add further considerations. In particular, we must begin to understand the market as a place of meaning and value formation, and we must appreciate the need for a general ethic of social responsibility promoting accessibility, diversity, reciprocity, and extensive resource distribution as fundamental to the concept of creativity. Creativity is indeterminate and convention breaking. It resides in the semiotic space beyond our traditional, conventionalized equilibrium models of economic analysis. Facilitating creativity, therefore, requires us to think beyond efficiency analysis and suggest that ethical norms and values beyond the efficiency criterion are wealth justified and wealth enhancing.

Within a semiotic understanding of the social exchange process, we can appreciate the idea that there are, indeed, alternative ways of structuring the value foundations of social convention. These alternative structures, serving as interpretive frames of reference, can be observed in competing approaches to legal and economic theory. Because semiotics understands the market as an exchange system, alternative legal and economic theories can be dealt with as competing propositional claims to the role of mediator in the process of interpretation.

Put differently, if the marketplace is understandable as a semiotic sign system or text it is subject to several possible readings depending upon one's position within any given interpretive community. It is not that the market has no objective characteristics or that the market has any subjective characteristics one may choose to identify. The market is simply understandable as a relational sign system in which signs represent an object or idea in some respects but not in all respects. People positioned in alternative interpretive communities have different experiences that ground their frame of reference and these references filter the understanding of the market exchange process. Even though we are all engaged in the exchange process and we are all working to understand it, we have conflicts based on disagreements related to facts and to values.

These disagreements need to be understood as such, and law and market economy offers a method of mediating between competing interpretive communities. It does this by first recognizing that the market exchange process is actually a community composition arranged by the continuously transforming networks and patterns of interaction between participants. In this context, alternative legal theories position themselves as interpretive frames of reference for describing the market exchange process. Their competing rhetorical strategies offer conflicting assumptions designed to influence and constrain individual market interpretation, but all of these strategies can be understood as attempts to assert authoritative influence over the allocation of scarce resources and the exercise of political authority. Law and market economy, by reference to traditional law and economic assumptions, makes it possible to mediate between these strategies.

Competing approaches to the relationship between law and market theory, therefore, are understandable as secondary sign systems that operate as competing rhetorical strategies for influencing the understanding of market economy.[54] They compete within the market framework for influence over the continuous mapping and remapping of social meaning and value. This means that they compete for control of the networks and patterns of exchange and of the process by which new ideas are evaluated or borrowed. They compete for influence over the process of moving from the predictive function of positive economics to the *ground*-shaping function of law and public policy prescription. They function, therefore, as interpretive lenses into the market process and each alternative theory positions itself as significant because of its ability to influence the real world by influencing the interpretive process of substantive choice and decision making. Consequently, law and market economy must be concerned to some degree with the process of sign making – with seeking to understand the implications of a variety of legal theories including critical, gender, and race-based theories, as these are interpretive theories that it must mediate.

In comparison to traditional law and economics, therefore, law and market economy presents a different form of inquiry. Rather than focusing on the problem of efficiency and economic calculation it directs attention to the networks and patterns of exchange. Examination of what is exchanged, with whom, and on what terms is considered vitally important to understanding the communities where people live and work. Likewise, it is important to know who engages in particular types of transactions and who is excluded. Consideration is given to matters of market accessibility, distributional inequality, and entrepreneurial opportunity as affected by such variables as race, gender, age, education, income, geographic location, ethnicity, and culture. All of this is important to examining the nature of the market exchange process and for understanding the meaning of market economy. A market economy involves decentralized exchange but the extent of authoritative participation in the exchange process may vary between communities and across alternative frameworks. Exploring the consequences of these differences rather than their efficiency is the key to understanding the concerns of law and market economy.

[54] *See generally* Kevelson, "Rhetoric"; Kevelson, *Peirce and Science*, at 63–80.

To illustrate the difference in focus between law and economics, and law and market economy consider an example from the field of real-estate transactions. In particular consider the borrower and lender relationship as it has been influenced by the emergence of a secondary market for mortgage investments.[55] Prior to the 1980s the federal government closely regulated the residential home mortgage market in the United States. The regulation was designed to stabilize the relationship between a lender's cost of funds (what the lender paid to investors to attract deposits) and its profit on lending activities (making mortgage loans and earning interest on the debt). The goal was to manage market outcomes so that mortgage lending would be profitable while simultaneously remaining accessible and affordable.

The primary lending institutions in this market were governed by regulations that established the terms upon which they lent mortgage money and by rules setting the interest rate they could pay to depositors. Local household savers provided the major source of lender deposits and were the primary beneficiaries of residential mortgage-lending activities. This arrangement favored a pattern of exchange between households and lenders that resembled the situation at the Bailey Building and Loan as depicted in Frank Capra's movie classic, *It's a Wonderful Life*.[56] Local lending associations dominated the residential mortgage market, collecting deposits from local residents and lending those funds to local homebuyers. These lenders held the mortgage loans they originated as long-term investments, earning a return from interest on monthly mortgage payments. The loan officers were likely to know their customers and since pricing was generally uniform as a result of regulation, competition between lenders focused on providing personal service and attention to the needs of individual customers and to the local community.

In the late 1970s and early 1980s the story of residential mortgage lending began to change. New investment opportunities emerged to attract the attention of savers. Such new ideas included the Dreyfus Liquid Assets Account as one of the first popular consumer money-market accounts. It appealed to household savers because it was generally considered to be low risk, required small deposits, was accessible like a checking account, and paid interest at a rate of four to five times the government-regulated rate for similar bank passbook deposit accounts. This was possible because high rates of inflation at the time

---

[55] *See* Robin Paul Malloy and James C. Smith, *Real Estate Transactions* 703–784 (1998).
[56] *See* Frank Capra, *It's a Wonderful Life* (1946); Jeanine Basinger, *The "It's a Wonderful Life" Book* (1986).

had driven up market interest rates. Federal regulations, however, continued to keep payment rates artificially low on regular saving deposits. Similarly, the market rate for home mortgages was rising rapidly to reflect inflationary pressures, yet the government kept rates low in an effort to maintain the traditional balance established in the earlier time period. This attempt to regulate a continuation of the status quo relationship proved to be unmanageable. Billions of dollars were rapidly withdrawn from the government-supported lending institutions. The money ended up in money-market accounts paying high returns but investing those funds in capital markets other than real estate. Thus, household savings were now funding capital markets and not being made available for local residential home mortgages. Local lending institutions were low on affordable funds for home mortgage lending and home mortgages became both expensive and scarce.

Eventually, the government recognized the need to respond to a dynamic and changing marketplace. Regulations were revised in the early 1980s to provide more autonomy to lenders in structuring their deposit accounts and mortgage offerings. Adjustable and floating-rate instruments were introduced and a variety of mortgage forms emerged to shift market risk from lenders to borrowers. At the same time the government also moved quickly to take advantage of new developments in an emerging secondary market for residential mortgages. This market involved the development of a complex set of legal relationships permitting lending institutions to originate and then sell residential mortgages to third-party investors. The investors could either purchase the mortgages directly or purchase stocks and bonds issued against the cash flow represented by numerous underlying home mortgages. In a relatively short time period this secondary mortgage market went from zero to billions of dollars of transactional activity.

The transition in residential mortgage markets briefly described above can be considered from a number of points of view. Using the approach of traditional law and economics one is likely to look at these events and analyze them in terms of efficiency. This would involve doing a positive analysis and comparison between the pre-secondary mortgage market situation (time period one) and the post-secondary mortgage market situation (time period two). It would involve a cost and benefit analysis of regulation and consider such things as alternative investment opportunities. Attention would also be given to the advantages of enhanced diversity and liquidity for primary mortgage market lenders as a result of secondary mortgage market activities. These are important factors to consider when looking at the market changes in question. Being able to buy and sell mortgages through this market meant that local lenders could have ready access to non-local money and that they could exchange local mortgages for ones from other parts of the country. This added liquidity and allowed for diversification so as to reduce the impact of swings in the local economy. Furthermore, the secondary mortgage market resulted in an expansion of the "pie" of money available for residential home mortgages because the issuance of mortgage-backed securities brought new investors into the real-estate related marketplace. Many pension funds and institutional investors, for example, were unable or uninterested in investing in mortgages per se, but were interested in buying the new securities being issued against such mortgages. Thus, an influx of additional funds expanded the money supply available for residential housing and worked to the advantage of home-buyers.

A law and market economy approach considers all of the above economic factors as important, but it goes beyond this to focus attention on other aspects of these developments. The law and market economist examines the meaning and consequences of such changes. A law and market economy approach seeks to understand these changes in terms of human practices. For example, attention is given to under-standing how secondary mortgage markets change the basic networks and patterns of exchange between different actors in the industry. Upon examination it becomes clear that changes have been significant in ways that would not generally be captured in terms of an efficiency analysis. First and foremost, residential real-estate activities have been rendered far less local in nature and character, and the relationship between the lender and customer has shifted to a new frame of reference. Lenders now typically sell the majority of loans that they originate rather than holding them as long-term investments. While this allows them to diversify and enhances their liquidity it also changes the nature of their business. Now they make a great deal of money from the fees associated with churning paper and processing loan originations rather than from establishing long-term relationships with local mort-gage customers. The lender's attention is directed toward a new set of customers – not homebuyers, but secondary mortgage market investors. Rather than concentrating on providing service and meeting the needs of local depositors or borrowers, lenders must now compete for profit-ability by responding to the demands of distant investors and institu-tions operating through the secondary mortgage market. In essence, George Bailey has been transformed into the self-interested and greedy Mr. Potter as he must pursue competitive pricing and cost structures that respond to impersonal and distant investor demands. The demands of such investors reflect a variety of considerations particularly with respect to global economic and monetary market trends. These investors are not, however, interested in the problems of local home-buyers. They are interested in profitable yields on investments and to that end they are indifferent as to the underlying activity supported by the investment.

Another consequence of this economically influential mortgage market is that concerns for efficiency and profit maximization may actually increase the incidence of racial discrimination in the market for access to home mortgages. This is evidenced in studies done with respect to differences in the success rate of mortgage applications when compared by race. For example, a study by the Federal Institutional Examination Council released on August 4, 1997 relied on data collected during 1996 to show that Asians enjoyed the highest rate of success in pursuing residential mortgage financing. Relative to the credit denial rate for Asians, whites were denied at almost twice the rate, Hispanics at about three times the rate, and blacks and Native Americans at about four times the rate.

This type of disparity has also been shown in other studies. Additional insight on this problem comes from a 1992 Report prepared by the Federal Reserve Bank of Boston and titled, *Mortgage Lending in Boston: Interpreting HMDA Data* (the "Boston Study"). This report found that loan approval rates between blacks and whites were virtually the same when both applicants had "clean" files, or virtually perfect credit histories. The Boston Study found a major divergence, however, when a file indicated a potential credit problem. Such a problem might relate to information on a credit report concerning a landlord and tenant dispute, or an assertion of an outstanding debt or fine. Typically, many of these problems can be cleared up without extensive effort if the loan officer pursues a telephone call or two, or does a little extra paperwork.

One way of understanding the difference in mortgage loan approval rates for black and white applicants with credit problems is that the loan officers use race as a proxy for deciding the amount of effort to put into preparing a file for ultimate loan approval. Since the loan officer generally works on a commission basis she has an efficiency and profit motive for processing as many successful application files as possible. Sending a file to the loan review board scores no points for the loan officer if it is rejected. Consequently, the pressure and incentive to produce may result in loan officers using race as a proxy for deciding about how much effort to put into preparing a file with credit history problems. The officers may be more willing to invest the time on white applicants rather than blacks because of a perception of an increased likelihood of ultimate loan approval. Because the secondary mortgage market promotes churning paper and because incentives are based on impersonal and volume-based loan processing, there is a perceived economic benefit to using race as a proxy for establishing how to allocate one's time in the loan origination process. This seems to work to the disadvantage of African-American loan applicants.

The same incentive structure causes some lenders and loan officers to reject applications for "small" mortgage loans. Low-cost housing is not as profitable to lenders that focus on churning paper because fees are generally based on the loan amount. Thus, small loans generate much less fee income, yet they cost just as much in terms of administrative time and overhead. Shying away from small loans and low-cost housing means that low-income borrowers are less likely to get service. Again, since income and race are correlated in the United States, race becomes a factor in successfully obtaining a home mortgage.

While more can be said about the secondary mortgage market, the important point for now is to see a difference in the focus of inquiry as between traditional law and economics, and law and market economy. Traditional law and economics examines the "facts" of a changing marketplace through an interpretive frame of reference grounded in positive economics. This promotes conclusions centered on measures of enhanced efficiency as between designated time periods in given market settings. It tells us little, however, about implications for values beyond efficiency, and it tells us nothing about the transformation process as a human experience.

Law and market economy, in contrast, tries to go beyond the traditional approach by referencing a broader set of factors as relevant to an understanding of market theory. Law and market economy seeks to understand the meaning and value-formation process as implicated by changing networks and patterns of exchange. In the secondary mortgage market, for instance, this approach directs attention to the changing nature of the relationship between lenders, depositors, and homebuyers. The "facts" defining the basic market activities are not so much in question as the value transformations represented by such facts. The emergence of a multi-billion to trillion dollar market in mortgages fuels a substantial realignment in the networks and patterns of exchange. Personal and local relationships are exchanged for impersonal and distant monetary contacts. Lenders redefine their customers and transform their work environments and product lines to reflect the interests of newly discovered and financially important secondary mortgage market investors. Relationships with local depositors and borrowers become less important to the lender's financial survival and the locals become less loyal to the lending institutions. Rather than seeing their relationship as an important network for connecting the lender and themselves, local depositors and borrowers come to view lenders as impersonal institutions bent on reducing services and cutting costs. The earlier relationships built on a complex set of human connections, like those depicted in *It's a Wonderful Life*, are replaced with much narrower relationships based on viewing others as mere means to a monetary end. In this way, multidimensional human experiences are reduced to one-dimensional relationships based on the pursuit of self-interested financial gain.

Looking only at the positive economic elements of this process, or giving primacy to an efficiency analysis of this process, prevents us from seeing the broader implications of the social/market exchange process. It restricts our ability to see how market changes influence social and cultural relationships, and it obscures the potential problems of increased racial disparity in accessing mortgage markets. This situation is particularly troublesome not only because racial discrimination is morally undesirable, but also because exclusion or restrictive access to these important financial networks unnecessarily reduces meaningful participation in social exchange. This in turn reduces the opportunity for extensive exchange networks and, as will be explained in later Chapters, has a negative implication for creativity and the process of sustainable wealth formation. Consequently, the traditional approach of law and economics simultaneously limits our ability to understand the transformation process and to imagine an alternative to it. Law and market economy, on the other hand, uses Peirce's notion of relational exchange to speculate about the market as a place of meaning and value formation. It directs inquiry to a number of factors beyond efficiency and presents a broader vision of market theory.

This, then, is a general overview of the more detailed argument that follows. In the succeeding pages I provide sufficient explanation for my approach. While some of my ideas may seem new to a legal economist, much of what I say is consistent with predicates found in earlier work in market theory. I will, for example, provide discussion on the relationship between my approach, using semiotic method, and a number of general themes expressed in the foundational work of Adam Smith. By way of textual and note references, I will also indicate connections between my approach and that of such people as Israel Kirzner and others. I shall also suggest, in my discussion of an ethic of social responsibility, and in my section on implications, some ways in which this approach might be used or implemented to enhance the legal economic analysis of pressing social problems. I know that some readers will demand more of an explanation, for this is always the case when presenting a new idea. I trust, however, that the interested reader will find sufficient material here for speculative inquiry concerning this new way of thinking about the relationship between law and market theory.

3   Law and market economy: further clarification

In order better to understand my approach to law and market economy I will clarify what I mean when I speak of markets and of the exchange process. In this section of the book, therefore, I will discuss the market as a place of meaning and value formation. I will proceed with two major lines of discussion. The first involves the idea that markets, as places of meaning and value formation, are inherently about communities in which individuals act by pursuing a notion of socially informed self-interest. The second involves an elaboration on the idea of the market as a process of semiotic signification facilitated by an infrastructure of law.

Market as community

Markets involve relational exchanges and, as such, they implicitly address the notion of community. The focus of market economy is, therefore, on the nature and consequences of the exchange process rather than on the allocative choice calculations of isolated individuals acting under conditions of scarcity and uncertainty. To understand this distinction better I will refer to an example that is similar to one used by James Buchanan.[1]

Consider the situation of a woman, Gina, isolated and alone on an island in the middle of a vast ocean. In her daily struggle for survival she must make numerous decisions. She must take action and make choices between alternative ways in which to use her time and energy. Should she collect fruit, gather firewood, or secure the day's supply of water? Should she rest, swim, or construct a shelter? These are all allocative choices that require her to make decisions. Traditional law and economics focuses its attention on the way in which she will make her choices within this framework. Assuming that she acts rationally, with good information, and in her own self-interest, traditional law and

---

[1] Compare James M. Buchanan, *What should Economists Do?*, 27–30 (1979).

economics would say that she will make a wealth-maximizing decision based on her best cost and benefit analysis of the trade-offs that confront her. While this type of analysis of her decision-making behavior may be important for some purposes within a given context, this focus of inquiry is not the central subject of law and market economy. A market, as a place of meaning and value formation, only emerges when someone else shows up on the island and begins to interact with Gina. In the absence of another party to interact with, Gina is not engaging in the market exchange process. She is making decisions, exercising choice, but the values and meanings that shape her selection process are all self-defined. In other words, things have value simply because Gina values them. Gina's values are formed individually, meaning that the symbolic, indexical, and iconic notions of wealth are all monologically informed and disconnected from the interactive process of social substitution and exchange.

This idea of an autonomous individual engaged in a science of choice is the focal point of traditional law and economics but it is not the central theme in market theory. Market theory examines the exchange process and positions the individual within a community. Market theory involves the relationship between individuals and their communities. Market theory involves relational choice based on the relationship between the individual and her point(s) of community reference. As Kevelson explains it:

although Freedom is the key term, or value, from which semiotic method derives its basic principles, Peirce is not concerned with the notion of "free individuals" but rather with freedom of individuals in community. The Peircean method of methods is an overt rejection of [C]artesian principles of inquiry, and therefore it rejects implicitly the notion of the individual as a referential model, or sign. It supports, instead, the kind of model which represents communal or dialogic inquiry. Its initial structure sets out a relational scheme between inquisitor and respondent (who, in turn, poses the question).[2]

Extending our example, let us assume that Gina is joined on the island by Giovanni, a man whose sailboat beached on the shores of the island after being blown off course by a storm. Gina and Giovanni are brought together as a community on this small and otherwise deserted island. There are still numerous decisions to be made concerning what to do each day and about when and how to do it. Now there is even the task of determining who should do these assorted things. In this context, it is the process of interaction and exchange between Gina and Giovanni

---

[2] Roberta Kevelson, *Peirce's Method of Methods* 11 (1987). *See also* Roberta Kevelson, *Peirce, Science, Signs* 1, 60, 88–90 (1996); Roberta Kevelson, *Peirce's Esthetics of Freedom: Possibility, Complexity, and Emergent Value* 140 (1993); Roberta Kevelson, *The Law as a System of Signs* 147, 208 (1988).

that is important to the understanding of law and market economy/
market theory.

With the introduction of Giovanni we have a market, an exchange
network, and now the question is not merely one of analyzing the
isolated and rational allocative choices of each individual actor, it is a
question of looking at their interactive dynamic. Now, the meaning of
value and of wealth are determined by a process of interaction.[3] The
exchange process itself influences and creates opportunities for understandings of wealth and of value that are not simply self-defined by each
individual actor. Some things on the island may, for instance, become
valuable to Gina only because Giovanni seems to value them. Giovanni
may introduce Gina to new ideas, new ways of thinking about the use of
resources, and as a result Gina may now have more choices revealed to
her as well as different orderings as to her own decisional preferences.
Similarly, Gina may well have this same effect on Giovanni.

Of central importance to law and market economy is the emergence
of a pattern of exchange between Gina and Giovanni – the way in which
they exchange and the positions they take in the exchange process. Both
are important to understanding the meanings and values of the market
process. Influencing the networks and patterns of their exchange can
also result in reshaping their choice interpretations and, consequently,
their course of action. They are part of a dialogic process of give and
take. Their decisions are relational and not isolated and atomistic.

The traditional legal economist, in contrast, may well see little
consequence from the introduction of Giovanni to our island example.
In fact, the traditionalist may well take the position that introducing
Giovanni to the island does nothing to change either individual's
decision-making behavior. All that happens is that the cost and benefit
calculations become more complex because of a variety of new variables
to be considered with the introduction of a second individual. None the
less, one can still assume that each individual acts rationally and in her
or his own self-interest to achieve a wealth-maximizing outcome. Consequently, the introduction of Giovanni does little, if anything, to change
the theoretical framework of law and economic analysis. Such a conclusion makes sense within the traditional law and economics approach.
This is because it assumes an isolated and atomized individual – in this
case, Gina – as the central semiotic sign of its discourse strategy. This
means that it positions the individual at center stage participating in a
drama in which the very act of participation fails to change the individual. Law and market economy, in contrast, reclaims the individual

[3] See Kevelson, *Peirce and Science*, at 18–21, 88; Kevelson, *Law*, at 147, 208; John K.
Sheriff, *Peirce's Guess at the Riddle: Grounds for Human Significance* (1994).

from her methodological isolation and places her back within the drama, as an integrated and relational part of the whole. This is important because the process of exchange itself affects the meanings and values of the participants. The exchange process is one of relational substitution and is an experience in which the individuals simultaneously leave their imprint on, and are imprinted by, the drama in which they participate.

The upshot is that there is no pure, absolutely autonomous "I" or self. No sign – or self – is an island, an entity unto itself and absolutely autonomous. We, all signs, are thoroughly socialized. The "I" addresses itself to its otherness, its social other as well as the other of physical "reality," both of which are "out there" in contrast to the self's own "inner" other. Part of that social otherness is that which is emerging and that into which the "I" is merging: the "I" is incessantly flowing into the otherness of which it is a *part of* and at the same time *apart from*. For, to repeat Peirce's words, "a person is not absolutely an individual," and at the same time, a person's "circle of society" is a sort of loosely compacted person.[4]

Value and meaning are, therefore, continually realigned as a result of both exogenous and endogenous forces. They are continually repositioned as a consequence of semiosis. This means that my understanding of the exchange process is different from that of Buchanan. While we both agree that the exchange process is the key to understanding market theory, I understand exchange as a diologic process, and such an understanding undercuts the primacy that Buchanan gives to methodological individualism.[5]

Even without invoking semiotic interpretation theory, however, one can still readily question the idea of methodological individualism in traditional law and economics. Ken Dau-Schmidt's work on preference shaping in economics provides another way of getting at some of the same basic problems.[6] He shows that once we look more closely at the way in which preferences are shaped it becomes increasingly difficult to

---

[4] Floyd Merrell, *Peirce, Signs, and Meaning* 61 (1997).

[5] My view is influenced by Peirce and rejects Buchanan's position. *See Philosophical Writings of Peirce* xiv (Justus Buchler, ed., 1955) (Peirce rejected methodological individualism).

[6] *See, e.g.*, Kenneth G. Dau-Schmidt, "Relaxing Traditional Economic Assumptions and Values: Toward a New Multidisciplinary Discourse on Law," 42 Syracuse L. Rev. 181 (1991); Kenneth G. Dau-Schmidt, "Legal Prohibitions as More Than Prices: The Economic Analysis of Preference shaping Policies in the Law" in *Law and Economics: New and Critical Perspectives* (Robin Paul Malloy and Christopher K. Braun, eds., 1995) at 152–180; Kenneth G. Dau-Schmidt, "Economics and Sociology: The Prospects for an Interdisciplinary Discourse on Law," Wisc. L. Rev. 389 (1997); Kenneth G. Dau-Schmidt, "An Economic Analysis of the Criminal Law as a Preference-Shaping Policy," Duke L. J. 1 (1990).

maintain assumptional barriers to the influences of endogenous as well as exogenous forces in exchange.

The problem with methodological individualism, therefore, is that it artificially abstracts exchange from the community reference points that make it understandable – capable of interpretation. Community-based referencing is of evident importance, for instance, in tort, contract, and property law. In tort law, for example, we think not only in terms of injury or loss to an individual involved in an accident, we also think of the pain, suffering, and loss to those closely connected to the victim or the event. We judge the degree of one's negligence not by an isolated review of conduct, but with reference to a community standard and expectation of care. Likewise, in contract law we interpret the terms of an agreement with reference to industry standards, course of dealing, and reasonable commercial expectations. In a similar way, we know that a piece of real estate is not priced or valued by an isolated consideration of its own intrinsic qualities but with reference to the qualities of other surrounding properties and uses. The value of any given property can be affected by its location – near a peaceful ocean beach or next to a toxic waste dump, in a high crime area or in a quiet suburban neighborhood.

Chief Judge Breitel explained this concept in connection to real estate, but his comments have relevance to exchange in general. He said in the case of *Fred F. French Investing Co. v. City of New York*:

It is recognized that the "value" of property is not a concrete or tangible attribute but an abstraction derived from the economic uses to which the property may be put . . . It would be . . . simplistic to ignore modern recognition of the principle that no property has value except as the community contributes to that value. The obverse of this principle is . . . no property is an economic island, free from contributing to the welfare of the whole of which it is but a dependent part.[7]

In studying the relationship between law and market theory we should, therefore, focus on the implications and consequences of *relational exchange*. It is insufficient to think exclusively or even primarily in terms of an imaginary individual exercising rational and scientific decision making on an island detached from the rest of human society. People, like property, are situated in and affected by their communities.

The networks and patterns of exchange in which we participate also shape our community point of reference for the process of choice. For instance, if a person is positioned within the welfare system most of his important exchanges will be ones of dependence and bureaucratic submission. This will influence his understanding of exchange and the

---

[7] *Fred F. French Investing Co. v. City of New York*, 39 N.Y. 2d 587, 350 N.E. 2d 381 (Ct. of Appeals N.Y., 1976), *appeal dismissed*, 429 U.S. 990 (1976).

way in which he relates to others in the exchange process. Likewise, if one is continually involved in the criminal justice system, or in situations where exclusion, submission, and feelings of inferiority are dominant, then these exchange experiences will influence the ground upon which interpretation rests.

On this point, Jeffery Harrison's work has also indicated that one's socio-economic class can influence the market exchange process.[8] He argues that class positioning influences an individual's assessment of value and self-worth in market situations. This is consistent with ideas in interpretation theory. It would also seem to indicate that being positioned in an excluded or despised group, for example as a consequence of racism, or living in a highly structured and bureaucratic one-party system, as in China or North Korea, influences the patterns and networks of exchange and informs the interpretive process of choice. In restrictive networks and patterns of exchange people are less likely to develop an alertness to creative potential and opportunity. This is because people in such situations are not likely to experience rewards for convention-breaking and habit-deforming ideas or actions. They are likely to develop innovative ways of dealing with regimentation, suppression, or bureaucracy but this kind of creativity needs to be redirected in order to enhance sustainable wealth formation. This is why social programs need to encourage positive and useful networks of exchange. It is why workfare makes more sense than welfare – it puts people into exchange relationships where they learn something about work, productivity, and positive participation rather than dependence and a sense of worthlessness.

In addition to these considerations, it is important to remember that when we speak of the rational allocative "individual" of traditional law and economics, we are merely addressing an idea or sign of the "individual" that stands in reference to a real person but is not the person to which it refers.[9] As explained, real people are affected by the environments in which they are situated and by the networks and patterns of exchange in which they participate. The idea of the individual, therefore, like that of "person," "alien," "family member," or "refugee," is continually evolving within the market context and is given coherence by its reference to a real person and also by reference to a

[8] See, e.g., Jeffery L. Harrison, "Class, Entitlements and Contract" 221–248 in Law and Economics (Malloy and Braun, eds.) at 221–248; Jeffery L. Harrison, "Egoism, Altruism, and Market Illusions: The Limits of Law and Economics," 33 U.C.L.A. L. Rev. 1309 (1986).

[9] Peirce said that man not only uses signs but that he himself is a sign. Karl-Otto Apel, Charles S. Peirce: From Pragmatism to Pragmaticism xxii (1995). See also Kevelson, Peirce and Science, at 165–178; Merrell, Peirce – Meaning, at 52–68.

particular community framework. When we forget the distinction between the idea of the individual and the real person to whom it refers, we collapse an essential element of their semiotic relationship and fall prey to the constraints of habitually blinding conventionalism that can deny us the possibility of envisioning further substitutional interpretation or change.[10]

We can also fail to appreciate simple distinctions, as in thinking that by embracing the idea of "capitalism" we can in fact become capitalists. Some of the Russian people misunderstood this distinction when they seemed to think that ending the Soviet Union and declaring themselves free-market capitalists would in itself transform them into an entrepreneurial society and raise their standard of living. While it is important to identify and name a new potential relationship one must also appreciate the implications of the human practice of exchange. For example, capitalism is an idea that stands for a particular way of experiencing and organizing relational exchange – it is learned, not simply given or declared.

When we collapse the idea with the real it represents, and we ignore or forget the difference between the two, we fail to appreciate our ability to implement change in law and social policy. We also fail to understand the process by which change occurs. Through the process of naming and renaming in law, for instance, we can continually recategorize ideas and create new potential for relationships. From these potentialities we can then move toward actualization of a new reality. For example, homicide can be broken down into degrees of murder, thus opening the door to multiple types and approaches to penalties or treatment. Similarly, fee simple ownership of real estate can be broken down into a variety of subclassifications and thereby create entirely new relationships between people and property while opening the door to additional market opportunities. Likewise, defining "people" can change by redefining the meaning of person – does person include, for instance, blacks, women, children, the unborn, immigrants, aliens, biological clones, or perhaps only white male property owners. When we say, for example, that all men are created equal or that the equal protection of the law shall be denied to no person, what/who do we count as a "person"? As long as we understand that the idea, or the sign, of "person" is something other than the person herself, we can comprehend the possibility of law and public policy changing over time and altering current understandings and relationships.

---

[10] *See* Kevelson, *Peirce and Science*, at 165–178; Denis Brion, "Naming and Forgetting," in *Semiotics* (J. Deely et al., eds., 1997) at 219–228.

This same idea or process is relevant to an understanding of market exchange. As long as we understand that ideas such as efficiency function as an interpretation of relational status within a framework of current conventionalized criteria, we can comprehend the possibility of an alternative interpretation. Efficiency, in other words, is simply a temporary and contingent idea grounded in a reference to a community-based system of convention and habit. Efficiency has no intrinsic value or meaning in the absence of a referential relationship.

In the approach of law and market economy, therefore, it is understood that the individual is not isolated or atomized but rather exists as an integrated part of a community in which she is positioned. Consequently, the individual and self-interest cannot be the key referential signs of the market discourse.[11] Within the framework of law and market economy, the individual self and self-interest are understood as dialogical concepts, and this means that the individual and her self-interest are always seen in relation to another or to others. Furthermore, it is understood that the individual is a sign, an idea given meaning as a result of a relationship with another, and the idea of self-interest implicitly references the public interest. These ideas or signs have relational meaning – they are not oppositional, they are reciprocal in a continuous process of semiosis.

Borrowing from the philosophical ideas of Adam Smith, we can envision this relationship between the individual and the community as related to the coevolutionary push and pull that exists between his reciprocal conceptions of self-interest and the *impartial spectator*.[12] Consistent with Smith's philosophy, I would suggest that there is, in traditional law and economics, an artificial dichotomy between the individual and the community. These two concepts are not in opposition but instead exist together as one, in a reciprocal relationship, each working to define the other in an ongoing reflective or referential process of semiotic synthesis.

Smith understood, for instance, that self-interest was an important

[11] *Peirce – Writings* (Buchler, ed.), at xiv (rejection of methodological individualism); Kevelson, *Peirce's Method*, at 11; Kevelson, *Peirce and Science*, at 28 (the individual is a relational sign); Merrell, *Peirce – Meaning*, at 52–68.

[12] *See* Adam Smith, *The Theory of Moral Sentiments* 71, 200–260, 352, 422 (E.G. West, ed., 1969) (discussing the impartial spectator). *See also* Robin Paul Malloy, "Adam Smith and the Modern Discourse of Law and Economics" in *Adam Smith and the Philosophy of Law and Economics* (Robin Paul Malloy and Jerry Evensky, eds., 1994) at 113, 122–126; Robin Paul Malloy, *Planning for Serfdom: Legal Economic Discourse and Downtown Development* (1991) at 21–24 (analysis and extensive cites to Smith): Robin Paul Malloy, "Invisible Hand or Sleight of Hand? Adam Smith, Richard Posner and the Philosophy of Law and Economics," 36 U. Kan. L. Rev. 210, 227–229 (1988).

element, or driving force, in human creativity.[13] He realized its importance to wealth creation. But he also understood that self-interest was
not the same thing as selfishness and that self-interest had to be
tempered with a respect for others. The individual was never to "prefer
himself so much even to any other individual as to hurt or injure that
other in order to benefit himself, though the benefit to the one should be
much greater than the hurt or injury to the other."[14] Pursuing self-gain
could not, therefore, be done at the expense of others even if it was
Kaldor–Hicks efficient, the winner gaining more than the loser lost.[15]
The pursuit of self-interest required a social ethic of responsibility in
which one respected others. Individuals and communities need, in other
words, to work together in order to create meaning and value; cooperation rather than domination is the key to advancing social prosperity
through market exchange. The objective of social organization, in a
Smithian sense, is to facilitate a value greater than economic efficiency
or wealth maximization, and this view was echoed in the words of
Milton Friedman when he wrote, "I would favor a free society even if it
were less productive than some alternative – say a slave society . . .
because my basic value is freedom itself."[16]

Smith's idea might be better understood by translating the notion of
"well-being" into a modern context. For example, every four years, in
the heat of a presidential campaign, we get a candidate who asks us,
"Are you better off now than you were four years ago?" I believe that for
most people this question invokes thoughtful evaluation that goes
beyond simple comparisons between pay stubs and bank account
balances. I believe that individuals naturally reflect on these material
and monetized measures of wealth, but they also think beyond them.
Being better off includes having a sense of optimism, a feeling of security
and progress, a sense of pride in one's work and community, and a
number of other intangibles.[17] Consequently, in the same sense that we

---

[13] See Malloy, "Smith and Modern Discourse," at 113, 116–127 (with cites to Smith);
Malloy, Serfdom, at 16–29 (with cites to Smith); Jerry Evensky, "Setting the Scene: Adam
Smith's Moral Philosophy" in Adam Smith and the Philosophy of Law and Economics (Robin
Paul Malloy and Jerry Evensky, eds., 1994), at 7–29 (with cites to Smith).

[14] Smith, Moral Sentiments, at 236.

[15] Id. See also Malloy, "Invisible Hand," at 228–229; Malloy, Serfdom, at 16–29; Malloy,
"Smith and Modern Discourse," at 113–127.

[16] Milton Friedman, "Free Markets and Free Speech," 10 Harvard J. Law & Pub. Pol'y 1
(1987). See sources above, in nn. 13, 14; Milton Friedman, Capitalism and Freedom
9–10 (1962).

[17] See, e.g., Floyd W. Rudmin, "Heider's Cognitive Theory of Property and the Problem
of Unnamed and Unrecognized Property Relationships in Law and Semiotics, vol. 3
(Roberta Kevelson, ed., 1989), at 321–334; "To Have Possessions: A Handbook on
Ownership and Property," 6 J. Social Behavior & Personality 1, 1–496 (F.W. Rudmin,
ed., 1991).

say, "We don't live by bread alone," we likewise do not tend to measure our well-being by simple reference to isolated and individualized forms of monetized wealth.

As social creatures, positioned in communities of exchange, we logically reference our own personal feeling of well-being with that of the "others" around us. We temper our pursuit of self-gain by reference to others as we come to understand that our own gain is, in part, one and the same as that of the community. This, it seems, is exactly the point made by Smith in his discussion of the impartial spectator. Being better off, in the context of community, refers to a measure of well-being that goes beyond purely self-interested calculations of material and monetized wealth. It includes indexical references to the communities in which we are positioned and reflects a sense of social prosperity that extends beyond the measuring methods of standard neoclassical economics.

Individuals may generally be moved to improve their own condition but this does not mean that they seek to maximize personal gain at the expense of others. Self-gain and community-gain need not be mutually exclusive. Nothing in the work of Adam Smith, for instance, suggests that people seek to maximize wealth in the way represented in the approach of traditional law and economics. To the contrary, I believe the better view is that people are motivated by the prospect of improving their position within the context of community and not necessarily to maximize wealth at the expense of others.

This view, in fact, would better explain results that I obtain each year when I play the "split the dollar" game at the start of my course on Law and Market Economy. This game involves giving each of three students, the initial players, five one-dollar bills and two quarters. Then the initial players are each assigned a partner. The deal is that the initial players must offer to split the money with their respective partner. If the partner accepts the offered split of the money both parties keep the money as agreed. If the partner rejects the offer the money comes back to me and they get nothing. If both parties to the exchange are purely rational and self-interested actors the initial player should offer the partner twenty-five cents and the partner should accept. Even though the initial player keeps almost all of the money the partner still comes out ahead by accepting any positive split. Both parties would maximize self-interest in this situation. In practice, however, the initial players almost always offer the partner between $1.50 and $2.50 as the split, and in the few instances where an initial player offered twenty-five or fifty cents the partner has rejected the offer.

This game indicates that people probably reference a number of factors when making a decision and that they seek to improve their own position but not necessarily to maximize it in a self-interested way. Likewise, rejection of a small offer by a partner seems to indicate a desire to punish the initial player for being "greedy" rather than having a strong connection to pursuing what would none the less be a small but wealth-maximizing gain. More importantly, these results seem to indicate that the choice process is an interpretive process. The players are referencing a variety of factors in the exchange process; they are not simply considering the efficient division of the resources that I have distributed to them.

Some traditional economists speculate that the results of this game might change when the allocation choice can be done privately or anonymously. I would suggest that the results might also differ as between players or groups with different social, class or cultural backgrounds. This is because they have different experiences and alternative interpretive grounds for understanding the exercise of choice. In fact, my own classroom experience has shown that in the several instances when I have selected graduate students from Latin American countries to play this game they have consistently made the most equal split possible, and on occasion have even given a larger share to the other person. Similarly, the splits tend to be more generous when I allocate the original money to a male member of the class and he must split his allocation with a female member. These outcomes may be aberrations or they may reflect the value differences of alternative interpretive communities. In any case, people must reference community standards when they contemplate the idea of being "too greedy" in any given circumstance. Likewise, they make interpretive reference when they consider gender or race issues in the context of differently composed settings. The allocation by a white male may be different when asked to split with a black male in a classroom of 50 other white males versus a classroom of 50 other black males. The point is that choice requires reference to community standards and values, and these references are complex. They are not simply based on factual disagreements concerning the appropriate calculation of costs and benefits. Moreover, they tend to be consistent with the idea that people can seek to improve their own position without necessarily feeling a need to maximize their wealth at the expense of others.

Returning from this example to a consideration of Adam Smith's work, we might think of Smith's analysis of the impartial spectator as an attempt to deal with this idea of pursuing gain in a community context. He was trying to reconcile self-interest, as a beneficial motive for creativity and invention, with its destructive tendencies toward power seeking and monopoly rents. Smith, I believe, feared that unconstrained self-interest, or selfishness, was destructive because it worked against the sharing of authority, it was antagonistic to competition, and it was destructive of community. Unconstrained self-interest could destroy creativity and inventiveness by oppressing the broad-based participatory input of others. Therefore, the necessary counterbalance and coevolutionary complement to individual self-interest was the community, and the community for Smith was reflected in the logic of the impartial spectator.

We might think of this as a form of enlightened self-interest where individuals understand that their own interest is promoted when they further the mutual interests of others. The impartial spectator, in this sense, serves as a metaphorical "otherness" that watches over the exercise of self-interest and imposes guidelines for judgment. According to Smith, each of us is judged by an impartial spectator in all that we do and we must measure our conduct by reference to the way in which we would imagine that an impartial spectator would view it. Seeking praise and avoiding blame from the judgment of the impartial spectator related to the way in which one's own self-interest was tempered and constrained. He said that we must "endeavour to examine our own conduct as we imagine any other fair and impartial spectator would examine it . . . and we must . . . soon become sensible . . . that others exercise the same criticism upon us."[18] In this way, we come to learn that our own merit and praiseworthiness is dependent upon the happiness and merit of others, and vice versa. As a consequence, each individual must reject a selfish "survival of the fittest" attitude and must act to maximize her own well-being within the guise and constraints of socially imposed mores and norms – mores and norms embodied in the otherness of the impartial spectator.

Consistent with the notion of a semiotic process of exchange, Smith also believed that we developed our individual sense of constraint on self-interest by a social process of experience.[19] By continually acting and interacting in a social/market context we learn of community norms and at the same time participate in the creation of new experiences, which themselves generate new possibilities for the reshaping of such norms. It is a dialogic process in which the conception of the self is shaped by each individual's experience with others (the community), while the community of others is also affected by its interaction with

---

[18] Smith, *Moral Sentiments*, at 205.

[19] Smith wrote that the general rules of how to act, of moral, ethical, and social conduct were grounded in experience. *See* Smith, *Moral Sentiments*, at 264.

each individual. The result is a socially informed notion of self-interest that is directly related to the social experience of the individual.

Self-interest is, in other words, contextualized by the community in which one is positioned, for the community helps define the idea of the self. For example, the community defines the limits of rights in our bodies and the other characteristics and property that might be "mine" and which might be used to define me. Likewise, the community helps define actions that may or may not be understood as self-interested actions, or permissible actions, or praiseworthy or blameworthy actions, or even legal or illegal actions. This is important to understand because it relates to the role of self-interest in the paradigm of law and market economy. When an individual pursues self-interest it should not be viewed as selfishly unconstrained. Likewise, it must be seen as a more complex idea than the mere pursuit of material gain, and, additionally, it must be understood that the concept of self-interest may differ from one community to the next, and change across time and context. Consequently, blacks, Hispanics, Asians, women, men, children, people in other places outside of the United States or North America, may all have different conceptions of self-interest based on different community-based experiences.

The exchange process is reciprocal and integrative. Meaning and value emerge, therefore, from a process that is dynamic and situational. As a consequence, we cannot simply extrapolate from the imagined world of the isolated individual capable of self-definition with respect to value and wealth. We must, instead, deal with the complexity of meaning and value forged from a dynamic or relational process of social interaction and exchange.

In focusing on the idea of the relationship between individuals and their communities Smith was thinking very much in the vein of Peirce's triadic logic. Smith's conception of the impartial spectator, as I have discussed, was one of contingent and continuously evolving meaning. It represented, in a contingent mode of thirdness, the product of an endless cycle of interspection, or process of semiosis, between the firstness of self and the secondness of community. Self-interest, while useful for thinking about some of the primary forces in human behavior, was to Smith an insufficient criterion for understanding social progress and prosperity. Something more was needed and that was a referential theory of community. Smith's concern for community was embodied in his conception of the impartial spectator and is expressed in my approach as a consequence of focusing on the interactive process of exchange.

Market as a process of semiotic signification

To legal economists the logic of semiotics should already be familiar even if they have never consciously considered it. Legal economists, for example, attach meaning and value to various relationships between supply and demand, or costs and benefits. They attach particular significance to points of equilibrium and assume that market actors respond to and interpret a continuous flow of constantly changing information. They use market models to think and talk about relative prices, opportunity costs, and comparative advantage, and all of these concepts involve drawing conclusions from a process of relational interpretive reference. They understand the ideas of substitution, complementary goods, and derived demand curves, and they think it normal to make interpretive predictions concerning future rates of interest, inflation, economic growth, and employment. All of these standard conceptions and ideas involve the process of interpretation, of meaning and value formation, and are the object/subject of semiotic inquiry. Semiotics allows us to consider the meanings and values that flow from particular conceptions of social organization and, therefore, my approach merely seeks to extend the scope and nature of our current practices. This extension is important because exchange processes create wealth and prosperity in ways that go beyond monetary measure, beyond coherent representation in tokenized dollar form.

In semiotics we understand these ideas and relationships in terms of *signs*. According to Peirce:

A sign, or *representamen*, is something which stands to somebody for something in some respect or capacity. It addresses somebody, that is, creates in the mind of that person an equivalent sign, or perhaps a more developed sign. That sign which it creates I call the *interpretant* of the first sign. The sign stands for something, its *object*. It stands for that *object*, not in all respects, but in reference to a sort of idea, which I have sometimes called the *ground* of the representamen. . . . A Sign, or *Representamen*, is a First which stands in such a genuine triadic relation to a Second, called its *Object*, as to be capable of determining a Third, called its *Interpretant*, to assume the same triadic relation to its Object in which it stands itself to the same Object.[20]

In its extended form the market is an idea or semiotic sign, and is, thus, a contextualized process of meaning and value formation. It is a sign and sign system – a creation of the human imagination – and it is an idea of significance because it has real-world meaning and consequence.[21] The idea of the market as sign is a theoretical way of understanding the

---

[20] *Peirce – Writings* (Buchler, ed.), at 99–100.
[21] *See* Kevelson, *Peirce and Freedom*, at 33; Kevelson, *Peirce and Science*, at 18, 32, 63.

interactive phenomenon of human behavior in a social process of exchange; exchange which continually references value relationships and meanings between people, their things, and the communities in which they are positioned. It does this through the process of substitution and permutation discussed above in Chapter 2.

By reference to relational positioning and substitution, the market, as a sign system, attempts to explain the dynamic phenomena of social organization in ways that are comprehensible. The market idea or sign, however, is not the actual real world to which it refers. The semiotic relationship that exists is *triadic*, which means that the market as an idea makes reference to real-world phenomena, which it "filters" in order to create meaning in the mind of a person. The triadic structure of the sign involves the object of inquiry (the real phenomenal world of interpersonal exchange) or what Peirce called a *representamen*, as a mode of firstness, the referential idea or Peircean *object* (the market idea or theory under investigation), in both its *immediate* and *dynamical* sense, as a mode of secondness, and, as a Peircean *interpretant* or mode of thirdness, the synthesis of meaning and value formation evidenced by their relationship in the understanding of a person (the individual who has learned, through social convention and therefore by reference to some other sign(s), how to understand the meaning of the real or dynamical world by way of the conventionalized code of market assumptions).[22]

This relationship can best be understood with an example. Economists can talk about the market for pork bellies, IBM stock, or apartment units in New York City. In any of these specific markets, data and observation can be brought together using certain standard equations, assumptions, and principles of economics. This database, inevitably partial, is said to represent the identified market. Evidence of each and every exchange in the database is significant because it affects, in some way, the meaning of the whole; just as the eventual interpretation of the whole will be read back to reassign meaning to each of the individual parts. The market is further explained and represented by referencing the data to particular mathematical functions and market diagrams. Standard supply and demand curves, for instance, can be drawn on a chalkboard or on a computer screen to portray a variety of relationships for each market, and perhaps even the relationship between these

[22] Peirce uses a triadic structure to analyze sign relationships. *See* Winfried Noth, *A Handbook of Semiotics* 39–47 (1995); Sheriff, *Peirce*, at 31–47; James Jacob Liszka, *A General Introduction to the Semeiotic of Charles Sanders Peirce* 18–52 (1996); Christopher Hookway, *Peirce* 106–174, 272 (1992); *Reasoning and the Logic of Things: Charles Sanders Peirce* 68–150 (Kenneth Laine Ketner, ed., 1992); *Peirce – Writings* (Buchler, ed., 1955) at 74–119.

markets. These equations and diagrams are not, however, the market(s) to which they refer. They merely refer to, stand in relationship to, are substitutions for, and are interpretations of, the real or dynamical practices of social/market exchange. Furthermore, the conclusions and inferences to be drawn from these market representations are dependent upon a set of conventionalized norms or codes of interpretation. The conventionalized code of market theory works to maintain a degree of continuity in the process of interpretation. At the same time, continual, dynamic change and the varying gaps that exist in the process of imperfect substitution result in a consistent element of indeterminacy. From this conflictive tension between continuity and indeterminacy, meaning and value emerges.

The above example can also be explained with specific reference to Peirce's three modes of logic. The individual data fragments collected are representamen in the mode of firstness. The diagrams, equations, and such, are used to analyze the data and serve as indexical codes of reference. As such, they are objects in the mode of secondness. The assignment of meaning in the completion of this process involves an interpretant in a mode of thirdness. The meanings, conclusions, and arguments to be drawn from this process are facilitated by reference to other signs and codes, which have been learned and which, through social convention, have been accepted as applicable to the under-standing of the relationships being investigated. In this respect the market process is a system of semiotic signification because it is an exchange process that is interpreted and which allows for a continuous process of meaning and value (re)formation.

Law is also a system of semiotic signification. Legal facts stand as observable data fragments in a mode of firstness. These facts are considered with reference to conventionalized legal rules and norms that serve as a source of indexical reference in a mode of secondness. Finally, in a mode of thirdness, arguments are formed and conclusions are drawn. These conclusions are then read back into the process and used to give further meaning and clarification to the basic data – to confirm or reconfigure the identification of "relevant" facts, and to sharpen the identification and application of governing rules. In this way, law and economics are both systems of interpretation – dynamic sign systems that shape meanings and values through the process of exchange, substitution, and permutation.

By understanding the triadic relationship of law and of the market sign one gains insight into the structure of social organization and the basis of wealth creation. One comes to see that our understanding of law and market theory is representational. Our understanding is an interpretation of the phenomenal world and because of the limitation of human ability it is of necessity always partial in some respect. Furthermore, the act of human interpretation of the relationship between the appearance of the real and the real itself is grounded in a certain set of social conventions, norms, codes, or laws. These conventions give coherence to the extensions of meaning attributed to the social exchange process and, like the concept of self-interest, they are formulated within a reciprocal framework of social interaction between the individual and the community. In this sense, the market, like law, is never static but rather dynamic, open, and continually evolving. Because interpretation is governed by social convention, the market idea is susceptible to reinterpretation and new meaning as a result of influences upon the generation of community norms. This presents an opportunity for facilitating real-world change and is of import for understanding the interactive function of competing legal theories concerning the allocation of scarce resources and political authority. This opportunity to mediate interpretation and to influence the networks and patterns of exchange, thereby affecting meaning and value, gives rise to a competitive struggle for ideological recognition and dominance in social discourse, and it is reflected in law by discursive challenges in the form of a variety of legal theories including critical theory and law and economics.

All of this is important to an appreciation of the relationship between the representational appearance of the market idea and the real to which it refers. The appearance is always partial, and since it is represented by an idea that is made coherent by social convention, norms, and law, there will always be a divergence, or incongruence, between the real or dynamical object and its representational appearance or representamen. I refer to this divergence or incongruence as a *semiotic space*. It is in discovering these spaces that wealth-enhancing potentiality is created and society is transformed.[23] To discover these spaces, however, one must be willing and able to challenge the accepted conventional norm. One must, for example, challenge the idea (the appearance) of an earth that is flat and dare to set sail, like Columbus, on a mission *around* the world. One must envision that which is not yet fully conventionalized, such as to first imagine the ability to communicate by wire, to fly, to reach the moon, and to store large amounts of information on tiny chips made of sand. It is by way of discovering the semiotic space between the

---

[23] Creativity within "spaces." *See* Robin Paul Malloy, "New and Critical Perspectives on Law and Economics" in *Codes and Customs* (Roberta Kevelson, ed., 1994) at 213–224; Stuart Kauffman, *At Home in the Universe: The Search for the Laws of Self-organization and Complexity* 180–181 (1995).

appearance and the real that wealth creation takes on its most meaningful conception.

The ideas discussed in this Chapter are important for a proper understanding of the relationship between law and market theory. This is because an understanding of the semiotic nature of law and market theory helps to direct our attention to three further points that I wish to address. These points involve: a two-level understanding of the interpretive process in law and market theory; an understanding of the need for interdisciplinary investigation methods in law and market economy; and a consideration of the key elements of an extensive exchange system.

The semiotic nature of both law and market theory indicates that each involves a process of interpretation. This means that legal conclusions, economic conclusions, and human action or choice always involves a process of interpretation – of observation or contact with the phenomenal world (a mode of firstness), an interpretive frame of reference for processing these observations and contacts (a mode of secondness), and the formulation of conclusions or arguments about our observations or contacts that facilitates our exercise of choice (a mode of thirdness). Understanding these systems of social organization as semiotic sign systems allows us to see that they are grounded in experience and that they are formed dialogically in relationships by and between people living in community with each other. This means that each system, law, and market theory is, at least partially, subjective, arational, and endogenously informed. Lawyers must take this into account, particularly when considering the policy prescriptions of traditional law and economics because these conclusions run counter to many assumptions in the methods of traditional law and economic analysis.

More importantly, as sign systems, we can understand the relationship between law and market theory on two interpretive levels.[24] First-level interpretation involves a simple understanding of an exchange relationship on its own terms. This is like reading a story for the story. In contrast, a second-level interpretation examines the exchange relationship to appreciate how the story works and to understand the extent to which it represents or signifies a broader set of meanings or values. This second-level interpretation is similar to reading a story not only for the story, but for how the story works as a broader representation of other stories and other narratives of social relationships. First-level interpretation involves, for example, gathering information on residential mortgage lending and determining the extent to which the market is

---

[24] *See* Umberto Eco, *The Limits of Interpretation* 92 (1990).

liquid and operating efficiently under some given set of conventionalized criteria. Second-level interpretation goes beyond this to investigate the meaning and value implications of using an efficiency criterion in the evaluative process, and to consider the significance of the various conventionalized assumptions employed. It asks what/who is included or excluded from participation and in what respects by virtue of the criteria used to validate particular elements of an exchange as relevant. Second-level analysis, therefore, generally goes beyond the boundaries of traditional law and economics, yet it is of fundamental importance for understanding law and public policy in a market context.

As a point of further clarification, consider the difference between first- and second-level interpretation in law. First, law is about more than the outcome of a given case, it is also about how a particular case reflects a broader set of issues and relationships within society. The O.J. Simpson murder trial, for instance, was, as a matter of first-level interpretation, merely a case about O.J. Simpson's innocence or guilt in the death of his former wife and her friend. As a matter of second-level interpretation, however, the case is a symbolic representation of a number of issues that go beyond the immediate story of the murders of Nicole Brown and Ronald Goldman. At this second level the case provides insight and commentary on matters of race relations, police practices, judicial process, media influence, and a variety of other matters extending far beyond the immediate facts and drama of the actual case. Similarly, the recent ordeal involving President Clinton and Monica Lewinsky is yet another readily apparent example of the same point. In each case the sophisticated lawyer understands that there is more to the story than the story of the case itself. In a similar way, law and market economy is recognizing that law and economics tells a story but the story is more complex and requires a broader interpretive perspective in order to be better understood.

A second significant observation that semiotics reveals about the relationship between law and market theory is that the market exchange process is dynamic and complex. The assumptions and static/determinate focus of traditional law and economics cannot fully explain how markets do, or ought to, work. Markets can be better understood by considering these economic observations in relationship to other interdisciplinary approaches. The idea behind this observation is simple. Markets are about a whole lot more than economics. Economic tools are concerned with only a small slice of human practice and experience. Any person who has been to business school or who has worked as a manager of a company knows that markets involve many issues that go beyond economics. Understanding how markets work involves reference to sociology, anthropology, cultural studies, human behavior, accounting, marketing, language, and a variety of other disciplines. The question then is why should lawyers feel constrained to think of law and market theory from within a traditional framework of law and economics. Law and market economy takes a broader view and suggests that one can study law in a market context without giving primacy to considerations of efficiency or wealth maximization. In fact, law and market economy demonstrates that a concern for sustainable wealth formation requires one to think beyond the confining and conventionalized assumptions of traditional law and economics.

A third significant idea revealed by applying semiotic method to law and market theory is that it indicates that both law and market theory are prototypical sign systems. Each is understandable as a sign system using Peirce's triadic theory of signs. This is important because sign systems exhibit certain characteristics when they function *extensively*, and these characteristics can help us analyze law and market theory from the point of view of sustainable wealth formation. I have identified three characteristics of sign systems that I believe help them operate extensively. These include the concept of the ground, the use of a referential framework, and the degree of exchangability.

The ground is an experiential-based point of view. Our philosophical outlook and our approach to understanding law and market theory are anchored in our experience. The idea of the ground is understandable in terms of a concern for stability and predictability in law and market economy. Stability centers around the concepts of habit and convention. Stability, therefore, carries with it an element of determinacy. This determinate factor gives rise to a level of predictability or bounded rationality. Simply because the world is dynamic, complex, and creative does not mean that it is completely indeterminate. Language, like law and like economic exchange, is also anchored in a reasonable degree of stability. Without a base or a ground we could not communicate – if words and rules of grammar changed completely and continuously every second there would be no basis for a comprehensible exchange – even though we must acknowledge that language is not completely static. Stability and predictability function to provide a degree of rationality and objectivity to an otherwise dynamic and indeterminate world. This is much the same role as is typically ascribed to precedent in law. Stability and predictability allow us to plan our actions and choices with some degree of confidence in the legal infrastructure governing the exchange. Similarly, a broadly shared ground allows communities to conduct exchange transactions in a reasonably predictable manner.

A referential framework is also important for a sign system to function extensively. The idea behind a referential framework is that sign systems, be they legal, economic, or language systems, need to be understandable and need to exhibit a reasonable degree of transparency. To be understandable, sign systems need to make reference to inter- pretive communities with a reasonably broad base of shared experience. Transparency makes a sign system accessible – it allows "outsiders" and newcomers to recognize, learn, translate, and participate within the system's framework. The more readily transparent a system the more accessible it is. Likewise, the more accessible it is the more under- standable, pluralistic, and extensive it can become.

Finally, we come to the concept of exchangability. Exchangability involves a concern for adaptation and tolerance. Where transparency invites others in – makes a system more readily accessible – adaptation fosters an ability both to export and import meanings and values between sign systems. An adaptive sign system is integrative, creative, and dynamic. This is the idea behind the concept of the US Constitu- tion as a "a living Constitution." The Constitution is said to be a living document because it is adaptive to changing times and circumstance – to variance in referential frameworks. Tolerance means that the system is open to change – is receptive to change and permutation. A tolerant system is less hierarchical than an intolerant system. It is more pluralistic and decentralized. It provides space for creativity and extensive author- itative participation in the social/market exchange process.

In looking at legal systems, economic systems, or language systems we can improve our understanding and enhance our influence by thinking of the semiotic structure of such systems. This allows us to think in terms of first- and second-level interpretive values and meanings. It permits us to approach law and public policy in a market context without feeling constrained to limit our frame of reference to traditional law and economics. Furthermore, it allows us to think about sign systems and sub-sign systems in terms of a few key characteristics that are important for extensive participatory exchange and therefore vital to sustainable wealth formation. With this in mind I shall now turn attention to a discussion of wealth as a process of creative discovery.

4   Wealth as a process of discovery: wealth, discovery, and imaginative choice

In the approach of law and market economy, wealth creation is linked to the process of discovery and is found in the expression of creativity, experimentation, and invention. This conception of wealth is not adequately captured by the standard equilibrium models used to calculate efficiency in traditional law and economics. Creative discovery emerges out of the semiotic relationship between continuity and indeterminacy. It cannot be achieved by simply pursuing efficiency because efficiency is grounded in convention and habit. Israel Kirzner also makes this point when he says that "entrepreneurial discovery consists not in achieving efficiency in dealing with a given situation but in alertness to the possibility that the true situation (with respect to which efficiency would be worth pursuing) is in fact different from the situation that had been assumed to be given."[1]

In this Chapter of the book, therefore, I will discuss a method of thinking about efficiency and creative discovery. I will do this by developing the concepts of *reactive* and *proactive* wealth and by relating these concepts to the discovery process and to the exercise of "imaginative" choice. Moreover, I will discuss the semiotic relationship between these two conceptions of wealth and show how they can be brought together to provide a standard for analyzing social prosperity.

The discovery process is one of investigation, experimentation, intuition, hunch, guess, accident, surprise, self-correction, and revision. Kirzner explains it this way:

What one witnesses in a market economy, at any point in time, are nothing but attempts by market participants to take advantage of newly discovered or created possibilities . . . The process is kept continuously boiling by the incessant injection of unexpected changes and surprise. The process of creative discovery is never completed, nor is it ever arrested.[2]

It is an ongoing process of trial and error and lends itself to wealth

---

[1] Israel M. Kirzner, *Discovery and the Capitalist Process* 157 (1985). *See also* Israel M. Kirzner, *The Meaning of Market Process* 39 (1992).
[2] Kirzner, *Capitalist Process*, at ix–x.

creation when new relationships, meanings, and values are discovered in the semiotic spaces between the conventionalized market idea and the real phenomenal world to which it refers.

Wealth, in such a system, is not merely a collection of capital goods or material resources because wealth formation involves more than the simple question of availability of tools and resources.[3] Wealth formation is a *process* that involves the way in which we use and relate to tools, resources, and each other. A collection of books, or computers, or scientific equipment does not make students well educated. The *process* of using these resources creates the potential for highly educated students. The same resources in different hands can lead to very different results. Merely equalizing spending or capital resources between communities will not produce equal outcomes. Wealth formation is really the product of the collective human practice of social exchange. It is, in a sense, a learning process where learning arises out of experience, and experience varies between individuals and with reference to culture, history, context, and other factors.

Through the human practice of exchange individuals and communities evolve and continually reshape or transform themselves. Decisions about what is produced, by whom, and for whom, and the terms and conditions of exchange and exchangability all reflect value choices within society. Americans, for example, spend billions of dollars every year on snack and junk food, pornography, and on sporting events. None of this is essential to human preservation, and while all of these billions of dollars are being spent in this way, people go homeless and die from lack of clean water, heat, from malnutrition, and from other preventable causes. Such behavior and exchange relationships give meaning and value definition to the idea of America and to the identity of Americans.

The market exchange process also reflects an interpretive exercise of choice and a continuous process of substitution and permutation. Individuals and communities are, therefore, continuously transforming meanings and values by the manner in which they interact as evidenced in the networks and patterns of exchange. Engaging in trade and learning how to replace imports with exports, for example, or how to develop new products and employ new systems of work relationships, are all illustrations of the transforming nature of the market exchange process. Likewise, the discovery and development of the printing press,

---

[3] *See generally*, Jane Jacobs, *Cities and the Wealth of Nations* 93–124 (1984) (development is a process and not merely a collection of capital goods). *See also* Robin Paul Malloy, *Planning for Serfdom: Legal Economic Discourse and Downtown Development* 113–141 (1991); L. Harrison, *Underdevelopment is a State of Mind* (1985).

the telegraph, the telephone, the fax machine, and e-mail are all exchange systems of communication that have altered the way in which social relationships are configured. Overnight-delivery systems, pagers, fax machines, cellular phones, and the internet have all changed working relationships by reconceptualizing the time horizon of work and by reconfiguring exchange networks and patterns – making it easier to communicate, or conversely making it more difficult to escape communicative intrusion into one's life. These systems of communication are also used differently and are accessible in different ways and degrees based, in part, on how people are positioned in society. Differences may arise based on occupation, education, income, geographic location, race, gender, or a variety of other factors. Regardless of configuration, however, the discovery and formation of new networks and patterns of interaction results in a dynamic process because we never know the full meaning or consequence of any particular action or inaction.

The development of the personal computer and the internet have enabled individuals to become effective disseminators of a vast amount of information at relatively little expense. Now a huge audience can be reached quickly without needing access to major publishers or regulated broadcast networks. This has allowed more ideas to be exchanged and it has diminished the ability of governments easily to control "unauthorized" communications within and between their borders. For example, it is now easier to communicate with individuals in China and for individuals to "leak" news items to the outside. Similarly, computer technology makes it easier for Chinese dissidents to communicate with each other and to produce and release information to a wider audience than was previously possible. This has resulted in new relationships between people in China and changed practices by the government in its efforts to control dissent.

In a like manner wireless communication systems also provide a good example of changing patterns and networks of exchange resulting from new technology. Less-developed countries, for instance, can now more readily provide communications to rural and distant communities because they can make use of cellular and digital telephone systems that do not require the miles of wire and infrastructure needed to reach these locations. Having a wireless telephone in one of these rural communities can influence a variety of exchange relationships. A family in such a town might acquire a telephone as an entrepreneurial venture and make money by renting time to others. Thus, a new business opportunity arises and new money flows emerge.

Contact with the outside world also means access to better and more current information and this can influence thoughts and preferences in rural areas. It can also change business practices. Prior to the introduction of the wireless telephone, for example, farmers and craftsmen might sell their production to urban suppliers with little information about the current market value of their wares. If the supplier visited once a month there might be little in the way of market information other than what the supplier quoted. The presence of the telephone means that the farmers and craftsmen can communicate with urban contacts to attain current market information and this improves their negotiating position with suppliers. Rather than relying on the supplier to provide a fair price, the villagers are now able to bargain with greater knowledge. This changes the market relationship between these parties in a dramatic way. The telephone may also open up the opportunity to learn of other suppliers willing to purchase the output of the village, or it might provide an opportunity to learn of demand for other types of goods that can be produced by village residents. In these and other ways the new technology changes the networks and patterns of exchange, and meanings and values are transformed.

Similarly, changes in legal and economic infrastructure influence the networks and patterns of exchange. Consider as an example the recent innovation in automobile sales centered on the concept of leasing. Now instead of having to purchase or finance the ownership of a vehicle outright, one can simply lease it for a stated term and pay for only that part of the market value depreciated over the term of the lease. This marketing and credit innovation, facilitated by law, has dramatically changed the automobile industry while generating a variety of exchange consequences. Both new and used car markets have been affected and the conversation used to close a sale has shifted to a new set of variables made possible by the lease arrangement. As a result of leasing, the market for luxury and larger vehicles has been dramatically enhanced. Consumers are "buying" more car and truck for their money and all indications are that they like it. The automobile companies also like it as it has helped to increase profits.

At the same time, however, leasing has resulted in the production of vehicles that have a greater negative impact on the environment and which pose a greater safety risk. These larger vehicles require more raw materials to manufacture and burn more fossil fuels. They also promote off-road use that aggravates the impact on wildlife habitats. Many of the automobile companies go beyond advertising off-road use and organize ownership groups that sponsor intrusive activities on hard-to-reach land areas. Another environmental impact arises from the size of these vehicles. As more people buy larger vehicles it puts added pressure on parking spaces in urban areas. These vehicles, especially sport utilities and trucks, also present a higher safety risk from roll-overs, and from the consequences of impact damage in accidents with smaller vehicles. On the luxury end, these vehicles also present a higher risk of theft and raise the cost of repair work. Such risks and costs have prompted changes in insurance industry standards and rates.

The point of this example is that this simple legal innovation of automobile leasing, just like the innovation of the wireless telephone, has changed a number of exchange relationships. We now deal differently when negotiating a new car "purchase," we have an entirely new market for "factory buy-back" used cars, and we have new businesses that deal with the leasing process. We are also becoming accustomed to occupying large gas-guzzling machines that redefine our understanding of and access to remote off-road areas. Similarly, we have new understandings about our relationship to the natural environment as we are told of our ability to conquer snow, sleet, rain, and mud. Ownership of these vehicles also redefines our self-image and our understanding of the type of people who do and do not own them. At the same time, people use leasing to acquire an automobile that would be expensive beyond their means if they had to buy it outright. This has allowed people to project a "false sign" or sense of wealth that they hope will be translated into an image of financial success.

In each of the above examples we see that discovery and innovation relate to networks and patterns of exchange. As a consequence of participation in these various dynamic exchange networks, people begin to think differently, new meanings and values emerge, and the potential for further creative discovery continues. These discoveries represent a breaking through of the semiotic space separating the conventionalized market idea from the real dynamical world to which it refers, and as stated earlier, this breaking through can result from trade, the introduction of new technologies, or the emergence of new patterns of social interaction. It might also reflect a sudden awareness of an idea or relationship, which, while already present, previously went unnoticed. Discovery may also arise by mere accident or chance as when scientists hoping to invent a drug to cure a particular disease end up with something that proves useful in a totally different and previously unimagined way (Viagra, for example). In any event, discovery, as such, involves a *process* and is not itself a particular good or resource that can be employed upon command.

As a result of its indeterminate nature, discovery cannot be adequately addressed within the traditional law and economics framework. Traditional law and economics, like the neoclassical economic foundation upon which it rests, is not process oriented, and it is understood, with rare exceptions, in terms of equilibrium models.[4] Thus, the traditional law and economics approach focuses on the analysis of states of equilibrium without providing an adequate theory of how the process of equilibration takes place. That is, it merely *assumes* that equilibration takes place instantaneously as the result of rational market forces. Such an approach is ill suited for analyzing the dynamic process of wealth formation through discovery. For example, when confronted with such market problems as lack of knowledge or information, the traditional legal economist tends to extend, rather than modify, the scope of the model's standard assumptions.[5] This means that market ignorance, lack of knowledge for example, is dealt with in terms of the costs and benefits of removing ignorance.[6] Ignorance, in other words, is just one more variable to be included in the equilibrium model.

In contrast to this approach, a process-based understanding of market exchange incorporates a concern for the indeterminate nature of discovery and is much less deterministic in its analysis of the situation. A process approach to market theory would recognize, for instance, that ignorance is not always understandable in terms of standard cost and benefit analysis. Sometimes ignorance is reduced or eliminated by indeterminate, non-rational, factors such as those resulting from discovery, surprise, chance, or accident. An equilibrium model, based on rational decision making, cannot comprehend or explain such dynamic and indeterminate aspects of the market exchange process.[7]

Israel Kirzner addresses the theoretical problem suggested in the above example by explaining the difference between the equilibrium and the process-based approaches to market theory. He suggests that we can understand this better if we think in terms of underlying and induced variables in market analysis:

in terms of (a) the *underlying variables* (UVs), identified conventionally as preferences, resource availabilities and technological possibilities, and (b) the *induced variables* (IVs), consisting of the prices, methods of production and quantities and qualities of outputs which the market at any given time generates under the impact of the UVs . . . equilibrium economics postulates that at each and every instant the actual market values of the IVs are those equilibrium values predetermined by the relevant values of the UVs. Any apparent discrepancy is explained away by postulating that some relevant UV has somehow been overlooked (as for example, the cost of overcoming ignorance had been overlooked in earlier equilibrium models). Market process theorists, however, claim that the movements of IVs in the market are *not* fully determined by the value of the UVs. The former retain a degree of freedom with respect to the latter.[8]

---

[4] Kirzner, *Meaning*, at 39.   [5] *Id.* at 38–54.   [6] *Id.*   [7] *Id.*   [8] *Id.* at 42.

In terms of the approach developed in this book, Kirzner's comments can be understood semioticly. Using his example, we can see that the UVs stand as the underlying *qualities or perceptible objects* of investigation, therefore; they are elements of a mode of firstness. The IVs, on the other hand, are *indexical references*. They are market signs that tell us something about the UVs; thus, they are in a mode of secondness. Finally, the equilibration process is a search for an interpretive *meaning* with respect to the relationship between the mode of firstness (the UVs) and the mode of secondness (the IVs). Therefore, equilibrium conclusions are meanings, in a sense of thirdness, which are deduced from the interpretation of market signs. In a Peircean sense, this means that the IVs represent the UVs in some respects, but not in all respects, and the IVs are indexical as they mediate between our understanding of the UVs and our conclusions with respect to the various stages of market equilibrium. These representations are, however, always partial, like the "maps" of our earlier discussion. Consequently, there are other elements at work, other values and meanings being generated as a result of these relational exchanges. Semiotic analysis, consistent with Kirzner's approach, suggests that market forces are only partially explicable in terms of standard and conventionalized equilibrium theory. In other respects, market forces display a degree of freedom, which is to say a degree of indeterminacy that cannot be expressed in a static system of equilibrium analysis. Kirzner expresses this idea when he writes:

To the extent that the market integrates existing scattered information concerning wants, technology, and available resources, it may be argued that the market's future course is determined by that existing stock of information. But to the extent that the market can, through long-run entrepreneurial discovery, transcend the limits of any existing constraints of knowledge, its future course becomes wholly indeterminate.[9]

Therefore, a "mapping" of the market exchange process will come closer to approaching the "real" world of social/market exchange if it can logically integrate elements of convention/continuity and chance/indeterminacy.

As should be clear from the above discussion, *creative discovery* is not simply an input item capable of static equilibrium analysis. One cannot,

---

[9] Kirzner, *Capitalist Process*, 163 (also consider at 150–168). *See also* Stuart Kauffman, *At Home in the Universe: The Search for the Laws of Self-organization and Complexity* (1995) at 17–30, 194–195 (chance, indeterminacy, and discovery in a complex system); James Gleick, *Chaos: Making a New Science* (1987) at 135 (degrees of freedom); Roberta Kevelson, *Peirce's Esthetics of Freedom: Possibility, Complexity, and Emergent Value* 1–5, 15–17, and 59; Roberta Kevelson, *Peirce, Science, Signs* 32–40, 105 (1996); John K. Sheriff, *Peirce's Guess at the Riddle: Grounds for Human Significance* 9–16 (1994).

therefore, set out to employ creative discovery in the same sense that a good might be considered for use or nonuse in traditional law and economic analysis.[10] Creative discovery is a process or indeterminate event, it is not a thing. As a result, one can only speak meaningfully about discovery by reference to the types of environment most likely to encourage creativity and innovation. Consequently, research and development departments of major firms may talk about investing dollars into creativity and discovery but to a significant extent much of this money is invested into *environments* thought to be conducive to the discovery process. Relaxed, integrative, well-equipped working conditions can promote discovery and creativity but this is not, in itself, a creative act. Many very useful ideas and inventions emerge from unlikely people working out of their garages and homes, without research support. Similarly, many discoveries result from research and development efforts aimed at completely unrelated objectives. The creative discovery process is complex and indeterminate. You cannot simply analyze it in the same way that you might approach the purchase of a hamburger or a six pack of beer.

Creative discovery is also related to the idea of entrepreneurism and should be discussed with reference to two different approaches to that concept.[11] One standard conception views the entrepreneur as a risk taker while the other speaks in terms of people exercising entrepreneurial alertness. As to the first, creative discovery can involve entrepreneurial risk but taking on risk does not mean that something new will be discovered. An entrepreneur, in this respect, may simply be a person with no creative ideas and a willingness to gamble on a risk that others avoid. To be sure, the entrepreneur can sometimes be creative or innovative and at times the willingness to take financial risk is the key to bringing a discovery to market. The entrepreneur, as risk taker, serves an important market function in a way that is similar to the research and development budget of a company. The willingness to engage in and finance risk, to invest in potentiality, is important but it is not in itself an act of discovery or creativity. It is important, therefore, to comprehend the creative discovery process as one that can involve chance, surprise, dumb luck, or happenstance. It is an indeterminate process not fully comprehensible within static equilibrium models. Thus, we must think contextually about the environment(s) most likely to encourage or facilitate experimentation, substitutional interaction, and unconventional thinking.

---

[10] *See* Kirzner, *Capitalist Process*, at 15–30.
[11] *See* Kirzner, *Capitalist Process*, at 6–10, 93–118. *See also* Jerry Evensky, *Economic Ideas and Issues* 286–290 (1990); Kirzner, *Meaning*, at 46.

A second view of the entrepreneur offered by Israel Kirzner focuses on the idea of the entrepreneur as a person exercising a special "alertness" to gaps in market knowledge and who pursues these gaps in the hopes of obtaining a "pure profit."[12] Kirzner's gaps are similar to my idea of semiotic space. In his approach, he distinguishes between a rational or deliberate act of learning to overcome ignorance or to exploit a particular market opportunity, and knowledge that is obtained by surprise. In the first instance, he suggests that standard market-equilibrium models can be used to address the cost and benefit considerations confronting the individual actor.[13] The key is that such an actor begins with an awareness of his ignorance – "an awareness sufficiently detailed to permit one to identify the specific items of knowledge that one lacks."[14] In contrast to this he asserts that a market process approach also concerns itself with a second kind of knowledge, "characterized precisely by the surprise involved by the discovery, and by the corresponding earlier unawareness of the nature of one's ignorance."[15]

To explain this distinction more fully he provides the following example.

Consider a market in which two prices prevail for the same commodity in different parts of the same market. Equilibrium theory, of course, would deny such a possibility outright and claim that it can be salvaged only by postulating *different qualities* of commodity (more carefully defined) or the existence of barriers separating the market into *separate* markets. For equilibrium theory such a barrier might be the presence of ignorance that is costly to remove. Market process theory insists that the possibility of the same commodity selling at different prices within the same market can be entirely accounted for by the phenomenon of costlessly removable unknown ignorance. Unknown ignorance is ignorance concerning which one is unaware. Suppose that one buys fruit for $2, when the same fruit is openly available for $1 in a neighbouring store which one has just passed but overlooked. Then it is clear that one might costlessly have been able to know where to buy the fruit for $1, and in fact paid $2 for it only because one did not know of the possibility of costlessly commanding the needed information – in other words, one has suffered from being unaware of one's costlessly removable ignorance. When one discovers that the fruit for which one has been paying $2 is in fact available for $1, this comes as a surprise. The discovery itself cannot, given the circumstance, have been undertaken deliberately; after all one did not even know anything existed to be discovered.[16]

He goes on to emphasize that the process of *deliberate* search is fully determinate, therefore it is understandable within an equilibrium model, but the process of discovery is not determinate.[17] This is because

---

[12] Kirzner, *Meaning*, at 46; Kirzner, *Capitalist Process*, at ix–40, 150–158.
[13] Kirzner, *Meaning*, at 45–49.
[14] *Id.*   [15] *Id.* at 46–47.   [16] *Id.* at 47.   [17] *Id.* at 48–49.

there is no guarantee that anyone will ever notice things of which they are totally ignorant: "the most complete rationality of decision making in the world cannot ensure search for that the existence of which is wholly unsuspected."[18]

The example of fruit prices, above, is akin to that feeling one gets upon discovering something new as a result of being forced to take a detour in driving to work. The detour disrupts and deforms habit and draws one's attention to valuable information – information that was previously unsuspected. It also draws attention to the importance of disruption in the patterns and networks of conventional exchange.

Kirzner's conception of entrepreneurism is compatible with and can be further developed by the use of semiotic theory. From a semiotic point of view we might say that markets have a tendency toward habit-forming patterns of meaning and value – of conventionalizing ideas and creating interpretive equilibriums. In part, these patterns can be made comprehensible by reference to hypothetical and provisional models of equilibrium theory. At the same time, however, markets, as ongoing exchange processes, express a potentiality for continuous revision and creativity. They contain an element of indeterminacy or freedom that cannot be captured or expressed by determinate models of equilibrium theory. In semiotic theory these two conflicting conceptions of the market, one based on habit, continuity, and determinacy, the other based on chance, surprise, and indeterminacy, are reconcilable. These two approaches are reconciled in a logic that rejects dualistic thinking, requiring acceptance of either theory "A" or theory "B." In a Peircean semiotic, speculative inquiry is triadic and proceeds in terms of both "A" *and* "B" as present in a third, "C." This gives rise to an "A1" and a "B1" present in a "C1," giving rise to an "A2" and a "B2" that are present in a "C2," and so on, all of which also hold out the possibility of creating something entirely new such as a "D" or an "E," in a continuous process of semiosis. The ideational image of this triadic way of thinking is *thought in motion*. Semiotic theory, as such, recognizes the relational positioning of all exchange processes, and that interpretation, at one and the same time, expresses habit/continuity and chance/indeterminacy. Therefore, meaning, belief, and argument are provisional and are subject to instability, fallibility, and revision.[19]

In semiotic theory discovery emerges from the identification and exploitation of the semiotic spaces between conventionalized codes of understanding and the unconventional positioning of something new

[18] *Id.* at 48.
[19] *See* James Jacob Liszka, *A General Introduction to the Semeiotic of Charles Sanders Peirce* 102–103 (1996); Christopher Hookway, *Peirce* 72–73, 152–172 (1992).

and different. This process of discovery is brought about in a number of ways, including investment in deliberate learning, chance, surprise, happenstance, and dumb luck. It results from being surrounded by and embedded within a universe of continuously unfolding networks of exchange – exchanges that position us in a dynamic and uncertain world, exchanges that force us to interact, evaluate, make decisions, and to participate in an ongoing community of speculative inquiry. These exchange processes are a natural part of any discursive, communicative form of social organization. Furthermore, they are all substitutional and, in the absence of any pure or perfect substitutes, they continuously generate new "shades" of value and meaning.

Every exchange, in other words, creates a surplus value or meaning, and this value is generated without the necessity of a deliberate self-interested search for economic profit. The generation of value is, therefore, conceptually distinguishable from its identification and economic exploitation. Consequently, in order to enhance wealth formation, we must facilitate the development of extensive and participatory networks of social/market exchange, *and* we must provide incentives for the act of discovery as a means of signaling the value to the community of any given act. In this framework, the market equilibrium approach of traditional law and economics remains of some importance. This is because it serves as an indexical referent allowing individuals (Kirzner's alert entrepreneurs) to judge or become aware of the presence and significance of some new value. In rewarding the exercise of such judgment we help keep people alert to the presence of creative potentiality embedded in the exchange networks that surround them, and by extending participation in these networks we add to the production of surplus exchange value.

Creativity, as I am discussing it, includes countless incremental changes in meanings and values as well as dramatic leaps from major events and discoveries. In all exchanges, private and public, creativity emerges from experimentation, and from the trials and errors of actors reasoning from experience in environments recognizable by convention and habit. The experiential nature of this process means that each individual brings a different perspective to bear on the exchange process. Experience represents the dispersion of knowledge throughout society and an environment that facilitates individual initiative promotes entrepreneurial alertness and sustainable wealth formation. It is this alertness to variance or incongruence between experience and convention that leads to discovery and the traversing of semiotic space.

The discovery process that I am discussing also leads to the identification of two different types of wealth, each of which is relevant to the market exchange process. The first I identify as *reactive wealth*. This form of wealth is related to the equilibrium approach of traditional law and economics. The second form of wealth I designate as *proactive wealth*. This form of wealth is related to imaginative choice and the process of discovery. Traditional law and economics attempts to measure wealth in physical or quantitative terms and does this by translating all of the human experience into monetary units of iconic or token value. Even love, marriage, and child-rearing fail to escape such monetization or token representation.[20] In this way, traditional legal economists stand ready to compare all aspects of life within an allocative framework given over to determinate calculation of optimal, equilibrating, relationships. This approach is incomplete and it errs in its failure to acknowledge that human experience is incapable of being fully unitized into readily comparable monetary form. This failure distorts the value of efficiency analysis and promotes a limited, determinate, and constrained conception of wealth maximization. It undervalues the role of individual freedom in the process of promoting sustainable wealth formation.

The traditional approach directs its attention only to the presentation of a theory of how to make the best use of what we think we already have. In contrast, the approach of market economy addresses this plus the indeterminate nature of the market's future – the creation of new wealth as reflected in the generation of new meanings and relationships in the exchange process. The traditional approach reflects or references a reactive theory of wealth and wealth maximization because it addresses itself to considerations of allocation within a particular and determinate opportunistic environment. Law and market economy, on the other hand, incorporates Peirce's notion of the possible as a real that becomes meaningful in the value (re)shaping and (re)formation process.[21] It does this by including a proactive conception of wealth and by addressing the environmental context in which future wealth is most likely to arise.

The distinction between proactive and reactive wealth can be further explained by reference to a classic example in the work of Adam Smith. Smith noted, for example, that it was not from the benevolence of the butcher, the brewer, or the baker that we received their services but

---

[20] *See, e.g.*, Richard A. Posner, *Sex and Reason* (1992); Richard A. Posner, *Economic Analysis of Law* (4th ed., 1991); Richard B. McKenzie and Gordon Tullock, *The New World of Economics: Explorations into the Human Experience* (1975); Steven E. Landsburg, *The Armchair Economist: Economics and Everyday Life* (1993); Gary S. Becker, The Economics of Life (1997); Gary S. Becker, *The Economic Approach to Human Behavior* (1976).

[21] *See, e.g.*, Kevelson, *Peirce and Freedom*, at 1–30, 39–43; Roberta Kevelson, *The Law as a System of Signs* 130 (1998); Kevelson, *Peirce and Science*, at 64.

rather from their concern for their own self-interest.[22] In traditional law and economics the point of this example is that individuals pursuing self-interest, acting rationally to maximize wealth, end up benefiting third parties. This much it seems is true, but the example raises an even more important question that goes unnoticed in the reactive analysis of the traditional legal economist. The real question of interest in this example, with respect to wealth creation and wealth maximization, is under what conditions did it come to be known that being a butcher, a brewer, or a baker would be a wealth-generating activity? In other words, what environmental context best facilitates imaginative choice and experimentation for creating a new product or service in the first instance? What alerts one to the potential self-interested profitability of a particular activity *before the appearance of* butchers, bakers, and computer-chip makers? Reactive analysis picks up at a point in the example that misses the most important theoretical problem – the problem of creativity, trial and error, and potentiality, the problem of imagining a profitable role in a position not yet created. This is precisely the problem that proactive analysis seeks to address. It is the same problem we observe in some lawyers and law students. There are those who are content to think in terms of what the law "is" versus those that understand the contingent nature of that conclusion and who appreciate the role that each can play in shaping and transforming law and public policy.

Coase Theorem

The distinction between reactive and proactive thinking can also be illustrated by reference to the standard Coase Theorem example used in traditional law and economics.[23] The classic scenario involves a polluting factory discharging waste into the environment. To explore this idea better, let us consider a situation where a factory discharges waste

---

[22] *See* Adam Smith, *An Inquiry into the Nature and Causes of the Wealth of Nations*, vol. 1, 18 (Edwin Cannon, ed., 1976). He discusses the idea of an *invisible hand* in a passage, *id.*, at 477–478, and also in Adam Smith, *The Theory of Moral Sentiments* 297–307 (E.G. West, ed., 1969). Smith also points out, however, that self-interest is not a proper motivation. *Id.*, at 71–72. He denounces Hobbes and his theory of self-interest and self-love. *Id.*, at 499–508. He explains that self-interest is different from selfishness. *Id.*, at 161–165.

[23] *See* Ronald H. Coase, "The Problems of Social Cost," 3 J. Law & Econ. 1 (1960) (Coase's original article). *See also* Robin Paul Malloy, *Law and Economics: A Comparative Approach to Theory and Practice* 34–38 (1990); Robert Cooter and Thomas Ulen, *Law and Economics* 79–93 (2nd ed., 1997). *See generally* "Symposium, A Response and a Reply to Whether Pigs Can Fly," 38 Wayne L. Rev. 1 (1991) (a forum on the Coase Theorem); Donald N. McCloskey, "The Lawyerly Rhetoric of Coase's 'The Nature of the Firm,'" 18 J. Corp. L. 425 (1993).

into a nearby river causing injury to six homeowners living downstream. In this situation we can assume, as is typically the case, that
several options are available for solving this externality problem. Let us
assume that the outcome options available to our community include:
(1) allowing the factory to discharge but requiring the payment of
damages to the downstream homeowners; (2) requiring the factory to
install a filter system at the point of discharge to eliminate the waste
before it enters the river; or (3) requiring the downstream homeowners
to install personal home filters in each home so that water intake from
the river will be cleaned at the point of entry into the home environment.
Assume further that there is a price differential between the above three
outcomes such that the filter at the factory point of discharge is the
lowest cost alternative at $300. This is followed by the collective cost of
an at-home filter system that each homeowner would have to purchase
at $75 each for a total of $450, and then by the amount of damages that
must either be paid by the factory to the homeowners or absorbed by
each of them if no filter system is used, assume $100 of damages for
each household and a total cost of $600.

The Coase Theorem holds that in a world of zero transaction costs,
the efficient (wealth-maximizing) choice alternative will be selected
without regard to the legal rule. That is, it makes no difference if (1) the
law permits the factory, as a landowner with riparian rights, to discharge
by-products into the river, or (2) the law protects the rights of all
homeowners to have clean water. Whether the legal rule grants the
factory a right to discharge (pollute) or it grants the homeowners a right
to clean water, the Coase Theorem suggests that the most efficient
outcome will be selected from the three options identified above. As
long as all parties are aware of the three options (as would be the case in
perfect competition) and there are few or no costs of transacting, the
lowest cost alternative – the filter for the factory – will be purchased
without regard for the legal rule. Under the first rule – permitting the
factory to pollute – the filter for the factory will be purchased by the
collective action of the homeowners and under the second rule –
providing for a legal right to clean water – the filter will be purchased by
the factory.[24]

The explanation for this is that under the first rule the factory has a
right to discharge – that is, it has certain property or use rights in the
river – some form of riparian rights, let us say. Thus, the legal burden
to provide clean water falls upon the homeowners and they must
correct the dirty water problem. Assuming no transaction costs, perfect

[24] *See* Malloy, *Law and Economics*, at 34–38.

information, and economically rational actors they will buy a filter for the factory (as a gift) because it is the cheapest way for them to solve their problem. The $300 filter for the factory costs each of them $50 as compared to the $75 for a personal home filter and $100 of damages for each. Similarly, if the rule is reversed and the homeowners have a right to clean water, making the factory legally responsible for the purity of the water, the factory will assess the situation and purchase a filter for the point of discharge because it is the most economically efficient way to act within the contextual constraints of the assumptions. Buying a $300 filter to install at the factory is cheaper than buying a $75 filter for each of the six homeowners ($450 total cost), and it is cheaper than paying each homeowner $100 in damages ($600 total cost).

The Coase Theorem goes on to suggest that transaction costs can change this outcome and cause the parties involved to make a less than socially optimal choice. If, for instance, the homeowners confront significant transaction costs in getting organized and acting collectively to deal with the pollution problem, they may opt to purchase their own personal filter system when the legal rule grants the factory a right to discharge pollutants. To understand this, let us assume that the cost of getting good information about the problem and the available corrective options, together with the difficulty of organizing all the homeowners and enforcing a contribution or collective agreement between them, is high – let us assume transaction costs of $80 per household. With transaction costs of this amount, homeowners might end up selecting the option of buying their own home filter system rather than working collectively to purchase a single filter system for the factory. The high transaction costs mean that they will not act collectively but will consider the individual options that they confront. Given this frame of reference the cost of the filter for the factory would be $50 plus $80 per household, or a total of $130 each. This makes the factory filter more expensive than the $75 personal home filter system and the $100 in damages.

Given transaction costs, the personal home filter system erroneously appears to be the best choice outcome, but this is not the most economically efficient outcome as can be seen by anyone capable of understanding all of the trade-offs and distanced from the problem of transaction costs. The factory filter costs $300 or $50 per household but the purchase of the individual units costs a total of $450 or $75 each. Because an inefficient choice is made, society wastes valuable resources. That is, as a community, the group spends more money than needed to correct the dirty water problem. It spends $450 rather than $300 and this means that $150 that could have been available for other activities is wasted. This is an inefficient outcome.

In our situation, with $80 of transaction costs per household, the socially efficient outcome, the least-cost alternative, will only be selected if the legal rule places liability on the factory by granting the home-owners a right to clean water. Under a clean water rule the factory is legally responsible, and since it does not need to coordinate with any other parties, its transaction costs are substantially lower than that of the homeowners. Thus, the factory will purchase the $300 filter for the point of discharge rather than pay $600 in damages or $450 to provide each homeowner with a personal home filter system. Consequently, the legal rule does make a difference when there are transaction costs.

The Coase Theorem also has an obvious implication for wealth distribution since the choice of legal rule, even under conditions of zero transaction costs, affects who pays for the corrective action. Even under a zero transaction costs assumption the choice of legal rule may be important. Remember we said that in such a situation it would not affect the outcome. It would, however, affect who pays for the filter and this raises distribution questions. If the rule places the burden on the home-owners and they happen to be poor they may lack the resources to address the problems they confront, without regard to the number of options available. In our illustration, for instance, they may lack the resources to purchase the individual filter units at $75 each. Therefore, this wealth effect may result in the least desirable social outcome because it means that the households will not take corrective measures, and each household will suffer $100 in damages. This outcome is the least efficient alternative in our illustration. On the other hand, if the rule places the burden on the factory owner one might argue that the factory could easily absorb the cost of corrective action or pass the cost on to customers, but competitive pressure from companies located in jurisdictions without these costly rules may prevent the passing on of such costs, and even if it can pass on the costs its customers may or may not be the beneficiaries of the clean water. Furthermore, customers may be located in different jurisdictions than either the factory or the home-owners. In other words, there may be transboundary jurisdiction issues with different legal regimes operating. All of this means that political trading may also play a role in these distribution matters and as a result it may become difficult or impossible to determine the real efficiency value of any given choice.

This analysis of the Coase Theorem further suggests that in order to reduce the inefficient use of scarce resources the law must attempt to clearly define private property rights and reduce transaction costs. It implies a course of legislative action if *experts* are better able than countless individuals to identify and overcome the choice and cost structure of alternative approaches. Naturally, if an expert can understand the relevant choices better than other non-experts he can overcome the problem of high transaction costs for each of the households. He can do this by delivering legislation, under our above assumptions, that adopts a legal rule in favor of homeowners and providing for a right to clean water. This rule promotes the efficient outcome by placing responsibility for clean water on the factory. The factory then makes the efficient choice and purchases the point-of-discharge filter. *Assuming* his cost and choice assumptions and constraints are correct, the expert can use law to move us in the direction of economic efficiency. The interpretation of his valuation choices is, of course, open to debate, but if he can shape the debate in one direction (toward the presence of high transaction costs) he will establish an economic basis for legislative action. On the other hand, if the debate can be shaped in the opposite direction (toward the presence of low transaction costs) there will be an economic basis for non-intervention. Thus, the discourse of transaction costs positions the dispute as one of fact and favors the use of "experts" and the exercise of government intervention in the marketplace.

The choice of legal rule also raises implications that go beyond questions of distributional impact and the role of legislative expertise. The rule itself changes the interpretive frame of reference for exchange. Rule choice, in other words, impacts on the meaning and value formation process of social organization and interaction. Consider our dirty water example. A rule that protects the homeowner's right to clean water imposes a duty on the factory. The choice is dualistic, and under our situational assumptions this leads to the "efficient" result of making the factory bear the cost of corrective action. Now, of course, to the extent that the factory can pass on its costs it will do so and the consumers of factory production will implicitly end up paying for at least part of the cost.

This approach, of placing the cost of corrective action on the producer, is one that represents the focus of the vast majority of environmental regulations in the United States. One problem with this type of rule, however, is that it denies the explicit role of the consumer in activities that cause environmental degradation. These rules, by focusing on producers, allow consumers completely to ignore the fact that they are involved in the entire process. The original rule choice was presented as dualistic and the rule selection process declared the producer, not the consumer, responsible. Consumers are allowed to feel absolved of responsibility and most of them accept this interpretation.

In my own experience I find that this view is reflected in general conversation as well as in the work of my students. Again and again, I hear complaints about corporate destruction of the environment, about irresponsible disposal of environmental waste by greedy businesses, about a corporate failure to use proper safety procedures, and about the desire of big business to exploit the environment and low-cost labor in all parts of the world.

I usually respond to such allegations by asking the inquisitors why it is that companies might engage in the particular activities being complained about. I usually get responses that include references to greed, selfishness, profit, and intrinsic evil. Following up, I ask if the desire to point the finger at the business world is not just a little too convenient and dualistic. It is as if the complainers envision a sharp and distinct separation between producers and consumers; as if each inhabited an entirely different world. They seldom seem to understand the relationship between production and consumption. They fail fully to comprehend that their demand for goods and services at low prices drives and influences production and producer action. Likewise, they seldom seem to make the connection between their environmental concerns and the fact that most American consumers simply want to pay the lowest possible prices for the products and services that they demand. For example, if a television set or a pair of running shoes will cost less when produced by child labor under conditions that require little regard for the environment, American consumers have generally shown that they will buy it. Feeling no direct responsibility for production, the consumer guiltlessly complains while all the time fueling the competitive pressure for businesses to cut corners and seek lower-cost methods of production. For the consumer it is the best of both worlds: high levels of consumption without responsibility.

To a large extent, the problem I am discussing involves a failure to understand that pollution and environmental degradation are as much consumption problems as they are production problems. In other words, exchange here, as elsewhere, is relational. One reason for this misunderstanding is that the selection of the legal rule raises implications for the meaning and value-formation process. The interpretive reference for most rules on environmental regulation imposes legal duties and responsibility on producers, and because of dualistic thinking this is translated into the idea that consumers must therefore be innocent. This message is harmoniously consistent with the general market assumptions of "the consumer is always right," and that individuals are detached from communities and social relationships. It is also consistent with many social narratives, from those found in James

Bond films with numerous corporate villains, to those beneath the most recent Star Wars epic with the evil "dark side" working through the commercial medium of the Trade Federation. These narratives depict the nature of business as greedy, selfish, and evil.

I suggest that if rule choices made consumers responsible, or if consumers had to pay an explicit environmental tax on everything that they consumed, meanings and values would be different. Consequently, the choice of the legal rule, even under conditions of zero transaction costs, makes a difference. It makes a difference not only in terms of distributional impact but also in terms of the interpretive framework and meanings given to particular exchange relationships.

Other interpretive issues are also raised by the Coase Theorem. Our Coase Theorem example, for instance, demonstrates thinking within a reactive framework and this type of thinking restricts the process of choice. In our example we were presented with three alternative methods for correcting the dirty water problem. Each method is known and each is given a price (factory filter $300, home filter $75 × 6 = $450, and damages of $100 × 6 = $600). Anyone who has the relevant information can easily calculate the most efficient way to allocate resources, and can, thus, readily select the socially optimal course of action. This example illustrates thinking within the status quo, within the context of identifiable constraints and options. Efficiency analysis, in traditional law and economics, takes this form. It is reactive in that it tells us how to make the best use of the resources we already know that we have, but it says little about the conditions under which new options might be facilitated and discovered. It also promotes a sense of certainty to the analysis of the problem because we can use simple math to calculate an efficient result. The numbers used in these calculations, however, are often "fuzzy" and based on debatable assumptions. This means that the calculus of efficient outcomes can be influenced by or manipulated with minor variations in assumed costs and benefits.

In comparison to traditional law and economics, law and market economy seeks to understand the current situation while also promoting the need for proactive thinking, thinking which attempts to direct our attention to that which we do not yet know, but which we might be able to imagine. Such imaginative thought is unconstrained by the deterministic approach of traditional law and economics. At the same time, it proceeds with reference to signs, symbols, and suggested meanings of the traditional approach. Imaginative thought, as speculative inquiry, is, after all, knowable as such by reference to convention and habit. Consequently, by challenging, testing, and confronting the constraints of the Coase Theorem, imaginative thought directs our attention to further creative possibilities, and to alternative choice options with different cost and benefit relationships.

From an imaginative or proactive perspective, for example, we might begin by asking why the Coase Theorem typically addresses problems such as pollution from within the language of *externality*. Why are these effects external or foreign to the activity of the factory? Why are the third party consequences of a manufacturing process not considered to be *internal* effects thereby expressing a value statement about the natural relationship between downriver consequences and the profit-seeking venture within the factory? How might this view change our thinking? Likewise, why is it that we are typically asked to consider choice options based on purely monetary cost and benefit trade-offs without consideration of the authority relationships, political relationships, and historical factors leading up to and contextualizing these choices?

This reactive way of thinking and positioning inquiry builds upon a conventionalized framework for addressing problems of social exchange. It reduces our ability to think alternatively or imaginatively about, for instance, an alternative form of production or the desirability of the factory's product in the first instance – or how and why we fail to value our own rivers, environment, and health from an alternative point of view such as "stewardship."[25] Questions of this type, validated as legitimate market process inquiries, could open up new networks of speculative investigation, and could promote the process of creative innovation.

The Coase Theorem, however, like much of traditional law and economics, has no satisfactory way of dealing with the idea of wealth and wealth maximization as emerging from the process of discovery. Instead, the traditional approach focuses on a given economic framework and then reacts by using law in an instrumental way to direct individuals in making a contextualized, rational, and self-interested allocative choice. Its assumptions lead to predetermined conclusions as if future events or outcomes are fully knowable in the present. Proactive analysis, under law and market economy, is less determinate and focuses on the *process* of exchange. It therefore opens up a broader range of speculative inquiry as legitimate within market theory, and this leaves open the very real possibility of people exercising imaginative, as well as rational, choice. Proactive analysis, in other words, recognizes that

---

[25] *See, e.g.*, Jeff L. Lewin, "Toward a New Ecological Law and Economics" in *Law and Economics: New and Critical Perspectives* (Robin Paul Malloy and Christopher K. Braun, eds., 1995), at 249–294; Alan Reder, *In Pursuit of Principle and Profit: Business Success Through Social Responsibility* (1994) (discussing alternative approaches to market success).

exchange is complex and dynamic. People cannot possibly account for all of the variables needed to calculate a truly efficient outcome. This is particularly true when the nature of their claim is really to assert what *will* be efficient. This involves a speculative conclusion about the relationship between current choices and future outcomes. At best this can only be an educated guess grounded in experience about expected possible outcomes. This means that there are a number of potential choices and outcomes that may all be equally justifiable as potentially efficient. This does not mean that we can never plan for the future. It merely recognizes that the process of planning is more complex and uncertain than is typically represented by traditional efficiency analysis.

The Coase Theorem raises yet another interesting issue when one considers its implications for the exchange process. Under an assumption of zero transaction costs an implication arises that the judgment of every individual is in some sense equal. There is perfect information, no barriers to market entry or exit, no problem with prior distributional or historical consequence, free and frictionless mobility of goods, services, and resources, and complete rationality. Personal experience provides no advantage or disadvantage in the exchange process. In such a fictitious world there would be no reason to give primacy to any particular individual's judgment, and choice would involve a simple factual calculation. On the other hand, the implication changes once we acknowledge the presence of transaction costs, externalities, and spillover effects as part of the real world.

Life in a world of more than zero transaction costs is life in a world of personal and subjective experiences that make a difference in the networks and patterns of exchange. There is imperfect information, there are barriers to entry and exit, there are problems of distributional and historical consequence, there is less than free and frictionless mobility of goods, services, and resources, and emotion, instinct, and other forces sometimes deform and distort the assumptional meaning of rationality. In such a world authoritative participation in the exchange process can be either more or less extensive. Issues of access and mobility, for instance, may vary significantly by such factors as race, gender, ethnicity, religion, education level, geography, age, family composition, and other variables. In a world of transaction costs these factors are important because different experiences mean that different fragments of knowledge are dispersed in an uncoordinated manner over countless individuals. Tapping into these knowledge fragments by facilitating extensive networks and patterns of exchange promotes creativity and sustainable wealth formation. It also reveals that choice is an interpretive process involving value considerations as well as factual assumptions.

A further implication of a world of positive transaction costs is that some people, "experts," may be deemed better situated than others to shape the decision-making process. This is easy to imagine. It is like the difference between making a decision about which road to take to work when you see the road from behind the wheel of your car versus from the position of a helicopter pilot surveying the traffic patterns from above. Driving on the highway, in your car alongside hundreds of other drivers, gives you a very different basis for decision making than that of the helicopter pilot who is able to see a multivehicle accident a mile up the road from your current location. Likewise, your ability to exercise some control over the speed and direction of your car is very different from the position of the person who rides the bus and submits to the judgment of a bus driver. Each of the people in this example – the pilot, the car driver, the bus commuter – have access to different information and have different experiences upon which to base expectations and make choices. In some sense, the pilot in our example is positioned like our fictional expert in the water pollution problem as confronted by our factory and six households in the earlier example. Somewhat removed from the immediate situation on the ground, the pilot can more clearly appreciate the options available and select a more efficient course of action for traffic flow than the drivers and commuters below. Furthermore, with an eye toward facilitating the overall flow of traffic for the benefit of the public at large she can make choices that are seemingly superior to those of the less-informed people on the ground. She can appreciate the lack of unity between the public interest and the individual driver's perception of self-interest in this situation.

In a world of transaction costs, therefore, "experts" would seemingly be given more authority than non-experts, and inequality between exchange participants increases as some are cloaked in expertise and others are not. It thus becomes important to consider the basis upon which one becomes an expert. What factors, in our example, place one person in the pilot seat while others are drivers and commuters on the ground below, and what elements of the human experience go unappreciated as a result of our expert's privileged position? These are questions of relational exchange, questions of law and market economy rather than economic efficiency.

Public choice

Communities frequently turn to the political process to address collective problems, problems that might be deemed difficult for individuals to resolve on their own or beyond the proper consideration of individual self-interest. Such problems, like our traffic-management problem above, might best be addressed by experts or by public bodies capable of considering a multiplicity of perspectives and points of reference. When decision making and regulation emerges from the process of collective action it is often times analyzed under the guise of public choice theory. Public choice theory, like the Coase Theorem, raises interesting issues for our understanding of the relationship between law and market theory.

If we reconsider the water pollution problem used in our earlier discussion of the Coase Theorem we can better appreciate the issues raised by public choice theory. In our illustrative fact pattern we saw how transaction costs might prevent the individual households from making the most efficient choice. As a consequence of transaction costs we saw that homeowners would select the individual home water-filter systems rather than the cheaper system installed at the factory. This decision resulted in spending $450 rather than $300 to correct the problem. The difference of $150 represents the inefficient use of scarce resources – resources that could have been used to provide other goods and services. The significance of this observation is that the choice of the legal rule does make a difference in terms of the efficiency of the outcome. In a situation where households confront substantial transaction costs, an expert might be able to see beyond this problem and work to achieve the socially efficient outcome by legislating a legal rule that granted homeowners a legal right to clean water. This legal rule, as we saw, placed the burden for clean water on the factory owner and promoted the efficient outcome. This raises an important question. How are we to interpret the meaning of legislation? Does a particular legal rule reflect an expert determination that overcomes transaction costs to provide a more efficient use of valuable scarce resources? Does the rule, therefore, reflect a public interest or purpose as well as an economically efficient choice? On the other hand, might the rule merely reflect the pressure and influence of special interest groups without regard for efficiency? Maybe the chosen rule reflects rent-seeking behavior rather than an assessment of the public good. Perhaps some labor unions and environmentalists joined forces with our six households in order to get a legal rule that simply placed the cost of corrective action on the factory owner, and no one ever considered transaction costs or efficiency. Similarly, the legal rule might simply be the product of incentives and disincentives within the internal structure of the legislative body – a product of horse trading and deal making done somewhat independently of any real deliberative consideration of the underlying issues in the specific situation at hand.

Since law and market economy is concerned with choice, as an interpretive process, the nature of public choice is important. The best place to begin an analysis of this matter is with Arrow's Impossibility Theorem.[26] Arrow's Theorem informs us that it is impossible to satisfy all of the conditions necessary for public decision making to reflect the preferences of the individuals comprising the society, and that public decisions may or may not be taken as attempts to promote the socially efficient rule. The Theorem maintains that four conditions would need to be met in order for social choices to reflect democratic decision making. These four conditions are: (1) social choice must be transitive (if x is preferred to y and y is preferred to z, z cannot be preferred to x); (2) social choices must not respond in an opposite direction to changes in individual choice (the fact that some people come to hold a certain preference cannot result in society rejecting that preference if society would otherwise have chosen it); (3) social choice must not be controlled by any one person inside or outside of the group; and (4) the social preference between two alternative choices must depend only on people's feelings with respect to those alternatives and not with reference to any other alternative. Arrow's research indicated, as one familiar with semiotics and exchange process would suspect, that it is impossible to maintain these conditions.

A simple example of the voting process reveals further insight. Suppose a given legislative body is considering legislation with respect to the legal rule to govern the issue of water quality as between our factory owner and our six households living downstream from the factory. To keep the example simple, assume that there are only three legislators (A, B, C) and three legislative proposals (listed below) to consider. Furthermore, assume that by good fortune we know the revealed preferences of each legislator in terms of how they rank each of the possible rule options. The options involve legislative proposals that reflect three alternative approaches described as:

(1) Dirty water rule. This rule protects the rights of all owners of land abutting a navigable waterway to discharge waste into the stream. Thus, there is no liability on the factory for a discharge.

---

[26] *See* Kenneth J. Arrow, *Social Choice and Individual Values* (1951). On public choice and Arrow's Theorem, *see generally*, Malloy, *Law and Economics*, at 42–45; Daniel A. Farber and Philip P. Frickey, "The Jurisprudence of Public Choice," 65 Tex. L. Rev. 873 (1987); Daniel A. Farber and Philip P. Frickey, "Legislative Intent and Public Choice," 74 Va. L. Rev. 423 (1988); Jonathan R. Macey, "Promoting Public Regarding Legislation Through Statutory Interpretation: An Interest Group Model," 86 Colum. L. Rev. 223 (1986); Mancur Olson, *The Logic of Collective Action: Public Goods and the Theory of Groups* (1971); James Buchanan and Gordon Tullock, *The Calculus of Consent: Logical Foundations of Constitutional Democracy* (1962).

Table 1. Rules preferences

Rank	Legislator		
	A	B	C
1st	Dirty	Clean	Contract
2nd	Clean	Contract	Dirty
3rd	Contract	Dirty	Clean

(2) Clean water rule. This rule protects the right of all residents to draw clean and safe water from all streams and rivers. Thus, polluters are liable for degradation of water quality.

(3) Contract rule. This rule leaves the matter to the individual owners of land abutting and using navigable waters and provides for them freely to contract with each other as to liability. This is basically a "hands-off" approach that appeals to those who would rather see the absence of a clean water rule and who prefer less government intrusion into the marketplace. Leaving the matter to individual contracting means that transaction costs will be a factor in reaching a final outcome, assuming one believes that transaction costs are significant enough to be of concern.

As to each of these rules the revealed preferences of our legislators is reflected in table 1.

Assume that for ease of discussion and voting the group has elected a voting procedure mandating that only two alternatives can be considered at a time. The alternative receiving the most votes is then considered relative to the third or remaining option in order to determine the final rule adopted. Following this simple procedure we can see what happens. If the legislators vote between Dirty water and Clean water, Dirty will win (two of the three rank the Dirty water rule higher than the Clean water rule). Then as between the Dirty water rule and the Contract rule, the Contract rule will win and be adopted by the group (two of them prefer the Contract rule to the Dirty water rule). If they vote first on Dirty water versus Contract, Contract will win and then compared with the Clean water rule, the final outcome will be the Clean water rule. If they vote first on Contract versus Clean water, Clean water will win and then compared to Dirty water, Dirty water will be the final rule. Given three different voting patterns we observe three different rule outcomes – three different path-dependent outcomes: in the first the Contract rule, in the second the Clean water rule, and in the third the Dirty water rule. Consequently, even under these assumptions we see that the outcome reflects authoritative influence over the voting process rather than a clear commitment to a particular "efficient" outcome. Such a situation directs attention toward an investigation of voter preferences so that one might strategically work to influence the order of the vote, and thereby have an impact upon the ultimate rule adopted.

From the point of view of law and market economy the above example illustrates an important concept. It informs us of the difficulty in assessing the extent to which a legislative rule has anything to do with efficiency. This is true even though legislative intervention may have been prompted by an assertion of numerous transaction costs that prevented the affected parties from achieving the most efficient outcome. Like the broader marketplace of which the legislative body is merely a smaller representation, decision making involves dynamic and complex variables. Neither the legislative outcome nor the legislative process can be fully governed by the deterministic constraints of efficiency. The future facts, variables, and legal disputes that might be implicated under any given rule are not fully knowable. Furthermore, knowledge is dispersed throughout society and not available in total to anyone. As a result, we unnecessarily limit our understanding of the relationship between law and market theory if we assume that all legislative actors act either to achieve a broad socially defined efficient outcome, or to maximize, through efficiency, their own personal benefits from the institutional incentive structure of the groups or bodies to which they belong.

The process of public choice raises further additional considerations. For instance, to the extent that legislative bodies represent the public, they operate within the guise of agency. As agents for others we need to consider the degree to which the agents either can or do represent their principals. As a collective and representative body, the legislative group is a symbol or sign of the public-at-large, but, like any sign, it can only represent the public in some respects and not in all respects. Thus, to understand the meaning of legislation, cloaked in the legitimacy of *public* choice or *public* interest, we must investigate the nature of the public that is represented by the legislative group. We must consider access, influence, and other factors as related to a variety of criteria such as gender, race, age, education, income, and geographic location, among others.

Furthermore, to the extent that the legislative group performs the role of expert, as in my Coase example of the helicopter pilot, we must again be concerned with how one attains this privileged position. Similarly, we must consider the extent to which our figurative pilot can know and appreciate the interpretive points of view of those who are positioned in dramatically different networks and patterns of exchange. This consideration takes on added importance when we remember that life, in a world of positive transaction costs, results in the dispersion of fragmented and subjective experiences and information. Tapping into these information fragments, through extensive exchange networks, facilitates creativity and sustainable wealth formation, but achieving this through a process of legislative agency requires a truly accessible, representative, and accountable system.

Further consideration of our clean versus dirty water illustration reveals that our public choice example invokes three currently defined voting options. Thus, like our Coase example, the traditional law and economics framework is positioned as static rather than dynamic. More importantly, deliberation concerning these three legislative choices will take place within a shared interpretive framework. This is generally the case as collective action requires some common ground, or shared conventions, in order for the participants to have a sense of stability and predictability that is required for understanding each other. This means that there will be some element of a common ground within the group, and the stronger and broader the ground, the more likely it is that matters of legislative dispute will be translatable into disagreements as to facts rather than as to values. Similarly, the more that a common ground is assumed by public choice analysts, the more likely that cost and benefit considerations will be used to describe and interpret the networks and patterns of exchange. This in turn will function to reduce input from alternatively situated interpretive communities.

Public choice, like individual choice, is in this way an interpretive process and it will be influenced by reference to a variety of exogenous and endogenous variables. Even when preferences are fixed and fully revealed, outcomes will be shaped by influence over the interpretive choice-making process. In other words, public choice, like private or individual choice, is influenced by those exchange participants who exercise authority over the positioning of the interpretive frame of reference through which values and meanings are translated and transformed. Therefore, the more extensive the authoritative participation in the social/market exchange process, the more likely it will account for diverse individual experiences and knowledge. In turn, this will lend itself to an increased potential for unconventional and habit-reforming relationships.

In this process, competition will exist between people positioned within alternative interpretive communities as they seek to influence the operative frame of reference. They will employ strategic rhetorics, to be discussed in Chapter 6, below, to influence the process of formal and informal decision making. They will seek to ascribe meanings and values to the decision-making process and its outcomes. This is important because influence over the interpretive frame of reference results in influence over the substance of social organization and exchange, and has consequence for the process of sustainable wealth formation.

In the framework of a system of law and market economy, therefore, law can be understood as providing a necessary infrastructure for the extension of meaning and value through the process of exchange. It provides a dynamic and referent sign system respecting the methods, processes, and consequences of exchange. It facilitates market exchange by establishing dynamic guide posts between which meanings and values are capable of being continuously shaped and reshaped. The legal system, like the market, is dynamic and open rather than static and closed, and each functions as a relational sign system providing interpretive "markers" for unlimited exchange opportunities within an openended universe of social interaction.

5   Social organization and the discovery process

As we have seen, the market process is a continually evolving idea or sign system. It involves the human practice of exchange and creates, through substitution and permutation, constant realignments in values and meanings between people, their things, and their communities. Markets, as such, exist in all social contexts and since they are the dialogic result of individual and community experience, they can have different appearances reflecting the different values and meanings of diverse communities. Likewise, since markets make reference to a particular legal system for coherence, diverse communities operating under different socio-legal arrangements may have different market structures. This raises the question of what form of social organization might best facilitate experimentation, creativity, and discovery. To consider this matter, I will present a market-based conception of social organization and discuss its implications for sustainable wealth formation. I will then suggest a particular set of criteria that might best serve as an initial guide for understanding an environment of creative discovery. These suggestive criteria make up what I tentatively refer to as an ethic of social responsibility.

The relationship between social organization and proactive wealth formation

Traditional law and economics generally assumes that social organization is contractarian in nature.[1] It understands community as emerging

---

[1] See generally, Randy E. Barnett, "A Consent Theory of Contract," 86 Colum. L. Rev. 269 (1986); Randy E. Barnett, "Conflicting Visions: A Critique of Ian MacNeil's Relational Theory of Contract," 78 Va. L. Rev. 1175 (1992) (with respect to theories of the firm); Paul N. Cox, "The Public, the Private and the Corporation," 80 Marq. L. Rev. 393 (1997) (discussing the conflict between contractual and communitarian theories of the corporation); Robin Paul Malloy, *Planning for Serfdom: Legal Economic Discourse and Downtown Development* 28–29 (1991) (Adam Smith's rejection of social contract theory). *See* Robin Paul Malloy, *Law and Economics: A Comparative Approach to Theory and Practice* 38–42 (1990). Contract and the limitations of such a theory, *see* Michael J. Trebilcock, *The Limits of Freedom of Contract* (1993).

from consent and it metaphorically invokes the construct of the social contract as its connecting web.[2] The invocation of the social contract is ideal for the traditional view because it is based on the rational and self-interested choice process of autonomous individuals. These individuals act rationally to come together as a community based on an understanding of the comparative advantages of limited forms of social cooperation.[3] They come together and work together by choice and consent. They do this by contract, which is a system of private rather than public law ordering, and they do this to achieve economic gain.

The social contract model makes reference to our understanding of contract law. As such, it is very much consistent with the idea of self-centered interpersonal arrangements for an economic purpose. It promotes a view of autonomy and consensual relationships that converge with a concern for wealth maximization. It also suggests that there is some "actual" (real or constructive) consensual agreement binding the individuals of the community together. Consequently, much attention is generally paid to the discovery and clarification of the "terms" of this agreement. Thus, constitutions and legislation are examined with a careful desire to identify and enforce the original intentions or core values of the drafters, and great pains are taken by traditional legal economists to explain these intentions and values as favorable to autonomy and wealth maximization.

In a broader sense, social contract theory presents a view of human action as predominately consensual, deliberate, rational, and self-interested. This results in a legal framework that translates these assumptions into the presumptive values and meanings of the market process to which it refers. The exchange process, therefore, and the relationships that emerge therefrom, are generally deemed to be the result of consensual, deliberate, rational, and self-interested choice. This is the presumptive norm to which violations are seen as aberrational. Such violations are often illustrated by reference to categories in law related to fraud, misrepresentation, and mistake, all of which raise conflict issues for a presumption of consent.

In most exchanges, social contract theory presumes consent and the burden of proof falls on those asserting the contrary. This leads to some interesting observations. For example, agreements meeting the formal requirements of contract law are presumptively valid and enforceable

---

[2] For a general discussion of contract in a semiotic context, *see* Roberta Kevelson, *Peirce, Science, Signs* 43–58 (1996); Roberta Kevelson, *The Law as a System of Signs* 137–150 (1988).

[3] *See* Richard A. Epstein, *Takings: Private Property and the Power of Eminent Domain* (1985); Richard A. Epstein, "An Outline of Takings," 41 Univ. Miami L. Rev. 3 (1986).

even when problematic, as in the situation of a surrogate motherhood contract. Similarly, racial equality is presumed the norm because unmerited racial discrimination is considered inefficient (therefore, economically irrational) and racism is thus made to appear as specific and discrete acts of transgression rather than as institutional or systemic.[4] Likewise, all sexual encounters are considered voluntary and only considered rape when the woman can overcome the presumption of her consent.[5] The purpose of law in such a setting is to define rights that are subject to exchange, to facilitate private ordering by reducing transaction costs, and to promote optimal social outcomes based on the exercise of sound, individual, rational, and allocative choice. In other words, law is used to promote a particular approach to the exercise of authority and the shaping of social meaning based upon a presumptive norm of mutual consent.

This presumption of consent is further embedded in traditional law and economics by reference to standards of efficiency that declare actual voluntary exchanges (Pareto-efficient moves)[6] and hypothetically voluntary exchanges (Kaldor–Hicks-efficient moves)[7] to be wealth maximizing. Pareto-efficient exchanges are ones that make at least one person better off without making anyone else worse off. A voluntary exchange under standard neoclassical economic assumptions meets this standard because both parties are assumed to be better off as a result of the trade. Kaldor–Hicks efficiency considers an exchange to be wealth maximizing when the person who gains from the exchange gains more than the loser loses. Kaldor–Hicks efficiency does not require a voluntary exchange but rather presumes one. This presumption seemingly rests upon an assumption that the payout to the winner, being more than the loss to the loser, justifies the presumption of consent because rational and profit-motivated beings would willingly make such trades. A failure to trade under such conditions indicates, therefore, the presence of transaction costs, irrationality, incapacity, or something else that stands in the way of a "proper" decision. Under these circumstances it is right to go ahead without actual consent because consent can be implied from the nature, circumstances, and assumptions that drive the situational analysis. The problem is, given the assumptions

[4] *See, e.g.*, Richard Delgado, "Recasting the American Race Problem," Cal. L. Rev. 1389 (1991); Ron Stodghill, II, "Get Serious About Diversity Training," *Business Week*, November 25, 1996, at 39 (Texaco racist practices); "Texaco to Pay $176.1 Million in Bias Suit," Wall St. J., November 18, 1996, at A3.
[5] Catherine A. MacKinnon, "Feminism, Marxism, Method, and the State: Toward Feminist Jurisprudence," 8 Signs: J. Women Culture & Society 635 (1983).
[6] *See* Malloy, *Law and Economics*, at 38–42.
[7] *See id.*

that can be made about the values being exchanged and the conditions under which exchange takes place, the desire to presume consent seems instrumental to the evaluation of any given outcome. It is the idea of consent in social contract theory that stands behind the concept of freedom of contract in law. This idea, as I have said, is also generally considered to be important to the approach of traditional law and economics. On this topic much has been written and it is not my intention fully to analyze or critique this body of work. Michael Trebilcock has done much in his recent book, *The Limits of Freedom of Contract*, to enlighten us about some of these matters.[8] In his book he presents important considerations that shed light on problems of consent and of divergence between consensual autonomy and wealth maximization. Similarly, Gillian Hadfield has made important contributions to our understanding of consent problems based on an analysis of feminist issues in contract paradigms.[9] Therefore, rather than explore these issues in detail, I intend to argue that the acceptance of social contract theory is simply not essential to an understanding of law and market theory.

I borrow from the philosophical insights of Adam Smith and argue for a broader view of market theory and social organization based on the concepts of *authority* and *utility*.[10] We might understand authority, in this regard, as a cultural and contextual exercise of power that is accepted or tolerated for a number of reasons, including the perceived utility or benefit that it brings.[11] Authority, as such, is reciprocal and positions itself in reference to a community.[12] It represents a pattern of bounded constraint from within which numerous points of freedom or exchange occur. Patterns of authority in social organization may be

---

[8] *See* Trebilcock, *Contract.*

[9] *See, e.g.*, Gillian K. Hadfield, "The Dilemma of Choice: A Feminist Perspective on the Limits of Freedom of Contract," 33 Osgoode Hall L. J. 337 (1995); Gillian K. Hadfield, "An Expressive Theory of Contract: From Feminist Dilemmas to a Reconceptualization of Rational Choice in Contract Law," 146 Univ. Penn. L. Rev. 1235 (1998); Gillian K. Hadfield, "Of Sovereignty and Contract: Damages for Breach of Contract by Government," 8 So. Cal. Interdisc. L. J. 467 (1999); Gillian K. Hadfield, "The Second Wave of Law and Economics," 46 Univ. Toronto L. J. 181 (1996).

[10] Smith rejected social contract theory as being unrealistic and problematic. *See* Adam Smith, *Lectures on Jurisprudence* 207, 311–330, 401–407 (R.L. Meek et al., eds., 1978). In its place he offered a theory based on *authority* and *utility. Id. See generally,* Malloy, *Serfdom,* at 23–29; Robin Paul Malloy, "Adam Smith and the Modern Discourse of Law and Economics," in *Adam Smith and the Philosophy of Law and Economics* (Robin Paul Malloy and Jerry Evensky, eds., 1994), at 114–122; Friedrich A. Hayek, *The Constitution of Liberty* 220–228 (1960) (general rules and Adam Smith's notion of freedom).

[11] *See* Smith, *Jurisprudence,* at 207, 311–330, 401–407.

[12] *See generally* Charles H. Long, *Significations: Signs, Symbols, and Images in the Interpretation of Religion* (1986) (a Black sign system within a White-dominated culture).

based on consent, but they may also arise from the absence of viable alternatives.[13] Authority may be based on a pattern of habit, convention, and tradition that goes unquestioned, or it may proceed on the basis of logic and reason – it may be provisionally accepted as useful even if not supported by consent; in other words, it may provide utility.[14] In this system of relationships utility encompasses the benefits derived from the exercise of authority.

This conception of authority and utility is consistent with Peirce's assumptions concerning a natural tendency toward habit and pattern formation.[15] Habit, according to Peirce, is convention and convention defines authority – the potentiality of authority thus gives rise to its actuality in the emergent patterns and habits of social convention and exchange.[16] The object of the exercise of authority, in such a system, is to effectuate a realignment of value and meaning within society. The exercise of authority is, therefore, the essence of market exchange, and the more dispersed and accessible the elements of authority within a society, the greater should be the potential for social prosperity. Stated differently, the more accessible the social exchange process, the more open and creative will be the meaning and value-formation process, and the more likely it is that proactive wealth formation will increase. Evidence to be discussed in the final section of this Chapter seems to support this conclusion.

The analysis of authority in social relationships differs from an analysis based on a presumption of mutually informed consent under a theory of social contract. Authority analysis does not presume that social arrangements are the natural product of consensual, deliberate, rational, and self-interested choice. To the contrary, it presumes that social relationships are the product of a number of factors – factors that may or may not be consensual.[17] For example, social relationships may be the product of evolutionary extensions of authority through the continual process of naming and renaming and of defining and redefining. In such a setting the idea of consent emerges out of conventionalized codes or norms of what it means to consent or act voluntarily, and these codes can demonstrate variance over time and between interpretive

[13] See generally Roberta Kevelson, *Peirce's Esthetics of Freedom: Possibility, Complexity, and Emergent Value* (1993), at 160 (authority through contract) and 174–176 (discussing Peirce's notions of the elements of authority). Authority is presented as provisional and as reciprocal. *Id.*, at 212.

[14] *Id.*, at 160–176.

[15] See John K. Sheriff, *Peirce's Guess at the Riddle: Grounds for Human Significance* 9–16 (1994).

[16] *Id.*

[17] See generally, Smith, *Jurisprudence*, at 207, 311–330, 401–407; Kevelson, *Peirce and Freedom*, at 160–176, 212.

communities. For instance, consider a few questions the answers to which seem to change with time, context, and interpretive point of reference. Consider the following questions as examples: is sex within marriage always consensual (meaning that there is no idea of rape within the marriage relationship); can a minor consent to sex (who is a minor and what acts constitute sex); does a minor need a parent's consent to obtain an abortion or birth-control devices; can a consumer consent to a sales contract under pressure or must there be a cooling-off period (consider the demise of caveat emptor in so much of modern contract law); and can a terminally ill patient consent to assisted suicide? As one can readily appreciate, the idea of consent in exchange is complex. A theory of exchange should, therefore, attempt to address a number of factors beyond those embraced by standard approaches to social contract theory and traditional law and economics.

Adam Smith's idea of social organization being based on the relationship between authority and utility is, in many ways, a more useful approach to the study of exchange than one based on social contract theory. Adam Smith used the ideas of authority and utility to develop a theory of social transformation related to different stages of social development.[18] In these stages he envisioned a series of coevolutionary or relational forces that governed all areas of life, such as language, science, art, law, ethics, and economics.[19] In his system everything is seen as dynamic and interactive.

Smith identified and discussed four different stages of social transformation; the age of hunters, of herdsman, of agriculture, and of commerce.[20] He assumed that society was on a progressive and evolutionary track through these stages, with a known or unknown aspirational goal of reaching a point, that I sometimes think of as "perfect harmony," where there would be little need for a coercive state.[21] Moving through

---

[18] *See* Smith, *Jurisprudence*, at 14–37, 200–290, 311–330, 401–407 (dynamics of the various stages and implications for law); Adam Smith, *An Inquiry into the Nature and Causes of the Wealth of Nations* (Edwin Cannon, ed., 1976), at 420–445 in vol. 1, 231–244 in vol. 2. *See also* Adam Smith, *Lectures on Rhetoric and Belle Lettres* (J. C. Bryce, ed., 1983) (similar analysis with respect to development in language). *See generally* Adam Smith, *Essays on Philosophical Subjects* (Oxford edition, 1980).

[19] *See* Malloy, "Smith and Modern Discourse," at 116–122; John W. Cairns, "Adam Smith and the Role of the Courts in Securing Justice and Liberty" in *Adam Smith and the Philosophy of Law and Economics* (Robin Paul Malloy and Jerry Evensky, eds., 1994) at 31–62 (four stages in connection to Smith's theory of justice and the role of the courts); Jerry Evensky, "The Role of Law in Adam Smith's Moral Philosophy: Natural Jurisprudence and Utility" in *Adam Smith* (Malloy and Evensky, eds.), at 199–220 (social maturation).

[20] *See* sources above, nn. 18, 19.

[21] *See* sources above, nn. 18, 19. I don't believe Smith was a "utopian." *See* Evensky, "Role of Law in Smith," at 199–219 (Smith's conception of a *real* and *ideal* society).

these stages and toward this imagined point of "perfection" required a number of things, but in particular it required a strong social ethic based on a highly developed and internalized notion of the individual as part of a community represented by the metaphorical positioning of the impartial spectator.[22]

I think Smith's theory of social organization and progress is useful because it establishes a basic framework for understanding market economy. In examining Smith's theory of the stages of social transformation, one discovers that the movement from his least developed to most developed stage involves the continual expansion of law and of the extension of meaning through the relationship between law and market theory. In each stage, Smith detected an increasing complexity to legal arrangements that corresponded to similar trends in social, political, and economic relations.[23] It is his idea of increasing legal complexity that is central to my theory of law and market economy. By this I do *not* mean creating more paperwork or making things more difficult. Increasing complexity involves creating more points of exchange and interaction in the sense of complex systems theory, as in the sense of the difference between a one-celled organism and a complex organism such as a human being.

This same idea of complexity can be understood, for instance, in terms of the added variety, creativity, and wealth generated from an increasingly complex system of property law. New types of property ownership such as condominiums, time-shares and cooperatives expand the market for real estate transactions and add to the variety and nature of wealth in the community. The same is true of the emergence of rights in views and vistas, air rights, water rights, and various zoning arrangements, as well as for the increasingly complex ways of dividing commercial real estate ventures so as to appeal to a variety of investor and lender interests. Similarly, the development of primary mortgage markets, secondary mortgage markets, and alternative mortgage documents has resulted in the creation of more, not less, wealth. All of these increasingly complex relationships in real property law facilitate creativity and promote wealth opportunities that are unavailable in simple systems of early law with only a few forms of property tenure. In the framework of a system of law and market economy, therefore, one sees that law provides a necessary infrastructure for the extension of meanings and values, and

---

[22] Jerry Evensky, "Setting the Scene: Adam Smith's Moral Philosophy" in *Adam Smith* (Malloy and Evensky, eds.), at 7, 15, 21–22 (duty).

[23] *See* sources above, nn. 18, 19. For an example of advances in property law *see A Property Anthology* (Richard A. Chusel, ed., 1997); John Edward Cribbet, "Concepts in Transition: The Search for a New Definition of Property," 1986 Univ. Ill. L. Rev. 1 (1986); Robin Paul Malloy and James C. Smith, *Real Estate Transactions* (1998).

the more complex and open-ended the legal infrastructure the more diverse and creative will be the system of exchange. Complexity facilitates the production of wealth as illustrated in the above examples. It also fosters a more extensive market exchange network and promotes an ever-increasing potential for value-enhancing relationships.

Smith's early observations regarding legal complexity were profoundly insightful but not even he appreciated the full implication of what he was observing. His observed extension of legal complexity provides a key to the broader understanding of the relationship between law and market theory. It also facilitates a better understanding of the continual dispersion of authority and utility within most of the stages described by Smith, the result being that there is generally more extensive authoritative participation in society as one moves from a lower to a higher stage. His one exception to this "rule" involved simple tribal society.

Smith thought that early tribal communities were very democratic but I question this in terms of the extensiveness of individual authoritative participation in the social/market exchange process.[24] While it may appear that in such societies the community is involved in collectively making many decisions and in "controlling" the community's "property," the fact is that such societies are not necessarily extensive in a meaningful sense, and observations about these groups may not be extendable to larger and more impersonal groups. This is because such groups tend to foster their own internal set of conventionalized norms and codes of conduct.[25] They generally share an interpretive framework and can easily marginalize proponents of deviant values and meanings.

Furthermore, Smith does not fully account for the informal hierarchy of such groups nor for the pressure for conformity, and the dependence of individuals on the group for "survival." When one is dependent on others for many things it is difficult meaningfully to challenge convention and the status quo. Independence is needed for convention-breaking action and for real democratic participation. We all know, for instance, that the Amish and other small and cohesive communities use shunning and other powerful social weapons to constrain deviation and to restrict the networks and patterns of social/market exchange. These groups also tend not to demonstrate much diversity. In many ways this tendency is easily illustrated by small groups of school children where peer pressure serves as a vehicle for conformity. I have observed the same process in law firms and on law faculties where the term "collegiality" can sometimes serve as a *code* word for conformity and not rocking the boat. In a small group or community it is difficult to ignore

---

[24] *See* sources above, nn. 18, 19.
[25] *See generally*, *Group Dynamic Law: Exposition and Practice* (David A. Funk, ed., 1988).

the pressure to conform – after all, you have to live and work with these people everyday, and, if they choose, they can make your life miserable.

The appearance of democratic process in such settings is questionable even when we observe group meetings with seemingly open democratic processes. Anyone that has ever been on a law school faculty knows that little of consequence goes on *in* a community meeting – the real decisions are discussed and "managed" outside of the meeting. This is how many groups function and voting processes within the formal meetings can be manipulated to favor prearranged outcomes even though they appear to be neutral on their face. Such are the considerations of public choice theory. These tendencies seem particularly troublesome when the instruments or signs of authority are not extensively distributed. This is why Smith errs when he suggests that small tribal societies may be exceptions to his general rule. This error, however, does not diminish or undermine the importance of his more general observation.

Based on my interpretation, I would speculate that small and cohesive communities would seemingly tend to be less inventive and less creative than more extensive and less cohesive groups. This is because authoritative participation within a group often depends upon having independent signs of authority and space for challenging the status quo. It is only with the expansion of legal rights, with the elaboration of, say, private property rights, contract rights, and human rights, that "space" is created for more and more individual creative activity. The elaboration of these rights furthers complexity and puts certain elements of authority into the hands of individuals and subgroups within the community. It disperses control and creates a source of independence capable of supporting diversity and experimentation within the group. In the absence of these dispersions, authority would be more likely to be centralized and to be used coercively to impose the will of a few onto that of the many. Consequently, it is the extension of legal meaning and legal form (be it formal or informal) that relates to creativity, sustainable wealth formation, and economic advancement through the stages of social transformation identified by Smith.

In the absence of legal complexity as evidenced in broad and dynamic concepts such as property, contract and human rights, the exchange process and, therefore, the process for the creation of social meaning and value are dominated by the few, with the power to shape and enforce the conventionalized norm, over the many, who are expressly or implicitly coerced into compliance.[26] Such a limited hierarchy acts to

---

[26] *See* Hayek, *Liberty*, at 11–22. *See also* Milton Friedman, *Capitalism and Freedom* (1962). *See generally* Malloy, *Serfdom*, at 30–44.

restrict the degrees of freedom within the system and this reduces the nature and extent of social/market exchange. Conversely, the more pluralistic and diverse the source and exercise of authority (definitions of property, contract, and of human rights) the more extensive will be the networks and patterns of exchange, and the more likely it is that society will advance by way of creative discovery; that is, break through the semiotic space between convention and potentiality.

In Smith's analysis a point of hypothetical perfection might theoretically be reachable when the exercise of authority and the receipt of its benefits are equally dispersed – resulting in the most extensive exchange network possible. For a Smithian this would probably not be communalism but rather the state of "perfect" balance between self-interest (private property and rights) and public interest (the impartial spectator). While Smith probably saw this process of dispersion as a linear and progressive evolution from one stage to the next (guided by the benevolent design of the deity), semiotic theory would likely view the process as less linear, with communities progressing and regressing at different points in time, sparked by multiple points of freedom within a complex system of social exchange. The process would also appear differently to people based on the position in which they are socially situated. In essence, this means that the interpretation and direction of a stage, or of a transformational point, may be subject to dispute. None the less, Smith's basic observations seem useful. Societies that decentralize authority and that disperse the benefits of authority, with or without reference to social contract theory, tend to be more creative, more complex, and generally produce more wealth and a higher standard of well-being.[27] As will be discussed later, these same basic tenets also seem to be relevant to wealth formation in individual firms and in particular business settings.

In a modern context we can apply Smith's insight to a consideration of social organization and speculate as to its implications for wealth creation. We can see that countries that are generally more democratic, provide more individual freedom, and that protect basic human rights (including the right to private property and to contract) tend to be wealthier, and their people enjoy a higher standard of well-being.[28] This is not to say that production and wealth accumulation cannot occur in less extensive (more restrictive) exchange societies.[29] History indicates that even dictatorships (Italy under Mussolini, for instance) can provide for wealth accumulation, but even among dictatorships, the sharing of

[27] *See* James Gwartney et al., *Economic Freedom of the World: 1975–1995* (1996).
[28] *Id.*
[29] *See generally* Friedman, *Capitalism*, at 1–21; Gwartney et al., *Economic Freedom*.

some authority and some benefits results in a more stable, predictable, and wealthy community. Dictatorships, one-party systems, and other forms of restrictive exchange societies generally suffer from a highly constrained process of social interaction. That is, they generally take a limited approach to the dispersion of authoritative participation in the social/market exchange process. This limits the potential for generating surplus exchange value, and the lack of attention to individual rights (property, contract, and human rights) deprives the system of a strong reward incentive for creative thinking and discovery.

Restrictive exchange societies generally express themselves in patterns of authority that are extensively coercive and driven by a determination to maintain a particular hierarchical structure. Many derive their wealth from activities and resources that are basic, meaning that they require low levels of creativity. Thus, they often find wealth in such things as natural resource extraction or in the fortuity of having, in the eyes of a wealthy society willing to pay, an important strategic geopolitical location. This was the case of Cuba in its relationship with the former Soviet Union. Because of their dependence on a limited or basic range of assets and activities, these countries do not perceive the need for extensive exchange systems and they are seldom considered modern and developed. This is true even when they use their wealth to buy "modern" products and to build contemporary buildings. Examples might include countries that export one or a few key natural resources such as oil, or countries with strategic political and military value based on their location in the world. Examples of both these types of situation can be found in the Middle East and elsewhere.

Another alternative situation involves the restrictive exchange society that opens up slightly, while retaining strong centralized control. This may be done, as in the case of China, in order to pursue progress by simulating the economic activity of other societies (countries). In this situation, wealth might be pursued through the development of what I call a "copy-cat" economy. By the term "copy-cat" economy I mean to indicate that it is an economy that does not itself actualize and produce many creative ideas or inventions. Such an economy can expand within a more open yet still relatively restricted exchange society because the need for creativity is constrained.

The copy-cat economy, for instance, attempts to generate wealth by producing, at a lower cost, goods and services invented elsewhere. This strategy can be effective for short-run development because it promotes new exchange relationships and patterns of interaction that generate wealth-enhancing value, while minimizing the need for original inventive action. At a certain point, however, it becomes evident that there are limits to economic growth from the copy-cat model. Countries that come to mind are China, Vietnam, and at previous times Japan, South Korea, and Taiwan. Such countries would have little interest in the protection of intellectual property while they are in a copy-cat phase. This is because they get more value from using other people's ideas and inventions and they have only a small relative share of their own economies tied up in local invention and creativity. At some point, however, localized inventiveness and creativity must take over. No matter what the source of its wealth, the restrictive exchange society generally lacks an environment conducive to the generation of real, sustainable, and long-term wealth. This is because such forms of social organization hinder rather than facilitate creative discovery; they constrain and discourage non-conventional thought and action and they are, therefore, less likely to be innovative. For instance, at the time I started writing this book I could not accurately have predicted the Asian economic meltdown of 1998, but its occurrence was no surprise since many of these Asian economies are restrictive exchange societies and lack a good environment for creativity and stable long-term sustainable wealth formation.

An environment conducive to creative discovery is important to the generation of wealth but it can vary in its form. Creative discovery occurs best in comparatively open and extensive exchange societies. This does not mean, however, that all market approaches must be the same. The United States, Canada, France, Britain, Germany, and Japan are all clearly comparatively wealthy societies, but they do not all share the same history or cultural outlook with respect to market theory. Each society is different, each has a different conception of the market and of self-interest, but all have embraced a form of social organization and exchange that is *relatively* extensive, open, inclusive, and pluralistic. Authority and the benefits of its exercise are comparatively dispersed. This creates space and opportunity for enhancing the process of creative discovery. Within this space there is room for differing approaches to social welfare, and there is room for variation in the balance between public and private interests in the economy.

Learning from Adam Smith's insight, we learn that the form of social organization is important to the generation of wealth, and that proactive wealth formation is advanced by the process of extending authoritative participation in the social/market exchange process. By increasing the nature and scope of meaningful exchange opportunities within and between communities, we expand and diversify the networks and gateways of social interaction. We facilitate the bringing together of fragmented and subjective experiences and information from within the community, and enhance the potential for creative exchange. This in turn enhances the production of surplus exchange value. By this I mean that as we multiply and extend the nature and scope of exchange we generate more variations, permutations, and shades of meaning. This is the result of the imperfect nature of substitution. The presence of this surplus value forms the potential for realizing actual value and fueling the process of sustainable wealth formation. Consequently, a prosperous society must be organized in such a way as to maximize the potential for creative discovery as well as to maximize the use of valuable resources within a given context. Proper attention should therefore be given to both proactive and reactive wealth formation.

An ethic of social responsibility for law and market economy

Every man is, no doubt, by nature first and principally recommended to his own care; and as he is fitter to take care of himself, than of any other person, it is fit and right that it should be so. Every man, therefore, is more deeply interested in whatever immediately concerns himself, than in what concerns any other man . . . Though every man may according to the proverb, be the whole world to himself, to the rest of mankind he is a most insignificant part of it. Though his own happiness may be of more importance to him than that of all the world besides, to every other person it is of no more consequence than that of any other man . . . When he views himself in the light of which he is conscious that others will view him, he sees that to them he is but one of the multitude, in no respect better than any other in it . . . [H]e must upon this, as upon all other occasions, humble the arrogance of his self-love, and bring it down to something which other men can go along with.[30]

As the above quote from Adam Smith's *The Theory of Moral Sentiments* indicates, we generally think most easily of our own interest, yet we must come to realize that self-interest is expressed within a social context. In this section of the book, I will focus on the social context in which self-interest is expressed by suggesting three standards or principles of evaluation that can tentatively serve as the basis for an ethic of social responsibility in a market economy. These three standards are humility, diversity, and reciprocity. These standards express an ethic that is fundamental to the nurturing of an environment that is conducive to the process of creative discovery. This is because they seem to enhance the opportunity for authoritative (meaningful) participation in the process of exchange. This ethic also promotes efficient allocation of resources within a given context by promoting conditions in which trust and cooperation can work to reduce transaction costs, including policing

[30] Adam Smith, *The Theory of Moral Sentiments*, at 161–162 (E.G. West, ed., 1969).

and monitoring costs, which are involved in the process of exchange.[31]
I, therefore, offer a general outline for an ethic of social responsibility
that must be understood in light of my prior discussion.[32] After out-
lining the three basic principles of my ethic, I will briefly address some
evidence that seems to support my provisional conclusions regarding the
relevance of such an ethic to the process of sustainable wealth formation.

Outlining an ethic of social responsibility

Proactive wealth, as I have argued, emerges from the exercise of
interpretive choice within a context of spontaneous and indeterminate
social exchange. It is the product of intuition, hunch, chance, experience, surprise, and discovery. Proactive wealth is difficult to measure by
traditional standards because it involves complex forces outside of the
boundary lines of conventionalized law and economics. None the less, it
should be clear that traditional law and economic approaches, linked to
the maximization of reactive wealth, are incapable of fully appreciating
the complexity of social exchange systems. Complex systems, even when
bounded by conventionalized norms, involve infinite points of freedom
or possibility and they are by nature unstable.[33] Within a limited and
constrained space of habit-taking convention, they involve, as Peirce
suggested, both continuity and indeterminacy.[34] Points of equilibrium
or rest within a complex system are never in the same space twice; there
are, in other words, no perfect substitutions, no way to revisit, in all of
its exactness, a moment that has passed.[35] Therefore, we must think not
in terms of points of efficiency but in terms of spaces of creative
potentiality. We must think in terms of the environmental processes that

[31] *See generally* Janet Tai Landa, *Trust, Ethnicity, and Identity: Beyond the new Institutional
Economics of Ethnic Trading Networks, Contract Law, and Gift-Exchange* (1994); Francis
Fukuyama, *Trust: The Social Virtues and the Creation of Prosperity* (1995); Malloy and
Smith, *Real Estate*, at Chap. 1 (the market context of real estate transactions).

[32] Other works on ethics, see, *e.g.*, Amartya Sen, *On Ethics and Economics* (1987); Amitai
Etzioni, *The Moral Dimension: Toward a New Economics* (1988); Frank H. Knight, *The
Ethics of Competition* (1935); Frank H. Knight, "Intellectual Confusion on Morals and
Economics," XLV Int'l J. Ethics 200–220 (1935); Jerry Z. Muller, *Adam Smith in his Time
and Ours* 63–176 (1993) (Smith's conceptions of a basic moral foundation to markets).

[33] *See generally* James Gleick, *Chaos: Making a New Science* (1987); Stuart Kauffman, *At
Home in the Universe: The Search for the Laws of Self-organization and Complexity* (1995);
Silvio Funtowicz and Jerome R. Ravetz, "Emergent Complex Systems," 26 Futures
568–582 (1994).

[34] *See* Sheriff, *Peirce*, at 138–140; Kevelson, *Peirce and Freedom*, 1–17, 59–69; Kevelson,
Law, 138–140. *See also* sources in n. 33, above (the same idea underlies complex
systems or chaos theory).

[35] *See* Kevelson, *Law*, at 3, 49 (no perfect substitutes); Smith, *Essays*, at 154–161 (we
never see the same thing twice). *See generally* Kauffman, *Universe*; Gleick, *Chaos*.

facilitate social prosperity rather than the collection of things that merely point to the evidence of the existence of such space.

A society, such as the United States, for example, is not rich merely because its people have accumulated a large number of *things*. These *things* are only outward evidence of an underlying social environment or exchange process that favors social prosperity through increasingly complex extensions of meaning and value. These extensions are made possible through law and the formal and informal development of property, contract, and human rights. The key to wealth, and particularly proactive wealth and social prosperity, is the underlying phenomena that defines the space of social organization, and not the physical representation of that phenomena in the things that it makes possible. Rich societies, in other words, are rich because of an environment favorable to the development of particular patterns of habit taking – patterns that encourage creative discovery and proactive wealth formation. Such environments derive from values and meanings embedded in the process of exchange. This is precisely why a country such as Japan can be "rich" even when it possesses comparatively few natural resources. Japan can be rich, not so much because of the "things" it possesses, but because of the underlying process of exchange that gives value and meaning to particular social relationships; social relationships that are relatively complex and extensive, and that are culturally and contextually positioned. Social conditions that are favorable to the dispersion of authoritative participation in social interaction, and that broadly distribute the benefits of the exercise of such authority, result in comparatively open or extensive exchange communities with an enhanced potential for creative discovery and the generation of wealth.

The ethic of social responsibility, to which I address myself, is really a multivalued *market ethic* based on an understanding of the dialogic relationship between the individual and the community. It is conceived in the recognition that people are motivated by self-interest yet attracted to, and positioned within, communities. The ethic I describe emerges from the acceptance of the semiotic synthesis of self-interest and public interest, and from the continual reflective interplay between Adam Smith's conception of self-interest and the impartial spectator. It is expressed in the human practice of exchange and the social meaning that it creates. This ethic is understandable as a sign or an idea observable in the human practice of exchange, which seemingly facilitates the process by which the merely possible becomes the actual – whereby creative potentiality becomes a "real" as evidenced in the signs of wealth accumulation and social prosperity.

The ethic of social responsibility is, furthermore, like any other semiotic sign, continually evolving and perpetually coming into being. In this sense, the ethic of social responsibility is, like the market itself, a sign that makes reference to a particular legal, economic, and social environment for its coherence and for its extensions of meaning. I think, however, that this ethic of social responsibility, this ethic of market exchange, can be given some sense of concreteness by reference to three key principles that, to me, seem relevant to creative discovery and the wealth-formation process. These three principles can be tentatively identified as *humility*, *diversity*, and *reciprocity*. The terms I use here are offered as ideational "spaceholders" and I ask that the reader try not to place too much emphasis on the particular words but instead focus on the dynamic and relational ideas that I seek to represent. As standards or principles of market economy, they offer a framework in which to consider environmental conditions suitable for the advancement of creative discovery. They serve as ideational placeholders for the concept of authoritative participation; participation made meaningful, in law, by such notions as property, contract, and human rights.

In addition to this, they may also function as important criteria in advancing the efficiency objectives of traditional law and economics. This may be possible if such an ethic can lead to: reduced transaction costs, including monitoring, policing, and information costs; increased respect for the property and rights of others; and the reduction of extreme opportunistic behavior of the type indicated by one-time exchanges or "games." If people act with *humility*, for instance, they will treat each other fairly, honestly, and as they themselves want to be treated. If they value *diversity* they will treat each other in an inclusive and participatory way, and if they act in *reciprocity* with each other they will be more likely to engage in cooperative transactional positioning. All of these factors should be relevant to increased efficiency as well as to creative discovery.

Humility

In my opinion, the real case for a free society and for freedom is ignorance - we cannot be sure we are right. If I cannot persuade people by reason and argument and talk, if I cannot persuade them to agree with me, what right do I have to force them? How can I be sure that I am right? In short, the basic virtue in a free society and the basic justification for a free society is humility, a willingness to recognize that no matter how strongly one may believe he is correct, he cannot be sure. Hence, he does not have the right to force his views on someone else.[36]

---

[36] *See* Milton Friedman, "Free Markets and Free Speech," 10 Harvard J. Law & Pub. Pol'y 1 (1987), at 8–9. *See also* Sheriff, *Peirce*, at 58; Kevelson, *Law*, at 102.

A key principle of my ethic of social responsibility is humility, which is itself a fundamental assumption of market theory. As the above quote from Milton Friedman indicates, humility involves the recognition of error, imperfection, and ignorance in human thinking. It addresses itself to the contingent and propositional nature of "truth." It reminds us that human theories are by their very nature speculative, partial, and fallible. It challenges us to seek the truth yet warns us to beware of the truth holders. Market theory likewise embraces the concept of humility in its focus on dynamic instability and competition. This is observable in the assumption of a competitive market in which every conclusion, every equilibrium, every truth value is continuously challenged and subject to revision. The idea of humility is to recognize the semiotic space between temporary points of equilibrium or truth value as well as between theories that represent the appearance of the real (the immediate object) and the actual phenomenon that *is* the real (the dynamical object). In the process of social exchange, humility means that the interpretive codes and conventions that define these propositional truths are continually subject to speculative inquiry and realignment.

The above quote also tells us something about our theory of authority. Since we can never be certain of our truth we have no right to force it coercively on someone else. We must reason and persuade. This means that the exercise of authority should be limited, should be open to change, and should be accessible. In acknowledging that even "we" can be wrong, "we" must hold open the possibility that others may be right. Consequently, space must be provided for others with different ideas. Providing this space for conflicting and competing ideas requires a dispersion of authority.[37] This dispersion is facilitated and made operationally meaningful by extending access to the legal infrastructure of exchange as embodied in notions of property, contract, and human rights. Institutional structures and exchange networks should be encouraged to facilitate this process.

Authority cannot remain dispersed, however, unless there is a system for ensuring that sources of authority reside in different locations. Stated differently, we must maintain countervailing sources of authority in society so that the potential for conflict or friction works against the tendency for concentrations of power in such forms, for example, as oligopolies, monopolies, or entrenched bureaucracies and ruling elites. The decentralization of power is indeed a primary justification for the dispersion of private property rights and for the ability of individuals to realign those rights through systems of contract and compensation law.

---

[37] *See* Malloy, *Serfdom* (particularly at 16–44, 53–60, 113–140).

It is from the process of instability within the boundaries of convention-alized space that freedom exists and discovery takes place. Instability itself is merely another way of expressing the dynamic of market competition. The constant push and pull of innumerable competing forces within the market continually move it to new equilibriums, or mediating points, of contingent and propositional truth value. The conventions of private property, contract, and human rights, together with institutional structures such as democratically elected governments subject to checks and balances, for example, help to ensure decentraliza-tion in the substitutional exchange process. Consequently, these con-ventions and culturally based norms help to reduce concentrations of power and work to create an environment conducive to extensive exchange networks, experimentation, and the potentiality of creating entirely new "truth" meanings and values.

In addition to the points of inquiry already suggested by a concern for the principle of humility, one further implication is also raised. This involves a concept that I call *spatial scaling*. In the context of complex systems, of which the social/market exchange process is one, scaling is important for focusing in on habit-taking patterns of interaction.[38] As a dialogic process, the market exchange system needs intermittent/vari-able scaling in order to get at the process of meaning and value formation as well as to explore the consequences of alternative market structures and conventions. In other words, it is necessary to think beyond the scale of atomistic individuals pursuing their own self-interest. We must think in these terms while also making inquiry into larger units of social organization and while focusing on the dynamic elements of community(ies) to which individuals are attracted and in which they find themselves situated. This means that law and market economy embraces, as a fundamental element of market theory, a multi-disciplinary investigation of a broad range of groups and environments in which individuals interact.

Examining groups and environments of varying dimensions raises the possibility of enhanced scaling and is important for presenting a more complete picture of the exchange process. Small groups and environ-ments such as families, churches, clubs, work teams, and professional or trade associations are significant because they tend to function as primary mediators for norm formation and habit taking. They are, therefore, central to understanding the interpretational references at work in the exchange process. They are also important when thinking about economic and public policy. This is because the key to such

---

[38] *See* Gleick, *Chaos*, at 83–186; Kauffman, *Universe*, at 17, 248–262.

programs as welfare reform or urban revitalization, for example, may have more to do with reaching and investing in community groups than it does in targeting individuals.[39]

Diversity

I have said that humility involves the dispersion of authority for it recognizes the contingent and propositional nature of truth. The point of dispersing authority and of creating space for the potentiality of a new "truth" is inherently connected to the principle of diversity. In other words, humility, or the dispersion of authority, implies, or makes implicit reference to, a need for social diversity in the market exchange process. Market creativity is enhanced by the multiplicity of buyers and sellers, and by competing individual preferences operating within the exchange system. Diversity is, likewise, important to an overall network of social exchange. In each instance, the more dispersed the exercise of authority in shaping social meaning, the more diverse will be the networks and gateways of social exchange.

The very ideational concept of a marketplace speaks to the notion of diversity – be it diversity in competition or diversity as an investment strategy. This is because market economy addresses the instability of a conventionalized status quo. Competition and exchange are all about reaching new points of equilibrium – new points of meaning and value. This instability involves indeterminacy and it is enhanced by dispersions of authority, which multiply the number of points of freedom/potentiality within a given system of conventionalized space. In a market economy this space is particularly important because it addresses the "outsider" and rejects the status quo. Market competition is driven by diversity and market theory promotes the need for new ideas and constantly changing hierarchies. Market theory embraces diversity by creating "space" for the merely possible, by speaking to the upstart, the outsider, and the imaginative agent seeking to move beyond the boundaries of the status quo. By providing space for the possible, market theory facilitates an understanding of how diversity promotes the transformation of the potential to the actual. It was, for instance, the upstarts, the outsiders, and the newcomers rather than the IBMs that launched the revolution in personal computer technology in the 1970s and 1980s.

A concern for diversity also suggests the need for an integrative approach to the *measure* of market competitiveness and the meaning of market outcomes. This measuring process relates to "scaling" and involves the idea of degrees of freedom within alternatively scaled

[39] *See, e.g.*, Robert L. Woodson, "Race and Economic Opportunity," 42 Vand. L. Rev. 1017 (1989).

windows of investigation.[40] In a complex system such as the market, various points of action or actors serve as degrees of freedom in the sense of the potentiality that each has for influencing or being influenced by patterns of habit taking; the degrees of freedom represent points of instability within the bounded universe of convention.[41] In law and market economy terms, the more we disperse authority, the more we expand the degrees of freedom within the system, and the more we enhance the potential for creative discovery and proactive wealth formation. Getting at these measures in a practical way presents some problems. Initially, however, this approach suggests a need to take a multidisciplinary look at social diversity. This can be done by going beyond standard measures of efficiency valuation to include hedonic and contingency valuation methods, the implications of the endowment effect, and by investigating market participation rates and distributional consequences related to particular economic predictions or public policy prescriptions. These investigations need to be done within and across a variety of scales. This form of inquiry would both broaden and enrich our study and understanding of markets. It also means that we must look more closely at the market implications of work being done in a variety of fields, including those of cognitive and behavioral studies.

Reciprocity

Reciprocity, like the concept of humility, involves the relationship between the ideas of self-interest and community. Reciprocity is present in a market economy because we are all at times buyers and at times sellers. We sell our labor and we buy the product of someone else's work, for example. It is also present in Peircean semiotics because we are all sign interpreters and at the same time sign makers. Our interpretations, in themselves, create permutations of prior signs and thus new signs. Reciprocity, therefore, means that the exchange process is a dialogic process. There is a give and take involved in social relationships and there must be a sense of responsibility, of accountability, of community, for this to benefit the process of creative discovery.

In its simplest formulation, reciprocity means that if a person is to share in the exercise of authority and in the benefits derived therefrom, she must also take responsibility for herself and she must extend to others the same sense of humility (uncertainty as to her own truth) and inclusiveness (commitment to diversity) as should be extended to her. Similarly, reciprocity involves the recognition of shared authority and

---

[40] *See* Gleick, *Chaos*, at 83–153; Kauffman, *Universe*, at 28–30 (unpredictable outcomes), 180–181 (diversity and sustainability), and 248–279 (scale, "patches").

[41] *See* sources above, n. 40.

responsibility. The practical implications of reciprocity can be illustrated with an example. Reciprocity means, for example, that all racial and ethnic groups are capable of racism and xenophobia. Arguments that artificially protect some groups while accusing others of such actions are unsupportable under a principle of reciprocity. Thus, the idea that whites are guilty of racism but blacks cannot be guilty of racism is one that lacks reciprocity. Likewise for the idea that blacks but not whites are justified in exercising jury nullification; the idea that racial preferences are acceptable when they benefit blacks, Asians, or Hispanics but not when they benefit whites; and the idea that one person is superior to another simply based upon the color of his or her skin.

In the broader sense, reciprocity involves the conventionalized boundary between continuity and indeterminacy. This is because conventionalized norms are always provisional and subject to the possibility of revision. They exist within an environment of instability. In an extensive exchange community these conventionalized boundaries are subject to doubt and challenge. This makes room for creativity and discovery. Reciprocity is important here because without reciprocity extended to others and to an unconventionalized "otherness," we would be attempting to enforce a status quo position. This would stifle change and hinder the dynamic exchange process, making conditions less favorable for creative discovery and social prosperity.

The metaphorical boundary line between continuity and indeterminacy is at the "edge" of social organization and provides the "fencing" that delineates the spaces of contextualized interpretive exchange. Activities beyond this contingent boundary are potentialities of what might be and are difficult to interpret prior to their actual coming into being. Temporary collapses of social organization, or conditions of anarchy and chaos, may occur but the demand for reciprocal exchange by and among people serves to bring us back to some social relationship, some unstable and dynamic reshaping of the relationship between the self and others, between the human practice of exchange and the meanings and values embedded therein.[42]

From the point of view of law and market economy we can try to get at issues of reciprocity by focusing on *positioning* within the exchange process. We can supplement our tools of scaling and measure by investigating and imagining particular market predictions and policy prescriptions from the alternative positionings of various individuals and groups within the system. If, for instance, we look at housing or

---

[42] *See generally* Gleick, *Chaos*, at 119–150 (strange attractors bring disrupted complex systems back into a pattern); Kauffman, *Universe*, at 277–279 (from chaos to habit and pattern formation).

mortgage markets from the point of view of a college-educated white or Asian-American male we will have a different view of the market than if we position ourselves as poor, black, and female, renting a government housing unit in the inner city.[43]

We will also see government intervention in the marketplace quite differently. Given years of intervention and access assistance, many middle-class white Americans enjoy comfortable rates of homeowner-ship, yet to them demands by members of "other groups" for more market intervention to expand access to these housing and mortgage markets seems inefficient, risky, and not based on wise business judg-ment. Naturally, most of them do not look back and attack their own access assistance, which was perhaps the subject of the same type of criticism in an earlier time period, but the expansion of market access to them and to others has facilitated authoritative participation in the market exchange process and has enhanced wealth formation and social prosperity. The point is that while almost any distribution of income or resources can be deemed economically efficient within a given contex-tual framework,[44] the principle of reciprocity calls upon us to examine the implications of these social arrangements from a variety of view-points.

For instance, we might be asked to determine the better social arrangement as between two different societies each of which has an economically efficient distribution of income. Assume our choice is between society "A" and society "B." We must determine which is "better" when both are deemed economically efficient. Society "A" has resources of $200 billion, of which $180 billion is controlled by 3 percent of the population. Society "B" has the same resources and same population but control of the resources is distributed almost evenly among all the members of the community. Depending upon our

---

[43] *See* Malloy and Smith, *Real Estate*, Chap. 15 (reporting on studies in the mortgage markets), Chap. 13 (housing markets). *See generally* Andrew Hacker, *Two Nations: Black and White, Separate, Hostile, Unequal* (1992) (data on market access and economic distribution based on race).

[44] *See generally* Gary Lawson, "Efficiency and Individualism," 42 Duke L. J. 53 (1992) (so many ways in which to assess efficiency that efficiency as a standard is incoherent); Nicholas Mercuro and Steven Medema, "Schools of Thought in Law and Economics: A Kuhnian Competition" in *Law and Economics: New and Critical Perspectives* (Robin Paul Malloy and Christopher K. Braun, eds., 1995), at 65–126, 103–105 (the contextual nature of efficiency – it can vary with the legal framework); Thomas S. Ulen, "Rational Victims – Rational Injurers: Cognition and the Economic Analysis of Tort Law" in *Law and Economics* (Malloy and Braun, eds.), at 386–433 (social science research and law and economics), at 387–434, 408 (economics provides no way of deciding between a negligence or strict liability rule – the choice must be made on non-economic criteria); Nicholas Mercuro and Steven G. Medema, *Economics and the Law* 118–121 (1997).

relational position within either one of these communities we might have very different feelings about the distribution, despite the fact that in each case it can be deemed economically efficient. How do we say which system is better, and if we start in one position how do we move to another, if at all?

If we rely on the efficiency criterion we will have a difficult time justifying a choice, but under my theory of law and market economy we can begin with the recognition that a more extensive distribution tends to facilitate a broader range of authoritative participation in the exchange process. Presumably, therefore, society "B" would be preferable to society "A" because it would be more likely to embrace an extensive degree of freedom and, thus, be more likely to facilitate a process of creative discovery and wealth formation. Law and market economy, as such, provides a wealth-based justification for favoring one form of social organization over that of another when a concern for efficiency is unable to do the same. This is an important distinction and it is one that is ripe for further empirical research. As it is, there is currently evidence to support this conclusion and I will discuss some of it in the section on "The ethic of social responsibility and wealth," below.

The idea of reciprocity can also be understood with reference to discussions of trade between the United States and China. Despite complaints about Chinese policy on the environment, human rights, and the use of child and prison labor many American politicians insist that trade with China is good because it will make China become more like the West. The argument is that trade and exchange will influence China and reform some of her policies so as to improve local conditions. This argument is almost always presented as a one-way flow of values – from West to East with a presumptive belief in the superiority of the Western approach. Trade and exchange, however, work in a reciprocal relationship. While it is true that interaction between the West and China will result in changes in meanings and values for China, it is also true that such interaction will result in changes for the United States and the West. Signs of the change in the United States are already evident as one observes added pressure to cut costs, to lower wages and reduce the living standards of American workers, to pressure people to work longer, harder, and produce more, and by rising pressure against the environment and attempts to protect it. Western values are shifting under the cost and exchange pressure of interaction with China and an expanding global marketplace. Our values and meanings are being influenced by the changing networks and patterns of exchange in which we are positioned. Reciprocity in exchange means that all parties continuously influence each other; it is not a one-way process.

Consequently, trade with China and other such countries reshapes our meanings and values at the same time as it does theirs. This is understandable from a semiotic approach to law and market theory, even though it remains unrecognized in standard approaches to traditional law and economics.

This completes my brief overview of an ethic of social responsibility. While my ideas are still in a preliminary stage, it seems clear that a new focus is called for in our consideration of the relationship between law and market theory. The ethic that I outline is designed to promote an extensive exchange process with diverse participation and an extensive distribution of resources and political authority. Furthermore, it is a market ethic because it promotes the values of competition in exchange and it facilitates creativity and the process of sustainable wealth formation.

The ethic of social responsibility and wealth: some supportive evidence

History, I believe, reveals that societies with a relatively integrated and extensive exchange process, including something similar to the market ethic or ethic of social responsibility described above, have generally been comparatively more creative, more wealthy, and more free than other societies.

Even within one country, such as the United States, we find that the more that it has advanced toward the achievement of these principles the more it has made progress in terms of wealth. The expansion of the right to vote, for instance, from a limited set of white male property holders to non-property owners, to women, to blacks, and to eighteen-year-olds has done nothing to reduce the wealth of the US. Likewise, the expansion of inclusion into the workforce of immigrants, blacks, and women has done nothing to impoverish America. In fact, despite constant fears of social and economic collapse, these changes have coincided with an environment of incredible creativity, productivity, and wealth formation. This is because the dispersion of authority and the expanded distribution of its benefits enhances the environment for creative discovery. It maximizes the opportunity for social exchange, interaction, experimentation, and surprise. It enhances the potentiality of creating new meaning and new value from an ongoing process of social realignment.

This point can be further illustrated by reference to recent studies at the macro level concerning national economies, and at the micro level by reference to particular business successes in the fast-changing global marketplace. At the macro level, for instance, a major study has recently been completed by the Frazer Institute, in which it reports on the relationship between economic freedom and economic well-being or social prosperity in a comparative study of 103 countries over a time period from 1975–1995.[45] The study focused on a seventeen-component index designed to trace key empirical measures of economic freedom. The seventeen components were, themselves, grouped into four major areas focused on a nation's laws and practices with respect to matters of: (1) money and inflation; (2) government operations and regulations; (3) takings and discriminatory taxation; and (4) restrictions on international exchange. This involved an investigation of private property rights; contracting, transferability, and exchange rights; and access to justice and equal treatment under law. The Institute's study attempted to create a global index of economic freedom, and put much weight on important elements of exchange such as the right to own private property, to exchange it freely, to invest and divest, to interact in currency markets, to avoid confiscatory takings of property or income by government action or regulation, and the right to participate in an open exchange process with reciprocal rights extended to all participants under a fair system of judicial administration. In other words, a multi-faceted measure of economic freedom was used to investigate the ease with which one could access the social exchange process and thus the report sheds light on the ability of individuals to participate authoritatively in the process of social meaning and value formation.

According to the report, there is a strong correlation indicating that the countries with the highest degrees of economic freedom consistently had the highest rates of growth and income. Similarly, the countries with the lowest ratings on economic freedom also were consistently among the poorest countries with the lowest rates of growth and personal income. Not surprisingly, countries with *extensive* market-oriented exchange processes based on concerns for private property, contract, and human rights were consistently the most prosperous countries. Most importantly, the report indicates that economic freedom *itself* (not just a concern for efficiency) is important to economic growth and prosperity. The freedom to own property, to contract and exchange it without fear of arbitrary exercises of coercive power creates

---

[45] *See* Gwartney et al., *Economic Freedom*; Alfredo G. Esposto and Peter A. Zaleski, "Economic Freedom and the Quality of Life: An Empirical Analysis," 10 Const. Pol. Economy 185 (1999). For micro level analysis, *see* Gary Hamel and C.K. Prahalad, *Competing For The Future* (1994); John Kao, *Jamming: The Art and Discipline of Business Creativity* (1996); Mathew J. Kiernan, *The Eleven Commandments of 21st Century Management* (1996).

space for individual action, incentive, and experimentation. Such freedom supports an environment favorable to creative discovery and, thus, the findings of the report seem consistent with my thesis on law and market economy.

When individuals have rights in property and are free to contract with a reasonable degree of freedom from arbitrary or coercive government intrusion (that is, they enjoy a reasonable degree of civil or human rights), they tend to be more likely to experiment, question convention, and foster creativity. The study by the Frazer Institute indicates that the legal system plays an important role in promoting sustainable wealth formation because it shapes the environment in which exchange takes place. When legal systems and cultural systems tend to support extensive rather than restrictive participation, the results seem to include both higher degrees of freedom and a greater level of social prosperity.

At the micro level a great deal is being written about the need for business to embrace new and innovative approaches for success in the fast-changing global marketplace.[46] The concerns expressed in these writings are also consistent with my thesis on law and market economy, and a review of several of the popular works in this area confirms the perceived need for a focus on creativity as a means of generating wealth. The emphasis in business today, we are told, is on flexibility, innovation, and creativity. The old rules based on "scientific management" and historical continuity are said to be no longer viable – the new rules are based on change and the establishment of a culture of continuous creativity.[47] The old rules of business planning are seen as reactive and contextually constrained – they focus on increasingly complex methods of analysis (such as those of positive economics) and are said to have "gotten more and more precise and sophisticated at measuring less and less."[48]

Successful businesses have come to realize that reactive performance measures, no matter how scientific, are all about history and not about the future. Simply trying to maximize efficiency or wealth in a given context will no longer provide a sustainable advantage in the marketplace.[49] Sustainable growth requires vision and the translation of potentiality into actuality. Cost cutting, restructuring, and merely improving one's competitive position *in the game* is not enough.[50] To survive and

---

[46] *See, e.g.,* Hamel and Prahalad, *Competing*; Kao, *Jamming*; Kiernan, *21st Century Management*.

[47] *See, e.g.,* Kiernan, *21st Century Management*, at 129–131. There is a need to develop and value potentiality. *Id.,* at 52–68.

[48] *Id.,* at 216.

[49] *Id.,* at 34–51; Hamel and Prahalad, *Competing*, at 1–24, 148, 163–193.

[50] *See* Kiernan, *21st Century Management*, at 34–38.

thrive beyond the immediate present, businesses need *to think beyond the game* – they need to create new rules, cross previous "boundaries," and *imagine entirely new game potentialities.*

Breaking the rules of convention, challenging, questioning, and breaking habitual practices – these are the keys to future growth, financial survival and prosperity.[51] This is because prosperity depends upon creativity that emerges from the continuous tension between past and present patterns of continuity and practice, and the dynamics of indeterminate future potentiality – this is the essence of exchange.[52] Some writers have identified this tension as "constructive contention" or "destructive creativity," and identify Honda (the automobile manufacturer) as just one example of a company embracing this viewpoint to foster constant questioning and rethinking – the goal being to find a proper fit between discord and harmony.[53] In terms of law and market economy, this process is simply an example of Peircean semiosis.

One key example that stands out as a metaphor for this entire approach involved the development of the very successful automotive product known as the minivan.[54] Chrysler Corporation received the credit for creating this entirely new line of automotive product and has successfully reaped huge profits by continually revising the concept. Interestingly, the original idea for the minivan is said to have originated at Ford. Upper management at Ford never approved of the minivan concept as a project, however, because they were concerned about the lack of proven demand and current market statistics for the vehicle. The information Ford executives wanted would be difficult to attain prior to the introduction of the product. Ford executives were basing their decision about the minivan concept on a reference to past and current market information in support of a product not yet available. Because there was no proven demand for the minivan, logic held that there could be no meaningful market for its production. Thus, Ford decided to pass over the project on the grounds of insufficient market demand. In the end Ford saw that it had made a mistake even if its decision could be said to have been efficient under the then given circumstances. Chrysler profited from Ford's mistake by hiring the concept designers and exploiting a vision of market potential rather than clinging to the imagined security of conventionalized market data.

---

[51] *Id.*, at 33–48, 103–128; Hamel and Prahalad, *Competing*, at 217–218 (leadership comes from imaginative potentiality); Kao, *Jamming*, at 15–19.

[52] *See* Kao, *Jamming*, at 17, 57–73, 75–94, 149–164.

[53] *See* Kiernan, *21st Century Management*, at 236–238. Honda "constructive contention." *Id.*, at 45–48. *See also* Kao, *Jamming*, at 38 ("creative destruction").

[54] Hamel and Prahalad, *Competing*, at 110.

In another example about creativity and behavior, more generally, an experiment is described in which a group of four monkeys are placed in a cage with a tall pole at the center.[55] At the top of the pole hangs a bunch of bananas. As the monkeys climb the pole and approach the bananas they are confronted with an unpleasant shower of water. Eventually they learn not to seek the bananas even when the shower is turned off. Likewise, when one monkey is removed from the cage and replaced with a new monkey the new monkey is trained by the remaining three monkeys not to seek the bananas. This restrained conduct was passed on to new monkeys and was observed even after none of the original monkeys were in the cage. This experiment seems to indicate that creativity and innovation can be suppressed in a hostile environment and that norms and semiotic codes may be established within a group, making that group less likely to innovate in the future. To the extent that this experiment applies to exchange processes more generally, it confirms the importance of environment in facilitating creative discovery.

Suggestions offered by various business consultants, for creating a culture of continuous creativity in business, seem to correspond to my own observations respecting an ethic of social responsibility in the social exchange process. To put into operation an environment of creativity, businesses are advised to establish a value system or an ethic that promotes the realization of potentiality.[56] Businesses are instructed to create "organizations of humility" where senior managers relinquish their hold on the role of "expertise."[57] Company structures should be "flattened" with authority and responsibility *extended* to more and more people throughout the organization.[58] Workspaces, technologies, and assignments should be open, flexible, diverse, experiential, cooperative, dynamic, and experimental.[59] Communications, access to information, expanded exchange networks are all to be encouraged as these are environmental conditions suitable to the advancement of creativity.[60] For example, the accounting department should be interacting with engineering and marketing – exchanging ideas and information. Working collaboratively across traditional boundaries within a firm will

[55] *See id.*, at 55–56.
[56] *See* Kiernan, *21st Century Management*, at 15 (value systems), 45–48 (value input from all levels), 135 (Levi Strauss Company example); Kao, *Jamming*, at 75–94.
[57] *See* Kiernan, *21st Century Management*, at 19–215 (Motorola example raised at 198); Hamel and Prahalad, *Competing*, at 102.
[58] *See* Kiernan, *21st Century Management*, at 129; Kao, *Jamming*, at 75–94 (promoting teams); Hamel and Prahalad, *Competing*, at 102, 144.
[59] *See* Kao, *Jamming*, at 57–73, 131–164; Hamel and Prahalad, *Competing*, at 102.
[60] *See* Kao, *Jamming*, at 57–73, 131–164.

challenge perceived constraints and stimulate new networks and patterns of exchange while facilitating new modes of thinking and creative interaction. Likewise hallways, workspaces, and "play" areas should foster a place for talk and unstructured exchange.

Numerous case studies are referenced in these new management materials in order to illustrate that success and prosperity actually emerge out of this approach; an approach that seeks to maximize one's present market advantage while continuously contending with the indeterminate potentiality of the future.[61] Businesses are instructed about the need to think in multidimensional patterns, and for learning to embrace ambiguity, complexity, and change.[62] The evidence and case studies examined indicate that when individuals cooperate in reciprocal environments of exchange they can experience more freedom, more stakeholder authority, and at the same time progressively advance their own prosperity along with that of their company or community. Examples in support of these conclusions come from a variety of sources, including such well-known companies as IBM, 3M, Ford, Chrysler, Honda, CNN, the Virgin Group, and a number of high-tech enterprises.

In arguing, therefore, that an ethic of social responsibility is an essential means for promoting creativity and prosperity in the social exchange process, I am stating a case that is supported by preliminary evidence at both the macro and micro levels of our economies. If, as legal economists, we are concerned with facilitating the implementation of wealth-promoting legal and economic infrastructure, we must take note of these new approaches. This requires us to cross additional interdisciplinary boundaries, going beyond the concerns of traditional law and of economics. It means that we need to develop a theory of market interpretation that is capable of embracing a constructive connection between efficiency and creativity, between continuity and indeterminacy. Thus, more empirical work needs to be undertaken to examine the relationship between creativity, efficiency, and sustainable wealth formation. Furthermore, this work must go beyond the social sciences to include the humanities in our understanding of the interpretive and sign-making process of exchange.

Ultimately, we are all engaged by the same complex forces that are causing businesses to reinvent themselves. We must, likewise, reinvent ourselves. In order to remain relevant in the discourse of law and public

---

[61] See Hamel and Prahalad, *Competing*, at 91–100, 252–261 (think outside or beyond established lines); *see generally*, Kao, *Jamming*.
[62] See Hamel and Prahalad, *Competing*, at 103, 107, 293–323; Kiernan, *21st Century Management*, at 194–215.

policy, we must broaden our understanding of the relationship between law and market theory, we must make space for new rules of play, imagine entirely new games, and we must internalize a culture of constructive contention and continuous creativity.

6   Implications of law and market economy

As we have discussed, law and market economy involves an interpretation of market meaning. It is an approach that builds on a number of concepts familiar to traditional law and economics but its focus is different. It is primarily concerned with exploring the networks and patterns of market exchange and it expresses an interest in facilitating the relational aspects of market activity and social organization. It identifies wealth maximization as part of an ongoing dynamic process consisting of reactive and proactive elements, and it employs an interpretive theory of semiotics to develop and explain the relationship between law and market theory.

The approach of law and market economy also shares a familiarity with recent ventures by Janet Landa and other legal economists who are investigating the law and economics of norms, values, kinship groups, and customs.[1] Their work is interesting, innovative, and useful but, again, it is different from law and market economy. The recent turn toward an economic analysis of norms has been dominated by a view that informal value-formation processes are implicit substitutes for more formal attempts at expressing, signaling, and serving the equilibrium models of traditional law and economic analysis. The work being done in this area generally applies the tools of traditional law and economics to informal settings. The legal economists involved in this area tend to argue, for instance, that more efficient norms win out over less efficient norms, and that better norms are more efficient and wealth maximizing than other norms. Thus, their recent investigations into norms broadens the scope of traditional law and economics by examining informal norms rather than focusing only upon formal legal rules, but this approach does not extend the fundamental nature of their market-based inquiry. It simply applies the traditional law and economics model to a new set of questions. The idea behind law and market economy, in

---

[1] *See, e.g.*, Janet Tai Landa, *Trust, Ethnicity and Identity: Beyond the New Institutional Economies of Ethnic Trading Networks, Contract Law, and Gift-exchange* (1994); "Symposium: Law, Economics and Norms" 144 U. Pa. L. Rev. 1697, 1745 (1996).

contrast, is that we need to explore new models as well as new questions, and this means that we need to extend the *nature* as well as the *scope* of our market investigations.

Even though this project on a theory of law and market economy is in its early stages, I believe it none the less offers promise for thinking about and developing an extensive theory of law and market exchange. In this Chapter of the book, therefore, I will discuss three important implications that flow from my theory of law and market economy. This discussion is suggestive in nature and attempts to establish a foundation for future work. It is offered as a further way of understanding the difference between my approach and that of traditional law and economics. The three primary implications I wish to discuss are: first, that the pursuit of economic efficiency does not maximize sustainable wealth formation; second, that the nature and extent of the distribution of scarce resources and access to the exercise of political authority influences wealth creation; and third, that alternative theories of legal discourse should be understood as normative rhetorical strategies competing for substantive influence over the market exchange process – over the networks and patterns of social interaction. Admittedly, these are not the only implications of my approach but they serve as good examples of the substantive significance of the theory.

Efficiency does not maximize wealth

The approach of law and market economy that I have been discussing focuses attention on people engaged in the human practice of exchange. It identifies the market as a semiotic system of signification, a place of meaning and value formation, and understands wealth as emerging from the tension between two interrelated modes of logic. The first mode depends upon maximizing the use of resources within a given context or set of constraints, and the second is based on the indeterminate nature of creative discovery. In this context, the pursuit of traditional economic efficiency will not result in sustainable wealth formation.

As discussed earlier in this book, such measures of efficiency, while helpful in some respects, fail to capture the dynamic and indeterminate elements of the market exchange process. This is because efficiency analysis concerns a calculatable measure of optimality based on a particular context and a conventionalized mode of logic. Creativity and discovery, on the other hand, are dynamic and indeterminate. Sustainable wealth formation requires that attention be paid to both of these elements – *efficiency and creativity.*

Efficiency analysis, none the less, remains relevant to creativity because it provides an important referential framework for signaling the presence of something *new*, and for providing an indexical system for rewarding the discovery process. Concern for efficiency drives us to a constant reconsideration of the human practice of exchange. It forces us to think about the future even if its methods are anchored in the past and the present. Efficiency analysis also asks us to consider continually the possibility that we could be doing better. This is important because it prompts us to be alert for potential opportunities for improvement. As a result we see that efficiency determinations, by themselves, are inadequate standards for promoting long-term wealth maximization and social prosperity. At the same time, however, it is clear that the process of thinking about efficiency considerations is not completely irrelevant.

The relationship between efficiency and creativity, between habit/continuity and chance/indeterminacy, can be understood within the framework of Peirce's three modes of logic. Using a Peircean approach, our actual human experience with the exchange process functions as a mode of firstness. It addresses our experiential contact and relationship to the networks and patterns of exchange in which we are embedded. With respect to this, the efficiency analysis of traditional law and economics as a sign of contextual continuity, convention, and habit, functions in a mode of secondness. It provides a frame of reference that we reflect upon in evaluating the nature of our own exchange experience. We reference the accepted convention in an attempt to understand its connection to, or convergence from, our own experience. Finally, the synthesis of these two modes of logic results in a third. This third involves, for our purposes, the construction of market meaning and of persuasive argument(s) for choice, and for law and public policy (in)action.[2]

In thinking about this referencing process we are confronted with a need to explore further the meanings of efficiency. We need to ask if efficiency is a certain and calculatable conclusion about an exchange relationship, or merely one of several ways of expressing a persuasive argument for a given course of action. We can pursue this analysis further with reference to what I call the "variance problem" in the use of the efficiency criterion for law and public policy making.

It is perhaps best to begin this discussion with reference to a point raised by Judge Richard Posner. Several years ago, in the course of a debate between myself and Judge Posner, he offered the argument that one of the real contributions of the economic analysis of law was that it

---

[2] Arguments as modes of thirdness. *See, e.g.*, Winfried Noth, *Handbook of Semiotics* 45 (1995).

provided a concrete method for resolving the vast majority of our legal/
social disputes and problems.[3] He implied, thereby, that positive economic method makes it possible for people to come to the end of the
day, sit down, and reach a calculated (calculatable) decision. In other
words, economics resolves and eliminates disputed areas of contention.
Economic analysis, therefore, was far more useful to people than moral
or philosophical discourse, which he positioned as hopelessly open-
ended and subjective. In essence, his concern with moral or philosophical discourse is that it does not solve problems since it is based on
subjective feelings rather than objective facts. The problem with this
rhetorical stance, however, is that it greatly overstates the case and it
implicitly assumes that the vast majority of our social disagreements are
merely ones of fact rather than of value.

In reality economics is a field of inquiry of which much the same
observation can be made of economists as is frequently made of lawyers;
put one hundred of them in a room, ask them to solve a complex social
problem, and you are likely to get one hundred different answers. The
point being that economics, even within the discursive community of
economists, cannot be used magically to solve our problems in the way
suggested by Posner. It can only serve to channel our method of inquiry,
to direct our attention to facts made relevant by its conventionalized
modes of logic, to suggest, within a constrained set of assumptions, a set
of possible alternative approaches to the resolution of difficult questions
of law and public policy.

The market, after all, is a complex system of social exchange with
large degrees of freedom. Thus, consistent with complex systems theory
it cannot, as such, be evaluated for a definitively optimal course of
action based on any one economic criterion.[4] It can only be analyzed for
a set or sets of plausibly good choice alternatives.[5] At the end of the day,
therefore, legal economic analysis does not provide us with a concrete,
calculatable, resolution to our disputes and problems. Nor does it
inform us of an optimal or definitive wealth-maximizing approach,
instead it merely provides us with a set of plausibly good paths for
decision making. To select from among these options, these plausibly

---

[3] Robin Paul Malloy and Richard A. Posner, "Debate: Is Law and Economics Moral?" 24
Val. U. L. Rev. 147 (1990), at 163 and 169–173 (wealth maximization is concrete and
fruitful), at 183–184 (nine out of ten times it will lead people to the same conclusion).
[4] Stuart Kauffman, *At Home in the Universe: The Search for the Laws of Self-organization
and Complexity* 248–262, 268–269 (1995). Trying to find the optimal course of action in
even a small set with few independent variables is impossible.
[5] *Id.* The idea is consistent with Eco's argument concerning the limitations to
interpretation. *See* Umberto Eco, *The Limits of Interpretation* 5–7, 32–42, 44–60,
148–150 (1990).

good alternative courses of action, we have to exercise interpretive judgment about the meanings and consequences of one way of approaching the problem as opposed to any other. We need a theory of interpretive reference to guide our logic in the meaning and value-formation process of social exchange.

The implication of semiotic theory and of my approach to law and market economy is that an ethic of social responsibility, as suggested in this book, is one useful way of providing this interpretive guidance. Law and market economy broadens our understanding of law and market theory by positioning speculative inquiry within a dynamic pattern of relational (re)interpretation rather than proceeding along an imaginary line of efficient calculation. This interpretive process allows the law and market economist to construct useful arguments, and it does this by including a variety of multidimensional factors in the analysis. These additional factors allow the law and market economist to move beyond the boundaries of static equilibrium analysis and into the territory of normative argument designed to influence the course of action for any particular legal or public policy objective.

The idea that economics provides no certainty, but only suggests plausibly useful choice alternatives, can be demonstrated with an example based on the question of whether or not prostitution should be legal. If we address our inquiry to only the immediate parties to the transaction, we might conclude that the seemingly voluntary and con-sensual nature of the exchange of money for sexual services is a wealth-maximizing move. Under such a scenario an efficiency-driven legal economist might argue for the legalization of prostitution. If, on the other hand, we change the *scale* of our investigation and look at the way in which these activities affect third parties we might reach a different conclusion. Assume that we include estimates of the "cost" impacts of this activity on the family and friends of the participants, the communities they live in, and the potential for extended health-related consequences across multiple communities. By including these third-party costs we change our efficiency calculations and, thus, we might reach a different set of conclusions. Scaling, therefore, raises the problem of what to count. Should we even worry about accounting for externalities, and if we do, then how should we decide on where to draw the line between impacts that count and those we deem too far removed from the transaction to be relevant? Depending upon how we choose to define the relevant scale, our conclusions will vary even if we profess a desire to operate at the most efficient point.

Still further problems can be raised when we consider alternative ways to *measure* the third-party impacts of these exchanges. How should we quantify such things as emotional, esthetic, and family values, for instance? Slight variations in pricing estimates, or in assessing distributive implications, may lead to significantly different outcomes.

Similarly, we can introduce *positioning* problems to our investigation if we relax the presumption that consent is evident in the exchanges being observed. Perhaps the market under investigation reveals that actions of the parties are not based on consent. Maybe there is historical, cultural, or institutional bias in the exchange, or some personal considerations that result in the woman feeling compelled to participate. Seen from the position of the woman, this transaction may have very different dynamics from those presumed under an assumption of rational consent theory. A change in positioning might, once again, change our conclusion.

In a complex system such as the market exchange process, factors of scale, measure, and position involve degrees of freedom or chaotic exchange and, as such, they suggest a theoretically infinite number of transactional influences. Consequently, efficiency analysis cannot solve the problem posed by our original question; should prostitution be legal? Efficiency analysis provides a useful way of thinking about issues that may be relevant to our inquiry but we need a normative, ethical, point of reference to guide us in the interpretive process of making market choices. Furthermore, we need to focus more attention on the dynamic nature of the networks and patterns of exchange that are being observed. We need to develop a better understanding, for example, of the way in which men, women, families, and communities interact. We need to transform our point of reference from one of concern for calculating economic efficiency to one that investigates the nature, scope, dynamics, and consequences of particular exchange relationships. We need, in other words, to inquire as to the manner in which prostitution affects the social/market exchange *process* and not merely as to the efficiency of making it legal.

Suggesting, as Posner did, that positive economic analysis can provide us with certainty becomes even more problematic when we consider that the field of economics has multiple measures of efficiency[6] and competing frameworks of analysis. The competing frameworks, for example, assign different value and meaning to the role of institutions,

[6] *See, e.g.*, Robin Paul Malloy, *Law and Economics: A Comparative Approach to Theory and Practice* (1990), at 38–42 (Pareto efficiency and Kaldor–Hicks efficiency); Nicholas Mercuro and Steven Medema, "Schools of Thought in Law and Economics: A Kuhnian Competition" in *Law and Economics: New and Critical Perspectives* (Robin Paul Malloy and Christopher K. Braun, eds., 1995) at 65–126; Nicholas Mercuro and Steven G. Medema, *Economics and the Law* 118–121 (1997) (efficiency is ambiguous because it varies with context and legal structure); Gary Lawson, "Efficiency and Individualism," 42 Duke L. J. 53 (1992) (efficiency is incoherent).

individuals, and groups.[7] Even simple concepts such as self-interest raise problems with respect to the manner in which self-interest is informed, and how it might differ based on culture, context, race, gender, or a variety of other variables.[8] These problems in economics are the same type of problems that frustrate the understanding of every complex system of exchange. They raise the same interpretive difficulties for market theory as they do for any other approach to legal theory. The point that this discussion illustrates is that economic analysis and the efficiency criterion are unable to provide us with absolute answers to our most pressing social problems. They are not, in other words, conversation stoppers or argument enders. They are what we would expect them to be – gateways and networks for channeling speculative inquiry. They are conversation starters. They point us in a useful direction. They embody a representation of individual and social experience that is relevant to our understanding of the relationship between law and market theory, but they are only partial and incomplete – they are fragmentary pieces in a continuously evolving mosaic of human relations. Therefore, we need a broader and more extensive approach to the investigation of law and market theory, and this approach must go beyond efficiency analysis.

Thinking in terms of selecting the most efficient outcome is also problematic because, in part, it suggests that one can predict a sequence of future events. That is, it implicitly assumes that future values can be identified and played back into our current decision-making process. This, of course, ignores the reality of our inability to know future states in a dynamic and complex system. It also overlooks the fact that actual value is always relational and relational meanings always change, in some way, with every choice or exchange. No piece of real property, artwork, or contract, for example, has meaningful value in an isolated and abstract sense. Value stems from the relationship that any act, thing, person, or idea has with respect to others. A parcel of real property, for example, has value based on the nature of other properties within its proximity (an ocean view versus a garbage dump), and in relation to transportation routes, schools, jobs, wildlife, air quality, climate, and a variety of other factors. When we make decisions about developing real

---

[7] *See* sources above, n. 6. *See generally, Law and Economics: New and Critical Perspectives* (Robin Paul Malloy and Christopher K. Braun, eds., 1995) (a variety of perspectives).

[8] *See, e.g.,* Jeffery L. Harrison, "Class, Entitlement and Contract" in *Law and Economics* (Malloy and Braun, eds.) at 221–248; Kenneth G. Dau-Schmidt, "Legal Prohibitions as more than Prices: The Economic Analysis of Preference Shaping Policies in the Law" in *Law and Economics* (Malloy and Braun, eds.) at 153–180 (to the extent that preferences can be shaped and have an economic impact it would seem that cultural context would be relevant).

estate or about approving applicants for a home mortgage loan we do not simply make decisions that are, strictly speaking, economically efficient. This is because it is impossible to select the most efficient future outcome when we know that dynamic exchange systems confront us with at least two levels of ignorance.

If people could actually predict the most efficient and wealth-maximizing moves they would make perfect decisions in the stock market and elsewhere and we would all become billionaires by using the same economic model. Inasmuch as this does not happen, it seems more likely that we think in terms of wealth improvements rather than in terms of wealth maximization. What we do, in a Peircean sense, is make choices based upon a wide range of experience. Some of this experience might readily make reference to economic criteria that have proven to be useful in either making or justifying prior decisions whereas other aspects of our decision-making process will draw on other parts of our individual and group identity. Consequently, because no two people have exactly the same life experiences, each will have slightly different insights or hunches about the potential quality or payout expected from any given exercise of choice. Therefore, rather than focusing so much attention on efficiency we should create extensive exchange networks that facilitate individual freedom to participate in and influence the decision-making process. In this way we enhance the value potential of diverse and scattered experiential knowledge and we tap into the creative discovery process that is important for sustainable wealth formation.

Concerns for efficiency can also make certain underlying value consequences less visible. I described this back in Chapter 2 when I gave the example of the impact of the secondary mortgage market on local home mortgage lending practices. There, I explained how one negative consequence of the secondary mortgage market was that it presented economic rewards and commissions to loan officers who processed high volumes of mortgage loan applications at a very quick pace. The pressure for production and the economic reward system seemed to drive many loan officers to use race as a proxy when making the subjective determinations of an applicant's likely ability and willingness to pay back a loan. Race was apparently used as a signal or sign of an applicant's likely ability or inability ultimately to get bank approval for a loan. As I explained, the data indicated that black and white applicants with clean files (no credit problems) were treated identically in the loan approval process, but when credit problems were evident in the files, whites were approved at a much higher rate than blacks. The loan officers were likely using race as a sign of a low probability of success on final loan approval and they were less willing to invest time in working with the black customers to clear up problems in their files. In this situation we can see that efficiency can have a negative implication by actually working to promote a pattern of racial discrimination in the home mortgage market. Such patterns are harmful because of the racial inequality that they perpetuate and also because they lead to unduly restrictive and less creative exchange processes.

In a similar way, I explained how small loans were also less likely to be approved because they resulted in the earning of small fees for the lender and loan officer. This is because fees are based on a percentage of the loan amount and even though small loans do not generate high fee income they consume almost as much time and paperwork as do large loans. This creates an incentive and an economic efficiency justification for avoiding small mortgage loans. The result of such an efficiency-driven practice is, once again, adverse to low-income applicants and for blacks and Hispanics who are more likely to be in these lower income groups. Thus, thinking only in terms of advancing market efficiency makes these issues less visible, and hinders the wealth-formation process by restricting from market participation people who would otherwise make an important contribution to the wealth-formation process.

We can also illustrate a further problem with efficiency analysis by exploring an example from contract law. For this example I offer the concept of the efficient breach. The idea of the efficient breach, according to traditional law and economics, is that under certain conditions the law should encourage people to breach their contracts. This action is justified in situations of Kaldor–Hicks efficiency where non-performance leaves the breaching party with an economic gain that exceeds the economic loss to the losing party against whom they committed the breach. A classic example of a fact pattern that illustrates the doctrine of efficient breach is found in the case of *Peevyhouse v. Garland Coal & Mining Company*, decided by the Supreme Court of Oklahoma in 1962.[9] In that case Willie and Lucille Peevyhouse, as owners of a farm containing coal deposits, leased the property to Garland for a five-year period for purposes of "stripmining" the coal from the land.

The stripmining process involved removing the coal by digging large pits into the surface of the land as opposed to coal-mining methods that involve digging underground mine shafts. The stripmining process leaves the surface of the land dramatically scarred and disfigured. In an effort to assure themselves that the surface of the land would not permanently remain in this exhausted state the lease agreement between

---

[9] *Peevyhouse v. Garland Coal & Mining Co.*, 382 P.2d 109 (S. Ct. Okla., 1962).

the parties required Garland to reclaim the land. The reclamation provision required restorative effort to return the land to a more natural and pre-mining state or condition. Garland operated under the lease and extracted the coal deposits. At the end of the lease term, however, it refused to restore and reclaim the land. Garland justified its breach of the agreement by presenting evidence that restoration work would cost $29,000 while expert testimony indicated that the value of the land would only increase by $300. In other words, the gains to Garland from non-performance readily exceeded the loss in value to the Peevyhouses. Thus, Garland argued that it would be a waste of social resources to spend $29,000 to achieve a $300 gain and therefore it should be allowed to breach the agreement. The court agreed, but it required Garland to pay the Peevyhouses $300 as damages representing the loss in value to the land from failure to reclaim it. This result is perfectly consistent with traditional law and economic analysis.

In contrast to the traditional view, I believe that the theory of efficient breach is suspect and should be rejected. Based on the arguments presented in this book, there are two key reasons for my position. One involves the recognition that contract exchanges involve meanings and values of social as well as personal consequence, and the second recognizes that dollar-based assessments of value unfairly exclude consideration of social values and objectives that are not easily quantifiable in monetary terms.

As to the first point, we have seen that exchange takes place within community and that it always results in the generation of surplus value and permutation. No exchange is isolated from the community and every contract raises implications for social meaning. Consequently a breach of contract raises implications that go beyond the two immediate parties to the exchange. Garland's ability simply to breach its contract with the Peevyhouses changes the nature and scope of such relational commitments. It also raises questions, for instance, about the extent to which we can value and act to protect the natural environment. These contract relationships are not removed from society – they are firmly embedded within the social fabric – but the theory of efficient breach implicitly assumes that these exchanges are isolated, autonomous, and detached events in which promises and their breach impact upon only the contracting parties. This assumption is incorrect and it results in a misunderstanding of the value of contract performance and of the cost of contract avoidance.

My second point addresses a further problem that is hidden within the concept of the theory of the efficient breach. Proposing that some breaches ought to be encouraged because they are efficient presumes that the value of non-performance can be quantified against an equally quantifiable notion of the cost of performance. We know, however, that this is a very problematic assumption. For example, not all environmental values can be reflected in an appraisal of the market value of a given piece of land. (How much is the Grand Canyon worth?) The value of land itself varies dramatically with relation to its permitted use, location, and other variables.

To claim that performance of a contract promise will result in wasted economic resources, as the court in *Peevyhouse* did, is to assume that all values can be monetized and measured in a way that is picked up by formalized markets. This is not true and it certainly is not a primary motivation in many exchanges. To take a simple example, consider the millions of people in the United States that every year spend billions of dollars on home improvements and redecorating. The majority of such expenditures are never recoverable in any market measure of the added value to the home. Should we allow homeowners to contract for $30,000 worth of home improvements and then pay only $7,000 for the work on evidence that $7,000 is all that shows up in the enhanced market value for the home? After all, the homeowner could employ the additional $23,000 in pursuit of other more economically beneficial activities. In substance there seems to be very little difference between the idea of wasted economic resources in the home improvement situation and that of Mr. and Mrs. Peevyhouse seeking to enforce their contract right against Garland after Garland had fully extracted the economic benefit of its undertaking. I believe, therefore, that the theory of the efficient breach is grounded upon erroneous assumptions that give undue support to behavior patterns that undercut a favorable environment for sustainable wealth formation. This is particularly true when we consider that the theory of efficient breach does not even require a showing of commercial impracticability or severe financial burden on the part of the breaching party. It simply promotes one-sided opportunistic behavior without giving proper consideration to the community context in which exchange takes place.

I understand that some people may find these arguments about the role of efficiency analysis in law and market theory to be difficult to understand. Being mindful of this I offer another way of thinking about the role that law and market economy ascribes to the concept of efficiency by making reference to the idea of precedent in law.

In law the concept of precedent serves as a referential guide to judicial decision making. It serves as a semiotic sign of a contextually positioned judgment about the meaning of law in a particular situation. Precedent provides an element of continuity, or stability and predictability, to law, but the function of law is not simply to render the same decision over and over again. Legal decision making is not a slave to precedent – the law is dynamic and expresses an indeterminate element of freedom in a constantly changing system of legal interpretive exchange. Precedent, in other words, establishes a "boundary" for plausibly reasonable decision making but it does not dictate the outcome of distinctly different points of tension or conflict within the legal system. Likewise, law and market economy makes reference to efficiency and standard equilibrium models in economics. Law and market economy recognizes, however, that market theory is no slave to efficiency. Market theory, like legal theory, involves elements both of continuity and indeterminacy; both are relevant to the way in which these systems work. Law and market economy seeks to understand and influence the meanings and consequences of a variety of legal economic relationships within the social/ market exchange process because the nature and scope of these relationships influences the environment of exchange and, thus, the dynamics of wealth formation. In this regard, efficiency analysis must be put in proper perspective.

Finally, the limitations to efficiency analysis become even more apparent when considered in the context of relational exchange. In a relational context efficiency can mean different things depending upon the objective of one's inquiry. For example, consider a meeting room at a large hotel. In this particular room there are ten tables and forty chairs. Imagine that you are asked to place the furniture in the most efficient arrangement for the room. In part, an efficient arrangement presupposes a desired outcome or purpose. The furniture might be arranged in different patterns depending upon the intended use. If the room is to be used for a lecture the furniture might best be arranged with a speaker's table at one end facing rows of participant tables. If the use is for an intellectual exchange in which thirty-five scholars will present papers and exchange ideas, the tables and chairs may be arranged in the round. If the room is to be used for dance instruction the furniture may all be pushed to one corner. In short, the efficient arrangement presupposes a particular agenda. Similarly, even though the content of the room never changes, the relationship between the objects in the room does change and these changes signal different purposes and influence the perceptions and exchange implications for the people who enter and use the room. Thus, alternative conceptions of an efficient relationship can signal different meanings and values. Efficiency, therefore, involves a reference to a predetermined or conventionalized framework and forces us to consider the nature, scope, and extent of authoritative participation in the agenda-setting process.

As should be evident from this discussion, the pursuit of economic efficiency cannot tell us how to maximize wealth. At best it can assist us in some aspects of speculative inquiry but there are limitations and problems with its use. This is because efficiency analysis is incomplete – it is not dynamic and fails to address the indeterminate nature of creative discovery that is important to wealth formation. In addition, the efficiency criterion is problematic because the results that it generates are subject to alternative interpretations based on a variety of factors and preconceived objectives. At the end of the day, therefore, efficiency analysis does little to relieve us from our obligation to engage in an ongoing process of social discourse and exchange. For this reason law and market economy positions itself as a *method of inquiry* for law and market theory rather than as a mechanism for generating specific answers to complex social problems.

An extensive distribution promotes wealth

I believe that an aspirational presumption in favor of extensive authoritative participation in the social/market exchange process is good for sustainable wealth formation. In this section of the book, therefore, I will discuss the value of extensive exchange networks and the relationship between these networks and the generation of wealth. I also discuss how this aspiration might reasonably be understood and made provisionally operational in the real world.

To begin with we need to keep in mind that law and market economy is about the way in which market exchanges are affected by changing points of reference in the interpretive process. Stated differently, law and market economy is about uncovering value differences in the exchange processes of people situated in and between particular interpretive communities. To understand market theory, therefore, one must appreciate it in the broadest sense, as a theory of continuous exchange and substitution giving rise to meaning and value (re)formation.

As we have seen, the exchange process in economics and in law is similar. In economics we have, for example, the exchange of labor for a wage, and the exchange of some portion of that wage for public services (through taxes), and for the purchase of goods and services. This process of exchange tells us something about communities and individuals, for it informs us about the nature and scope of things able to be exchanged, by whom, and on what terms. Also, through the "token" use of money we are given a proxy for equating the exchange relationship between these various reference points. In law we also have exchange. We have a legal rule, for instance, and we seek to apply it to a new case.

In so doing we think about the origin and fact pattern that gave rise to the rule and we substitute the new facts and circumstances and draw a conclusion. Likewise, we have trials where both sides present a version of the facts and the jury substitutes its view of the facts for that of the parties, and sometimes the judge substitutes her view, notwithstanding the verdict of the jury. These exchanges tell us much about the meaning and value-formation process because they provide social markers of relationships.

Furthermore, since there are no perfect substitutes, we know that with every exchange there is some element of a meaning or value "misfit" or an exchange surplus on at least one side of the equation. In saying, for instance, that an Italian Chianti is like a California Zinfandel we learn something about the taste relationship between two different types of wine, and simultaneously we lose something of the distinction between these wines. The exchange is not an exact fit and it creates a new meaning or value relationship between the two things equated. At the same time it sheds light on the nature and scope of things that are exchanged and the degree of differentiation of wine types, agricultural products, and growing climates. A market that distinguishes wines by type, region, flavor, and aging is very different from one that offers only classifications of red or white. It also reveals an opportunity to extract value and meaning from subclassification and market segmentation.

The imperfect nature of exchange gives rise to surplus value that is present but often goes unnoticed. The opportunity for capturing and creating value from this surplus is present but is often lost in the inattention caused by conventionalized ignorance. By way of convention and habit, we tend to think in terms of the familiar and we focus on rational and logical choice within a given set of exchange relationships (efficiency calculations). In a community identified by its convention of recognizing only red or white wine, for example, we might find that people react with some surprise when they are informed of interesting and unique subclassifications of each. Their surprise is likely to be further heightened when they learn that each particular subclassification makes reference to particular foods and that knowledge of such classifications makes further reference to one's social class. Being told of these differences, however, is not the same as discovering or creating them with reference to one's own experience. Discovery of new values and meanings, new relationships in exchange, requires imaginative choice, thinking beyond the ordinary while using the available reference points as a ground.

Expanding the pie of market progress depends upon the ability of people to uncover and create new value and meaning relationships. This uncovering process requires a conventionalized market understanding as a reference point for identifying that which is new (an experience at variance with the suggested convention). Furthermore, the experience of something new informs and transforms habit and convention. Thus, communities provide conventionalized points of reference from which individuals can participate in the making of something new. The opportunity/potentiality is always there but the individual is not always alert, does not always recognize it – there are those who look for, recognize, and seize the opportunity and then there are those who simply wait. The beauty of an extensive exchange process is that it seeks to draw inclusively upon the fragmented experiences of countless individuals and thereby increase the potential for discovering something new.

Implicit in this discussion, of exchange and the creation of value from substitution and permutation, is an important insight concerning the distribution of scarce resources and political authority within society. My argument is that the process of exchange, by itself, creates value even when that value goes temporarily unrecognized. Every exchange creates a potentiality for something new. Consequently, the greater the number and the more varied the nature of exchanges within society, the more potential there is for actual wealth formation. This means that there is at least a two-step process to wealth formation and social prosperity. The first step involves exchanges that generate value, and the second step involves the realization of that value by a creative act of discovery. This means that our system of social organization, in the manner discussed previously, should favor decentralization and should allow for extensive authoritative inclusion in the process of exchange.

The presumption of extensive authoritative participation embraces an aspirational ideal of participatory equality of opportunity. It does not, however, express a requirement of equal outcome or sameness.[10] Equality of outcome would seem, in fact, to be entirely inconsistent with the idea of the market as a dynamic and complex system of exchange. This is because, as an interpretive matter, outcome equality presumes the theoretical possibility of innumerable individuals passing through the same point an infinite number of times. Complex systems, however, display just the opposite tendency. That is, the market as a complex system of imperfect substitutional exchange and permutation presumes that no individual or group can pass through the same point twice. Equality of opportunity must be understood, therefore, as directed at participatory access to the creative process and not as the substantive

[10] *See* Roberta Kevelson, *The Law as a System of Signs* 174–180 (1988); Roberta Kevelson, *Peirce, Science, Signs* 71–85 (1996).

equivalence of participatory outcomes arising from the process. Creativity and wealth formation are promoted, in other words, by diversity and difference rather than by conventionalized notions of duplication and repetition.

The importance of the distinction between equality of opportunity and equality of outcome is also implicit in my earlier discussion concerning creative discovery and the role of entrepreneurism. There it was suggested that we should encourage extensive exchange networks as a way of generating more surplus exchange value from the process of substitution. At the same time we concluded that there was a need to encourage the practice of speculative inquiry or entrepreneurial alertness, which plays an important role in directing attention to creative opportunities in a market economy. Consequently, we identified the need for a reward system. Such a reward system, in order to be meaningful, must return benefits to those people who successfully transform potential surplus exchange values into actual recognized social value. This reward process will most likely result in differentiation, rather than sameness, as between particular people across the community. This result does not appear unreasonable and it seemingly promotes the continued actualization of creative potentiality because it gives incentive to the process of transforming the possible into the actual.

This result can also be made even more politically acceptable when we embrace two additional and related points. First, in order to act as suitable incentives, rewards for creative discovery should not have to be equal to the full economic profit attributed to any particular act. Economics is unable to represent the full value of any exchange and ample incentive should exist when a substantial portion of the economic benefits of discovery and creativity are returned to the entrepreneur. Second, and following from the first, some of the economic profit generated by a particular act of creative discovery may reasonably be used by the community to support the infrastructure necessary for the presence and continuation of extensive exchange networks. In other words, since creativity is facilitated by particular environmental factors, such as the presence of a well-developed market ethic of social responsibility and a complex legal infrastructure, it is fair and reasonable for entrepreneurs to contribute some portion of their profit to the support of the communities that facilitate the possibility of profit-rendering opportunities.

The full implication of this position is that the presumption in favor of extensive exchange networks must be balanced against concerns for rewarding individual acts of creative discovery. In the real world of decision making and policy shaping, we must, therefore, construct some reasonably useful way of operationalizing our concerns. Quite simply, we can do this by referencing experience to traditional law and economic models. Our concern for appropriate reward structures can *begin* with a consideration of the various alternatives that might be suggested by traditional law and economics. This could provide us with a set of plausibly useful conventions from which to make an indexical or referential value judgment relative to a ground based on experience. This would then require us to make a speculative inquiry into the suggested options. From there we could *select or imagine* responses capable of facilitating our concurrent objectives of considering elements of both reactive and proactive wealth formation, and of extending authoritative participation in the social exchange process.

In essence, we would seek to be mindful of currently perceived economic constraints, but economic efficiency or some imagined point of profit maximization would not be our only, nor our primary, objective. Our primary objective would be to go beyond this conventionalized point of reference and focus on the ways in which market access and resource distribution can be extended. In some respects we would proceed like a not-for-profit institution in that we would obviously need to be mindful of the conventionalized market context in which we were operating, but our primary guiding principle would not be profit maximization, at least not in the traditional economic sense. Other objectives and values, ones unable to be fully monetized for traditional economic analysis, would guide us in our approach to decision making and policy shaping. An ethic of social responsibility and the aspiration for extensive inclusion in the exchange process are two such values that would influence our inquiry. By continually reassessing the plausible courses of action suggested by efficiency analysis and extending them by reference to these other values we would constantly push and extend the networks and patterns of exchange; we would validate a wealth-based space for the importance of a variety of social exchange values. These values would then be plugged back into our evaluative process in an attempt to generate new sets of "efficient" guideposts, and so on in a continuous process of semiosis. As with the development of the common law and with discovery in general we would proceed by informed trial and error. Adjustment and revision would be continuous.

In my approach to law and market theory, therefore, distributional matters related to authoritative access and participation are of central importance. This is because the broader and more extensive the distribution, the greater the likelihood that creative discovery and wealth formation will be enhanced. Consequently, an extensive distribution of resources and of participatory authority are not only matters of fairness, they are of primary importance to a theory of sustainable wealth formation.

Rhetorical strategies

A theory of law and market economy, as a new jurisprudence of exchange, must provide a mechanism for thinking across interpretive boundaries. By understanding market theory as a process of relational exchange, engaged in for the purpose of continually bringing about realignments in value and meaning relationships, law and market economy positions itself as an interpretive undertaking. It allows us to comprehend alternative styles of legal argument as competing rhetorical strategies attempting to effectuate relational exchange outcomes by influencing the process of interpretation in the exercise of market choice. In a market sense, legal argument becomes part of a persuasive rhetorical strategy directed at the (re)shaping and mediating of author-itative positioning with respect to the referential filter or screen used in market interpretation. In this way rhetorical strategies compete for influence over the networks and patterns of social interaction and, as a result, they have a substantive impact on the market exchange process. In this section of the Chapter I discuss the value (re)shaping function of alternative forms of legal discourse.

Understanding the rhetorical strategy of alternative discourses is important for analyzing arguments and for constructing arguments in pursuit of advancing a particular proposition or agenda. In a very real sense alternative legal rhetorics are all about law and market theory because each operates strategically to influence the allocation of scarce resources and political authority within the exchange process. The substantive consequence of referencing any one approach rather than another is that meanings and values change with different referential grounds, as do the identity of decision makers and the nature of the decision-making process. Therefore, an important consideration of law and market economy involves mapping out the different consequences that flow from employing one particular rhetorical strategy, or interpre-tive frame of reference, rather than another.

In addressing the interpretive implications of competing rhetorical strategies I will first consider how law and market economy can help us better understand the consequences of different frames of reference within the rhetorical strategies of traditional law and economics. I will then briefly consider, for comparative purposes, the implications of rhetorical strategies in some critical approaches. My discussion here is a refinement and modification of earlier work. In particular, some readers

will recognize its relationship to my early exploration of these ideas in
Law and Economics: A Comparative Approach to Theory and Practice
(1990), *Planning for Serfdom: Legal Economic Discourse and Downtown
Development* (1991), and a variety of law review articles and essays that
followed.[11] I therefore undertake to provide a brief and suggestive
discussion of how these competing rhetorical strategies might be understood in this new jurisprudence of exchange.

We can start by considering the basic idea of efficiency in law and
economics. Some legal economists focus on Pareto efficiency while
others use Kaldor–Hicks efficiency.[12] Pareto efficiency gives presumptive validity to consensual exchanges between transactional parties.
Pareto-efficient exchanges occur when at least one person is made better
off while no one is made worse off as a result of a trade. This means that
the parties themselves exercise authoritative roles in the decision-
making process, relatively unencumbered by third-party control or
censure. This is because voluntary exchanges are assumed to be advan-
tageous, or at least not disadvantageous, to the parties. Kaldor–Hicks
efficiency, in contrast, makes room for a series of justifications for
coercive trades because it is based on the assumption that an exchange is
efficient if the winner wins more than the loser loses. The Kaldor–Hicks
test, therefore, does away with the need for mutual consent and really
provides a basis for third-party influence over the exchange process. It
can authorize an exchange where the parties have not, themselves,
agreed to it. Under this test, if an exchange will generate more gains for
the winner than the loss to the loser the legal system should encourage
or coerce the transaction in order to achieve a Kaldor–Hicks-efficient
outcome.

Authority in the meaning and value formation process thereby shifts
by merely changing the choice of the efficiency criterion. As a form of
strategic rhetoric, the shift from a Pareto to a Kaldor–Hicks efficiency
test results in a substantive consequence. It shifts decisional authority
away from individual traders required to achieve mutual consent and
transfers it to third-party observers, regulators, and interpretive agents
who can establish that the winner will win more than the loser(s) will
lose. Functionally, this means that "experts" become empowered to

---

[11] Malloy, *Law and Economics*; Robin Paul Malloy, *Planning for Serfdom: Legal Economic
Discourse and Downtown Development* (1991). *See, e.g.*, Robin Paul Malloy, "Towards a
New Discourse of Law and Economics," 42 Syracuse L. Rev. 27 (1991); Robin Paul
Malloy, "Letters from the Longhouse: Law, Economics and Native American Values,"
Wisc. L. Rev. 1569 (1992); Robin Paul Malloy, "A New Law and Economics" in
Malloy and Braun (eds.); sources in Chap. 2, n. 13, above.

[12] *See* Malloy, *Law and Economics*, at 38–42; Mercuro and Medema, *Schools of Thought*, at
65–126; Robert Cooter and Thomas Ulen, *Law and Economics* 1–54 (2nd ed., 1997).

force exchanges in situations where their calculations produce a numerical justification. Setting aside the difficulty of making such calculations, it is important to see how channeling discourse through one efficiency approach rather than another may lead not only to a different decision but also to a different decision maker.

We can see this distinction more readily by revisiting our earlier example of *Peevyhouse v. Garland Coal & Mining Company*. In that case Garland was able to breach its contract promise to reclaim the land because the cost to reclaim the land exceeded the value that would be added to the land as a result of the work. If that fact pattern is considered under a Pareto efficiency test Garland would not be able to use a theory of efficient breach to justify avoidance of its contract performance. Under the Pareto criterion a move is efficient only when someone is made better off while no one is made worse off. In this case, even though Garland greatly improves its position, the Peevyhouses lose. Since the Peevyhouses have a loss of value from the breach, the breach cannot be justified as efficient under a Pareto criterion. In contrast, *Peevyhouse* presents a classic example for the theory of efficient breach under the Kaldor–Hicks criterion. Inasmuch as the gain to Garland more than offsets the loss to the Peevyhouses the outcome of non-performance is efficient in Kaldor–Hicks terms. Therefore, not only should Garland escape punishment for such a breach, the law should encourage the breach in an effort to promote efficient outcomes. Thus, the authoritative positioning of one criterion over the other changes the nature and the substantive outcome of the situation at hand.

In similar fashion, legal economists bring multiple approaches to other aspects of their undertaking. Some legal economists, for example, focus attention on the two most prominent parties to an exchange in assessing its efficiency, while others worry about transaction costs and third-party externalities. Consider the example discussed earlier in this Chapter with respect to the question of legalizing prostitution. If one focuses primarily on the "buyer" and "seller" in the exchange, the analysis and conclusion can be very different from that of a person looking at a broader set of third-party actors and variables. The third-party referencing strategy allows one radically to change the nature and meaning of the exchange process. In shifting to a consideration of third-party impacts, the determination of the optimal social outcome can be changed. Outcomes that appear efficient, wealth maximizing, and socially optimal when considering only the perspective of an immediate buyer and seller, for instance, may become non-optimal when overwhelmed by considerations of "relevant" third-party impacts and market distortions.

In addition to the prostitution example just mentioned, we might also consider the example of surrogate-motherhood contracts. In setting the scale, measure, and positions for analysis, what and who should be included? Some legal economists frame their analysis around the primary parties to the transaction: These would be the surrogate mother and the couple contracting for her services. A cost and benefit analysis framed around these parties would be very different from one that included them plus the child to be born, the public that will provide schools, healthcare services and other support systems, and the grandparents. As we can see, traditional law and economic analysis gives us a way to start our inquiry but no way of justifying one frame of reference over any other plausibly relevant frame. So even if we could all agree that a cost and benefit analysis is possible and appropriate we can still have very different outcomes depending upon how we shift through multiple frames of scale, measure, and position. Conversely, depending upon the outcome we desire, we can select the most useful rhetorical strategy for framing our analysis.

The implication of rhetorical strategies involving such ideas as transaction costs and externalities under the Coase Theorem, as discussed in Chapter 4, is that they too can be used to shift authority within a given context of exchange. They can be used to promote arguments in support of identifying numerous transaction costs preventing individual exchanges from reaching a truly efficient outcome. They thereby hold out a potential for justifying or shifting decisional authority away from individuals. In the place of countless individual decision makers, hindered by the blur of transaction costs, we can substitute the opinion of experts capable of knowing just where to draw the arbitrary line between relevant and irrelevant externalities, and equipped to quantify and calculate all critical trade-offs so that the truly efficient outcome emerges.

These examples, concerning efficiency and externalities, illustrate the consequences of employing particular rhetorical strategies within traditional law and economics. They depict dynamic refocusing with respect to matters of scale, measure, and positioning. This process of scale, measure, and position shifting within law and economics is not without purpose. The use of different rhetorical strategies promotes different assumptions about underlying social relationships, facilitates change in the networks and patterns of social interaction, and changes fundamental meanings and values. The real or dynamical world consequence of this rhetorical gamesmanship is observed in the different pieces of social information that are deemed important, the potential change in the suggested outcome to the question of optimal resource allocation, and in the opportunity to shift decision-making authority to different locations within the community. For this reason we must be careful to consider the meanings and consequences of alternative approaches to legal economic relationships in the social/market exchange process. Law and market economy can help us understand the strategic nature of alternative approaches and facilitate their use in advocating particular legal and public policy agendas.[13]

As a further example of employing rhetorical strategies to influence the frame of reference for interpretive communities, consider the invocation of cost and benefit analysis in making public policy decisions, such as in the environmental area.[14] The concern expressed here is that a cost and benefit approach to environmental decision making is inappropriate because there are so many variables that are difficult or impossible to calculate.[15] Speculation as to the value of some environmental or esthetic factors can lead to divergent guesstimates on the nature of a given set of trade-offs and thereby justify, as optimal, a wide variety of opposing alternatives.

In the realm of the Environmental Protection Agency (EPA), for example, cost and benefit analysis is alleged to have resulted in a presumption favoring agency *inaction* when potential input items are too uncertain to establish a clear computational benefit from government regulation.[16] When social and environmental values are difficult or impossible to quantify they cannot be recognized or counted. This results in the privileging of values and meanings that are easily monetized. In such a situation, the strategic role of a cost and benefit analysis requirement is to limit agency action. In essence, it does not matter if cost and benefit analysis gets us to any optimal point of efficiency; what counts, in terms of strategic rhetoric, is that it works to channel social interaction along a conventionalized path of agency inaction. It thus facilitates a shift in authority and supports a particular political agenda. With respect to environmental values that cannot be "properly" (meaning conventionally) quantified, authority is shifted away from government administrators and the interests alleged to be represented by the EPA. Consequently, we see that cost and benefit analysis, like our

---

[13] *See, e.g.*, Malloy, *Law and Economics*; Malloy, *New Discourse*, at 1–30.
[14] *See, e.g.*, Jeff L. Lewin, "Towards a New Ecological Law and Economics," in *Law and Economics* (Malloy and Braun, eds.), at 249–294; Daniel H. Cole, "Environmental Protection and Economic Growth: Lessons from Socialist Europe" *in Law and Economics* (Malloy and Braun, eds.), at 295–330; David M. Driesen, "The Societal Cost of Environmental Regulation: Beyond Cost-Benefit Analysis," 24 Ecology L. Q. 545 (1997).
[15] *See* sources above, n. 14.
[16] Driesen, "Societal Cost."

earlier examples, has a strategic role to play in mediating and shaping our understanding of the market exchange process. The form of rhetorical strategy, in other words, is significant because it influences real-world outcomes.

Shifting our attention, briefly, to rhetorical strategies outside of a traditional law and economics framework also leads to similar insights and conclusions. We will see, once again, that the form of the rhetorical strategy shapes the substance of legal and economic relationships by influencing the interpretive frame of reference for exchange. As a basic illustration of strategies outside of traditional law and economics I will refer to positions in critical theory. This is not meant to be a detailed analysis of critical theory but rather to be a simple illustration of some of the issues raised by alternative interpretive frameworks. In so doing I will first make some general comments about critical theory as it relates to traditional law and economics and then I will provide an example.

Critical, gender, and race theories (collectively "critical theories") generally reject the relevance of market-based analysis and thereby position themselves as the counter-signs of the traditional law and economics paradigm.[17] Their critique of the current networks and patterns of market exchange are usually referenced against an interpretive framework that rejects the ideas of objectivity, neutrality, rationality, equality, and self-interest. These critical theories, although they position themselves as oppositional signs to law and economics, are none the less a part of the broader undertaking of law and market economy. This is because critical theories function as referential screens or indexical guideposts in the process of meaning and value formation. They operate in a "mode of secondness," to use Peirce's term. Therefore, critical theories provide a frame of reference for particular interpretive communities and function as the interpretive filter through which these communities understand the complex process of social/market exchange. In this way they operate like the shifting rhetorical strategies

---

[17] *See* Mercuro and Medema, *Economics*, at 157–170 (with related notes); Daniel Farber and Suzanna Sherry, *Beyond all Reason: The Radical Assault on Truth in American Law* (1997). *See also* Malloy, *Serfdom*, at 61–83; Malloy, *Law and Economics*, at 60–103; Robert L. Hayman and Nancy Levit, *Jurisprudence: Contemporary Readings, Problems and Narratives* (1994), 213–264 (critical legal studies), 325–382 (feminist legal theory), 383–451 (critical race theory); *Critical Legal Studies* (Allan C. Hutchinson, ed., 1989); Mark Kelman, *A Guide to Critical Legal Studies* (1987); *Feminist Legal Theory: Readings in Law and Gender* (Katherine T. Bartlett and Rosanne Kennedy, eds., 1991); Catherine A. MacKinnon, *Toward a Feminist Theory of the State* (1989); Catherine A. MacKinnon, "Feminism, Marxism, Method, and the State: Towards Feminist Jurisprudence," 8 Signs: J. Women Culture & Society 635 (1983); "Symposium: Women in Legal Education – Pedagogy, Law. Theory, and Practice," 38 J. Legal Educ. 1 (1988); Guyora Binder, "On Critical Legal Studies as Guerrilla Warfare," 76 Geo. L. J. 1 (1987); *Race-ing Justice, En-gendering Power* (Toni Morrison, ed., 1992).

within traditional law and economics. They function as interpretive devices that influence choice in the process of exchange.

The rhetorical strategies of critical theory, when used as interpretive or indexical mediators, can lead to conclusions that differ from those of traditional law and economics. For example, in Chapter 2, I discussed how a Chicago School approach might find a perfectly competitive market, without a need for government intervention, in the examination of data that might lead a critical theorist to reach the opposite conclusion. I suggested that this might occur when a group of sellers produced similar products and sold them for similar prices and on similar terms. I showed how the critical theorists might view this data and concluded that the networks and patterns of exchange were not competitive but dominated by the hegemonic practices of powerful corporations – a situation requiring significant structural intervention. Competing interpretations, such as these, lead to very different policy prescriptions. The practical consequence of critical theories, therefore, is that they compete with other approaches in an effort to obtain authoritative influence over the interpretive networks and patterns of exchange so that they can have a substantive impact on social organization and the process of meaning and value formation.

As strategic rhetorics, critical theories raise some concerns for the process of creative discovery. To the extent that they are grounded in conceptions of the personal – revelation, higher consciousness, inequality, and power – they express a potentially restrictive and non-reciprocal meaning, which functions as a screen against extensive authoritative participation in the social exchange process. This is because appeals to the personal – revelation and higher consciousness, for example – invoke a subjective privileging of personal opinion and situational positioning that cannot be accessed or tested by others who are differently situated.[18] A personal revelation involves the revealing of a personal truth and personal truths do not function well as social mediators. Personal truths, like efficiency calculations, presuppose a desired objective or outcome and a shared set of values. They are not very helpful in addressing social conflicts arising between alternative interpretive communities with different values, different experiences, and different frames of reference. For this reason critical theories tend to be restrictive and end up promoting a conventionalized code or habit accessible only to those who subscribe to a shared set of meanings and values on such things as race, gender, and class. Challenges to these critically prescribed conventions are generally discouraged, classified as

---

[18] *See* Farber and Sherry, *Beyond Reason*, at 12–13, 26–33, 35–50.

a form of denial, used as evidence of one's poor character (evidence of being a racist, for instance), or dismissed for lack of *authenticity*.[19] These aspects of critical theory raise concern for the concepts of reciprocity and humility in the ethic of social responsibility.

In critical theory the market sign of the individual is also presented differently. Rather than being a key referential part of the exchange community, the market-oriented individual is positioned as a greedy, exploiting, and selfish antithesis of community. Self-interest in the critical approach is translated as selfishness and placed in opposition to the public interest, rather than seeing the individual and the community as a relational part of a fully integrated process of dialogical exchange.

Critical theories also raise restrictive concerns to the extent that they reject reciprocal respect for the actions and thoughts of people that go against the interpretive revelations and instincts of critical theorists. For example, when distinguished African-Americans such as Supreme Court Justice Clarence Thomas and economists Thomas Sowell or Walter Williams criticize positions taken by critical race theorists on matters such as affirmative action, they are often said not only to be wrong but to betray their race. Likewise, when a woman such as Professor Ellen Frankel Paul challenges the insights of critical feminists on such matters as comparable worth she is said not only to be in error but also to lack authenticity as a woman. Such a discourse strategy operates to restrict authoritative participation in the social/market exchange process because it denies, as an interpretive presumption, the possibility of error in its own referential point of view. It denies the possibility of difference between alternatively situated individuals and dehumanizes the messenger along with the message. As such, it also works against the process of creative discovery since it seeks to restrict rather than extend the space for authoritative interaction and participation.

Critical theory also uses other concepts of concern in its rhetorical strategy. It tends, for instance, to focus attention on the concepts of "power" and "indeterminacy" in its analysis of law, market theory, and the social exchange process.[20] The critical position on these matters is oftentimes non-integrative, in a semiotic or law and market economy sense, for two reasons. First, it fails adequately to account for the fact that in a complex system authoritative influence is distributed and exercised in multiple directions. Sign relationships, according to Peirce, are multidirectional and as such it is difficult, for example, to speak of a

---

[19] *Id.* at 72–94.
[20] *See* above, n. 17 (in particular, Mercuro and Medema, *Economics*, at 157–170). *See also* Lawrence B. Solum, "On the Indeterminacy Crisis: Critiquing Critical Dogma," 54 U. Chi. L. Rev. 462 (1987).

distinctively feminine or African-American "voice."[21] Sign relationships
are more complex than that and the failure to account for this can result
in misconceptions. The "world" and the "market" are not, in other
words, simply "constructed" by the isolated actions of easily defined
individuals or groups such as men, whites, or capitalists. The world and
the market are integrative concepts that express themselves in signs
emerging from the relational exchanges of numerous variables, forces,
and points of reference. They are communities in which self-interest,
public interest, authority and power are always multidirectional. It was,
after all, an all-white and male US Congress that had to vote in favor of
giving the vote to women, and a white power structure that agreed to
various voting rights and civil rights for blacks and other minorities. In
some respects, therefore, these acts involved a response to countervailing sources of power and authority.

Signs, meanings, and values in these communities reflect a variety of
dynamic forces. Women, African-Americans, and everyone else play a
role in influencing the formation and reformation of these signs. From
the point of view of law and market economy the focus should be on
authoritative participation in extensive exchange networks and not on
giving primacy to the idea of power that implies coercive and one-
directional control. The role of power analysis should not be over-
emphasized any more than the role of efficiency. We must be careful,
therefore, not to have power analysis construct an interpretive descrip-
tion of many things while, at the same time, functioning to explain very
little about creativity and the nature of the social/market exchange
process.

A second weakness in the critical approach is that it typically fails to
recognize that all complex systems, including the market exchange
process, are at one and the same time determinate in some respects
(habit and convention based), and indeterminate in other respects
(influenced by chance, surprise, and creative discovery). Consequently,
there can be little meaningful criticism of law or market theory in
pointing out their indeterminate characteristics. Indeterminacy is an
element of all theory, including critical theory.

In seeking to influence the formation of values and meanings, critical
approaches tend to promote outcomes that differ from those suggested
by traditional law and economics. In particular, critical theories tend to
promote the concept of equality of outcome as opposed to equality of
opportunity. This means that they tend to interpret unequal outcomes

---

[21] See Kevelson, *Peirce and Science*, at 104–106. *See generally* Charles H. Long,
Significations: Signs, Symbols, and Images in the Interpretation of Religion (1986) (counter-
sign system and sub-systems).

as evidence of power, bias, and discrimination.[22] In a complex system, however, equality of outcome, as discussed earlier in this Chapter, is impossible. This is because it is impossible, in a complex system, to pass through the same point more than once, and an extensive market exchange network with multiple degrees of freedom is an extremely complex system. Any hope of making the idea of outcome equality coherent requires us to focus on a temporary (if it is ever attainable) idea of sustained static equilibrium – an impossible conception in a dynamic and complex system, short of death or extinction. Any attempt to maintain such an equilibrium would be futile and would require constant and continuous interference with the social/market exchange process.[23] Such an objective therefore implicates the need for a restrictive and controlled environment, and this type of environment does not facilitate the process of creative discovery.

At this point it may be useful for me to offer an example that might help clarify the nature of critical strategic rhetorics. For this example I refer to an article I wrote several years ago. In the article I used a law and market economy approach to examine the meanings and values of exchange from the perspective of Native American Indians in central and northern New York State.[24] My project involved talking to native people about their reactions, their feelings, and understandings respecting the five-hundredth anniversary celebration of the "discovery" of America by Christopher Columbus. I managed to get a number of native people to put their thoughts down in letters that I included in my article. I examined the content of the letters from an interpretive law and market economy approach, and found that the letters revealed a set of referential or mediational assumptions grounded in elements of critical theory.

Four major themes emerged from these letters and demonstrated their relevance, not only as part of a general belief system, but also as strategically useful rhetoric in the defense of Native American interests with respect to various land claim and other disputes against the state of New York, the United States, and Canada. In summary, these themes involved: (1) a belief in instinctive, emotive, and revelational decision making based on a connection to nature, rather than an appeal to rationality; (2) the rejection of the idea of private ownership and free transferability of the natural environment, the natural environment being held in a capacity of stewardship by the entire Indian community,

---

[22] *See* Farber and Sherry, *Beyond Reason*, at 52–71.
[23] *See generally*, Robert Nozick, *Anarchy, State, and Utopia* (1974); Friedrich A. Hayek, *The Road to Serfdom*, 77–87 (1944).
[24] *See* Malloy, *Longhouse*.

and playing an integral part in the material and spiritual definition of the Indian people; (3) the rejection of the privileging of the written word over that of a personal and "authentic" oral tradition; and (4) a belief in an original emergent connection to specific geographical space, including a rejection of the idea that native people might have arrived in North America as part of an earlier migration of peoples out of Asia.

An initial review of these four themes reveals a clear conflict with several standard assumptions in traditional law and economics. This conflict is evident in the rejection of rationality, the rejection of extensive individual private ownership, and the rejection of the free transferability of elements of the natural environment. Seen as rhetorical strategies, these value assumptions serve an important interpretive function by offering support for a referential ground upon which to defend Indian land claims against the state of New York and the governments of the United States and Canada.

First, by rejecting the idea of private ownership and free transferability of the natural environment, they ground the Indian assertion that no "transfers" to Europeans or Americans ever took place. A provisional and conditional sharing of the land and natural environment was misinterpreted, they believe, by the power-seeking white people who came to North America.

Second, by rejecting the privileging of the written word and of rational logic, they ground their assertion that Indian oral tradition is clear and contrary to the written record of land transfers. They assert that their land claim disputes and other rights need not be rationalized nor resolved by appeal to unfavorable written treaties, codes, and case decisions collected and indexed by non-Indian people. Favorable written treaties, codes and cases may, however, be used to their advantage. Thus, they use a non-reciprocal logic of picking and choosing for themselves sources that are legitimate and authentic.

Third, by believing in a spiritual emergence from a particular geographical place, and by rejecting a theory of Asian migration, order, coherence, and a sense of timelessness are brought to their argument. Indian people are not, in other words, simply people who migrated to a land at an earlier date; rather, they originate from, and are entrusted to preserve, a specific geographical place in the natural environment. Indian people are not only earlier in time, they are the first and original owners of a land that they believe was not and cannot be transferred to non-Indian people.

Fourth, and finally, by rejecting a role for rational or logical inquiry and replacing it with an instinctive, emotive, and revelational connection between Indian people and the natural environment, they make their uniquely positioned point of reference inaccessible to all "outsiders" who are not of the same "body" or "mind." Their assumptions, as part of a rhetorical strategy influencing meanings and values, leads to an alternative conception of property, of ownership, and of resource allocation, as well as to a different set of authoritative criteria for dispute resolution. We see, therefore, that the form of strategic rhetoric is of substantive import.

The Indian argument outlined above presents a strategic rhetoric more closely grounded in critical theory than in any frame of traditional law and economics. As a consequence of this positioning we see that the Indian argument is also strategically transformed into a personal one. Challenges to the Indian position, therefore, may be easily translated into personal attacks rather than seen as legitimate elements of social discourse or exchange. Consequently, much care must be taken to avoid having alternative views unfairly characterized as making ad hominem and racist arguments. The ability to personalize the argument, as well as to shift its interpretive framework, can be very effective as a form of strategic rhetoric, but it can also severely restrict the process of exchange. This is because it is difficult to mediate conflict between competing interpretive communities when their opposing positions are based on individual revelations and personal truths.

The point of this example is simple. Critical theories, like alternative approaches within traditional law and economics, operate as rhetorical strategies, and these strategies are important because they function as interpretive frames of references in the social/market exchange process and have substantive consequences in the real world. The approach of law and market economy helps us to understand these strategies as part of a dynamic process of exchange.

From our examination in this section of the Chapter, I believe that critical theories may be helpful in speculating about considerations of *scale*, *measure*, and *position* in the relationship between law and market theory, but they may also be more restrictive than other approaches. This raises some concern with respect to the process of creative discovery and sustainable wealth formation. In the context of the highly complex and impersonal structures and institutions of modern public life (as in government, business, and other organizational networks), critical theories seem less likely to promote extensive, diverse, and unconventional exchange networks. This is because such organizations are too large and complex to operate with extensive authoritative participation in the absence of a commitment to an ethic of social responsibility. In complex and diverse exchange communities, of the type that affect most people on a pervasive basis every day, exchange and creativity are more likely to be furthered by extensive access to exchange mechanisms that promote humility, diversity, and reciprocity, rather than by approaches grounded in the primacy of restrictive concepts such as authenticity, instinct, emotion, and revelation.

In the process of constructing persuasive arguments for law and public policy prescription, therefore, alternative rhetorical strategies can be understood as competing for the role of referential (indexical) mediator in the meaning and value formation process. They are not just exercises in fanciful word play, they are invoked for purposes of facilitating a substantive consequence in favor of one particular group or outcome, rather than another. As normative facilitators of interpretation, each of these rhetorics is of interest to law and market economy because each suggests its own implications for resource allocation and authority over the political process. In this regard, careful consideration must be given to the likelihood that one set of approaches may be better than another for purposes of advancing the values of an extensive and participatory social/market exchange process.

7   Conclusion

In many ways this book represents a new beginning for understanding the relationship between law and market theory, so it is difficult to formulate concrete and definitive conclusions. None the less, it is possible, and I hope useful, for me to comment on some of the key points addressed in the book and to explain how I use my approach in teaching. In particular, I will comment on the way in which this approach informs my teaching of law and market economy, and real estate transactions. I hope that these examples will give others a better understanding of how to translate some of the ideas from this book into practice.

First and foremost, I have attempted to explore a theory of law and market economy that is concerned with the process of sustainable wealth formation as emerging from the human practice of exchange. In doing this I benefited from a reference to the humanities, by way of semiotics. This allowed me to speculate about a new understanding of the relationship between law and market theory. In using semiotics to think about the meanings and values of exchange, I was led to three important observations. First, semiotics permitted me to explore the concept of efficiency in a new way. In doing so it became clear that the concept of efficiency was problematic for reasons that went beyond traditional concerns. It was problematic because it was unable to address issues of creativity, and creativity is vital to wealth formation. Semiotics allowed me to explore the nature of creativity in exchange and this led me to conclude that paying undue attention to efficiency does not promote a process of sustainable wealth formation. Second, in response to traditional critics of the efficiency criterion, semiotics directed my attention to the issue of a conflict between efficiency and justice or fairness. In contrast to traditional critics I was able to reframe the tension as one between efficiency and creativity. This triggered a variety of new ideas and questions. Third, I realized that the human practice of exchange and the exercise of market choice involve a process of interpretation. Therefore, I concluded that a useful approach to the relationship between law and market theory must account for some theory of interpretation.

Responding to these three related observations, I have offered a way of reinterpreting the values of traditional law and economics, and of envisioning a new field of inquiry. Admittedly, my ideas and conclusions are speculative in nature and I offer them as a framework for further investigation and conversation.

My analysis has led me to revise a number of assumptions in traditional law and economics and to suggest three important implications that I address in Chapter 6. First, I explain that the pursuit of economic efficiency, as a standard used in traditional law and economics, does not maximize sustainable wealth formation because it cannot adequately deal with the process of creativity and because it is context dependent. Second, I argue that the nature and extent of the distribution of scarce resources and access to the exercise of political authority influences the process of sustainable wealth formation. Here, I suggest that the more extensive the networks and patterns of exchange, the greater the potential for creative discovery and for wealth formation. Third, I suggest that alternative approaches to legal discourse can be meaningfully understood as rhetorical strategies competing for substantive influence over the social/market exchange process. These rhetorics function as interpretive references for influencing market choice and, thus, impact on the meaning and value formation process of market exchange. The discussion of these implications in Chapter 6 helps to illustrate a number of points made throughout the book.

Having, thus, broadly summarized some of the key elements of the book, I now offer a brief illustration of how my approach influences my work in particular teaching areas.

First, my course in law and market economy involves working through the various points and arguments addressed in this book. The central tenet of the course is that we want to study the process of sustainable wealth formation, explore its benefits, and figure out how best to organize society to facilitate its continuous enhancement. I take it that sustainable wealth formation is generally considered a positive thing inasmuch as we benefit from such things as improved healthcare, education, housing, and expanding networks of opportunity. Likewise, it seems safe to assume that most people do not want to fall into a pattern of ever-increasing poverty. Given this, however, I take the position that the meanings and values of this process, along with the consequences of alternative approaches to it, are all up for grabs. In this regard I expect my students to learn the basic terminology and concepts of traditional law and economics while addressing its interpretive implications. They must also deal with the process of creative discovery and develop an ability to think about how these various concepts are used in law.

This includes understanding how and why a lawyer might use or reject particular market concepts in best representing a client or in advocating for or against a given public policy position. For example, I not only want my students to know the basic tenets and critiques of the Coase Theorem, I want them to explain when, how, and why they would strategically use it. In other words, they need to know how Coase influences the networks and patterns of exchange – how it influences substantive outcomes in law and social relationships. Similarly, when I present them with fact patterns or hypotheticals built around concepts such as the Coase Theorem I expect them to identify the types of arguments and evidence that will be needed either to advance or undercut the use of Coase in the given situation.

I also want my students to be able to read or listen to an argument and learn how to disassemble its economic assertions. I want them to think about the underlying value assumptions that are necessary to make the assertions logically understandable in a given market context. Then I want them to learn how to develop rhetorical strategies that both support and defeat the underlying values that they discover. Finally, I ask them to map out how the decision makers, the decision-making process, and the beneficiaries of the process change with alternative interpretive references.

In order to work on these skills I assign my students readings and problem sets on a variety of issues including property and contract law disputes, affirmative action, healthcare delivery systems, and the Americans with Disabilities Act, among others. Sometimes they work individually and at other times in groups. To the surprise of some of my colleagues I also have them view and discuss scenes from a variety of film clips. These clips can include a discussion of urban gentrification and the market exploitation of African-Americans from the movie *Boyz 'n the Hood*, or a discussion of reverse discrimination in hiring from the movie *Jungle Fever*. Similarly, I have used clips from *Do the Right Thing* to explore the claims that a community has upon businesses operating in a given neighborhood. I have also found very useful scenes in such diverse films as *My Dinner with André*, *Class Action*, and *Disney's Pocahontas*.

Two films that I like to use very early on in the term are *Wall Street* and *Other People's Money*. Scenes from these two films are straightforward and easy to work with even when students are just beginning to learn the subject matter. The scenes I select from these two movies both involve a corporate stockholders' meeting in which there is a takeover bid by an investor seeking to break up the company as a way of enhancing stockholder value. The lead characters in each film make appeals to the stockholders, and their appeals raise fundamental questions about the nature and purpose of market exchange.

In *Wall Street* the character of Gordon Gekko, played by Michael Douglas, tells stockholders to vote in favor of his takeover because he will make them rich. He tells them that greed is good, greed simplifies, greed clarifies, greed in all of its forms makes the marketplace work. Similarly, in *Other People's Money*, Danny DeVito, playing Larry the Liquidator, makes an appeal to stockholders to vote in favor of his takeover bid because he will make them money. He tells them that the company, while profitable, is worth more dead (liquidated) than alive. He tells stockholders to vote for making the best return on their money and that they have no obligation to the employees of the company or to the community where its factory is located. Their only obligation is to make the best profit for themselves. In contrast to these views Gregory Peck, playing the role of the eighty-one-year-old founder and president of the New England Wire and Cable Company in *Other People's Money*, argues that a company is worth more than the value of its stock. He says that a business is about people. It is about people who work together pursuing a common purpose and who share the same friendships and live in the same community. He cautions the stockholders to avoid selfish and greedy actions and instead asks them to vote with their feelings. He asks them to vote for the continuation of a profitable business that is more than a collection of capital goods, it is a community.

In reviewing these scenes we get a close-up look at the real tension between two different visions of the market. We get to hear the argument and see the speaker as if he had come into our law office or we had attended the meeting. We also get the sights and sounds of the film that impose the director's interpretive imprint upon the arguments of the characters. This is very different from reading a law review article or working on a problem set. Here the student must listen, as if to her own client, and understand the meanings and values at play in these different approaches to understanding the market exchange process. In exploring these scenes we consider each character's appeal to different types of evidence and competing interpretive references in making his argument. We examine the nature and structure of the rhetorical strategies being used, and we discuss the implications of the alternative views for law, legal institutions, and social organization. We see that the disagreements are as much, or more, about values as they are about facts. This allows us to start exploring the major themes of the course.

The point of these exercises is that students need to develop an understanding of the interpretive frames of reference at work in legal and economic exchange. They need to know how to decode messages and encode counter-messages using a variety of rhetorical strategies. In this way they learn about the dynamic and creative process of exchange, and about the substantive implications of particular interpretive references. They also learn that the market is easily understandable as a place of meaning and value formation. The implication, of course, is that gaining authoritative influence over the interpretive framework of meaning and value formation carries with it the ability to have a substantive impact upon a variety of legal and economic relationships.

While most students readily grasp the significance of these ideas, some students inevitably have difficulty. This is particularly true with respect to understanding the relationship between the interpretive process and market exchange. For the benefit of these students I provide a few additional examples that are more directly related to their own experiences. I find that these examples usually bring the point home. For instance, I ask them to think about their experience in using computers. I ask them to consider the importance of the operating system. I tell them that the operating system actually functions as an authoritative interpretive lens or screen for organizing their interaction with the computer. This interaction involves a complex exchange process or sign system and in this regard is very much like the market process discussed in this book. Moreover, by making reference to Microsoft and its Windows operating system I get them to think about the relationship between operating systems and individual programs. They all understand that individual software programs need to be compatible with the operating system. They also understand that having a strong market position over the operating system means having authoritative influence over the way in which software products will be designed. Consequently, they appreciate the idea of value related to influencing the interpretive framework of exchange. Just as software must be compatible with the operating system to function properly, so too legal, economic, political, and social exchange must be compatible with an authoritative framework in order to be effectively "heard" or "understood." In other words, there is a great deal of competition for controlling an authoritative interpretive screen (an operating system for social organization, so to speak), because it functions to conventionalize a particular way of doing things. Furthermore, this creates value and influence for the people benefited by such conventions in the same way that Microsoft profits from its market position with respect to computer technologies.

Using a related example I ask my students to think about all of the information and data fragments available on the internet. I ask them to think about the vastness of all of this information, about the potential value present in this information, and about the difficulty of finding the specific information one needs to solve a particular problem. I ask them how they go about accessing useful elements of this information and this usually leads us to a discussion of search engines such as Netscape, Yahoo, Microsoft Explorer, and Excite, among others. In pursuing this discussion we inevitably talk about how the various search engines provide slightly different ways of accessing information and how search results can vary between them. Some students offer advice about the best search engine for a particular type of question. Likewise, some students offer their opinion about the comparisons between the Lexis and Westlaw legal research systems. From this discussion I ask students once again to consider what is at work. The search engines that they use actually function as interpretive frameworks or screens. In this sense they act as the gateways for access and understanding of the data and information available on the internet. Controlling these screens or gateways creates value, both economically and in terms of social understanding. These search engines, I tell them, are like the rhetorical strategies used in law and market theory. They compete for authoritative influence over the exchange process – they compete for an authoritative position in conventionalizing the interpretive process and the exercise of market choice.

The lessons learned from a course in law and market economy can also be applied in other substantive areas. In addition to teaching courses in law and market economy, for instance, I am actively involved with the subject matter of real estate transactions and my approach to real estate transactions is market driven.[1] I use the ideas and concepts of law and market economy to help structure my approach to teaching in this area because I believe that successful transactional lawyers must be familiar with much more than the legal rules that govern a given area of practice. While the law provides basic tools and infrastructure, lawyers must understand transactional relationships as part of a broader market exchange process. In order to be successful at real estate transactions, therefore, I tell my students that they must learn the relevant legal rules *and* they must understand how these rules relate to market theory. They must understand the networks and patterns of exchange, and the motivations and dynamics of market interaction, as well as the problems of risk and ignorance. They must understand the meaning and value-

---

[1] *See e.g.*, Robin Paul Malloy and James C. Smith, *Real Estate Transactions* (1998).

formation process because it informs the understandings between the parties, and it shapes the market-based expectations of the exchange.

My approach focuses on understanding the market context of exchange rather than on assessing the efficiency of any particular legal rule. Instead of merely studying the types of housing products available, for instance, we consider accessibility to housing and mortgage markets. We look at income distribution, mortgage availability, and patterns of exchange by race, age, gender, and other factors. We consider the emergence of new forms of housing and finance, and we evaluate the impact of alternative housing market assumptions. We look at how changes in basic assumptions and in exchange patterns can influence outcomes and redefine efficiency.

In a similar vein I tell students that they cannot fully understand real estate mortgages unless and until they understand how lenders operate and make money. Simply knowing the rules related to five or ten different types of mortgages tells one very little about when and how to select the proper type of mortgage for any given circumstance. Likewise, until one knows how a lender operates one cannot appreciate which terms in a mortgage are negotiable and which are essentially fixed. When one appreciates the lender's objectives and constraints it is then possible to negotiate. This is because one cannot reasonably hope to eliminate terms that go to the heart of a lender's profit center. At the same time, however, we must appreciate the nature of rapidly changing business practices in these mortgage markets. Therefore, we must think proactively as well as reactively in planning and structuring such transactional relationships.

Examples of how market considerations inform real estate transactions are numerous.[2] One cannot hope to practice law successfully in this area without understanding the various networks of relationships and patterns of exchange that make up the market. Investigating what is exchangeable, by whom, when, and on what terms is central to understanding real estate law in its market context. One must think beyond rules that define property rights to consider alternative conceptions of ownership, and to investigate the relationship between these rights. One must be aware, for instance, of the relationship between real property law and a variety of other areas of law, including: human rights, civil rights, contract, mortgage, title, corporate, environmental, regulatory, bankruptcy, securities, and administrative law, among others. One must also consider the relationship between these rights and a variety of social, political, and economic issues. One must inquire about the

[2] *Id.*

meanings and values of such relationships from the point of view of alternative interpretive communities.

The market for real estate transactions, like other markets, must therefore be understood as restrictive or extensive with an appreciation for the implications of particular legal rules, institutions, and infrastructure. The market must also be examined for its potentiality – for its ability to promote creative opportunities. Importantly, much of this examination can be done without focusing on the efficiency of any particular rule or legal arrangement. While efficiency considerations remain relevant, they must be put into proper perspective. We need to think about a variety of potentially good or efficient arrangements and about the criteria and implications of making any particular choice between them.

The market can also be examined by looking at the way in which new legal rules and legal infrastructure transform the networks and patterns of exchange within a community. Changes in these relationships will have substantive impacts for market participants – on who participates, on what terms, in what relationships, and to what ends. New computer technologies, new laws on race relations, new banking hours and outlets, new down-payment and credit criteria, are just a few of the types of changes that can have a dramatic impact on market exchange. All of these changes influence the networks and patterns of exchange and reframe individual social experience. In undertaking to practice or to study law, therefore, we should examine the potential exchange implications of the legal and economic relationships involved. Again, we can do a great deal here without making economic efficiency our primary touchstone consideration.

As an example of this approach one can refer back to my discussion of the secondary mortgage market at the end of Chapter 2. There we saw how changes in the networks and patterns of exchange dramatically affected the nature of a variety of relationships within the community. These changes are important because they have a significant influence upon the market exchange process and because they transform the meanings and values of a market economy.

As another example I refer to my 1991 book, *Planning for Serfdom: Legal Economic Discourse And Downtown Development.*[3] While my theory has advanced since writing that book, the basic underlying approach is consistent with the theory of law and market economy. In that book I examined the trend toward public and private partnerships as ways of

---

[3] Robin Paul Malloy, *Planning for Serfdom: Legal Economic Discourse and Downtown Development* (1991).

revitalizing downtown urban areas in a number of American cities. These partnerships involve various ways of mixing private and public resources and ownership forms in an effort to plan and rebuild urban downtowns. My investigation involved a look at how the types of partnerships and methods of planning influenced the networks and patterns of exchange within a given community. I was not so much interested in whether particular approaches to urban redevelopment were efficient, as I was concerned with the way in which meanings and values were reshaped within the community as a result of these new arrangements – the basic idea being that communities promoting a great deal of public planning and extensive public and private partnering were different in kind than communities that did not engage in such exchange relationships. I concluded that communities with extensive public and private partnering had different understandings of the state, private property, and the individual than communities that rejected this approach. It was important, therefore, to think about, to understand, and to evaluate such differences – to ask not only if a given set of relationships was efficient, but to also consider the types of communities promoted by their meanings and values.

In all of the situations that I have considered in this book, the relationship between law and market theory reveals itself as dynamic and complex. It is not easily characterized as merely positive, efficient, and wealth maximizing, or as exploitative, chaotic, and oppressive. The truth is more likely to be that it is simultaneously all of these things and more. This is precisely the reason why I believe that we must seek better to understand this relationship.

To do this, however, we must think beyond the boundaries of traditional law and economics. We must go beyond a static system of analysis grounded in the values of detached and isolated individuals, individuals who exercise purely rational and self-interested choice in worlds disconnected from experience, and from the communities in which real people live, work, and play. We must embrace a broader form of inquiry, one that places the individual back into a community context linked to experience, and one that understands that wealth-promoting exchanges are sustainable only in so far as they are embedded within dynamic and multivalued interpretive communities.

In this book I have speculated about such an approach. In doing so I am fully aware of the tentative nature of my undertaking. Ultimately, therefore, my effort has been suggestive more than exhaustive and serves as a prolegomenon to a larger and ongoing research project. It has been designed to indicate the possibility, and the potentiality, of an alternative framework of analysis. It has been offered on the assumption that current approaches to understanding the relationship between law and market theory are inadequate. My hope is that this framework will be useful in providing yet another vehicle for understanding the world in which we live, and for imagining a world that is *continually coming into being*.

Index

adoption, 26
Ahonen, Pertti, 25–26
amoral, 10
Arrow's Impossibility Theorem, 101
authenticity, 160, 163
authority, 4, 10, 14, 21–22, 27, 31, 38,
    41, 49, 68, 73, 98–99, 102, 104,
    108–118, 120, 122, 124–125, 127,
    129–130, 133–134, 137, 147–148,
    150, 152–154, 156–157, 159–161,
    164–165, 167, 170–171

Balkin, Jack, 24
barter, 31
Brigham, John, 24
Brion, Denis, 24–26
Buchanan, James, 37–38, 57, 60

Calabresi, Guido, 8
chaos, 1, 21, 32–33, 126, 141, 174
Chicago School, 40–41, 159
China, 12–15, 38, 62, 80, 116–117,
    128–129
choice, 5, 9, 12, 15–16, 35–37, 41, 43, 47,
    49, 57–58, 62, 67, 74, 76, 79, 93–94,
    96–101, 104, 138–141, 143, 149,
    154, 159, 166, 173
    imaginative, 39, 41, 43–44, 46–47, 78,
        89–90, 97, 152
    interpretive, 13, 119, 149
    objective, 3, 4
    rational, 4, 10, 37–38, 43, 57, 59, 61,
        97, 107, 110, 149
Clinton, William (President), 75
Coase, 103–104, 168
    Coase Theorem, 20, 90–93, 96–98,
        100, 103–104, 156, 168
code, 15, 47, 71–73, 87, 110, 113, 159,
    163, 170
complex systems, 5, 21, 27, 32, 112, 115,
    119, 123, 125, 139, 141–142, 150,
    161–162
complexity, 27–30, 59, 69, 76, 112–114,

    120, 131, 134, 139, 158, 161, 164,
    170, 174
continuity, 3, 15, 27, 32–33, 43, 47, 72,
    78, 84, 126, 138, 146, 147
contract, 25, 61, 102, 106, 108–109, 111,
    114–116, 119, 121–123, 130–131,
    142, 144–146, 156, 168, 172
    freedom of, 109
    social contract, 20, 107, 109–110, 115
convention, 3–4, 10–11, 19, 30, 32–34,
    39, 42–44, 46–48, 62–64, 71–73, 76,
    78–79, 84, 88, 96–97, 104, 110, 113,
    115, 119, 123, 125–126, 138–139,
    149–152, 159, 161
cost and benefit, 3, 5, 13, 33, 37, 44–45,
    51, 58–59, 67, 70, 83, 86, 96–97,
    104, 156–157
creative destruction, 132
creative discovery, 11, 18, 21, 27, 36,
    43–44, 77–78, 82, 84–85, 106, 115,
    117–118, 120–121, 125, 128, 131,
    137, 143, 148, 150, 152, 154–161,
    167, 168
creativity, 2–4, 18, 21, 36, 38, 44, 46–48,
    55, 65, 67–68, 77–78, 84, 87–88, 90,
    98, 104, 106, 112–117, 124, 126,
    129, 132–135, 137–138, 151, 161,
    165–167
credit, 30, 39, 81
critical theory, 20–21, 27–28, 41, 73, 109,
    153, 158–162, 164
    critical, 20, 49, 158
    gender, 20, 49, 158, 160
    race, 20, 49, 158
Curran, Vivian Grosswald, 24

Dau-Schmidt, Kenneth G., 60, 142 (n.8)
determinate, 1, 3–4, 47, 75, 87, 89, 97, 103
dialogic, 29, 38, 58–60, 64, 68, 74, 106,
    120, 125, 160
discrimination, 53, 55, 108, 130, 173
diversity, 3, 7, 21, 33, 44, 48, 51, 114, 118,
    121, 124–125, 151, 165

Eco, Umberto, 34
efficiency, 1–7, 10–11, 18, 20, 22, 26–27, 36–38, 44, 47, 49, 52–55, 64, 75–76, 78, 89, 91–94, 96, 98–100, 103, 108, 119, 121, 127–128, 132, 136–138, 140–148, 152, 155–156, 166–167, 172–174
    Kaldor–Hicks efficiency, 65, 108, 144, 154, 155
    Pareto efficiency, 108, 154, 155
efficient breach, theory of, 144–146
endowment effect, 125
entrepreneurism, 20, 49, 63, 78, 80, 84–88, 151
environment, 1, 15, 18, 38, 42, 44–45, 54, 81–82, 85, 90, 94–97, 106, 117–121, 123, 128, 131, 133–134, 147, 151, 157, 162–163
equality, 27, 158–159
    of opportunity, 150–151, 161
    of outcome, 150, 161–162
equilibration, 20, 83–84, 89
equilibrium, 11, 20, 21, 33, 36–38, 43, 44, 48, 70, 78, 83–86, 88–89, 119, 122–124, 136, 140, 147, 162
ethics, 3, 5, 10–11, 21, 44, 48, 111–112, 119, 141
    ethic of social responsibility, 11, 21–22, 36, 44, 48, 55, 65, 106, 118–122, 128–129, 133–134, 140, 151–152, 160, 164
    market ethic, 120
exchange, 4–5, 17–18, 21–23, 26–31, 35, 37, 39–41, 43–44, 46, 49, 57–58, 61, 63–64, 71–73, 77, 80–84, 88–89, 96–98, 106, 113, 115–116, 118–120, 122, 124, 130–134, 139, 141, 147, 150–151, 157, 159, 160, 163, 164, 166, 170–171
externality, 91, 97–98, 140, 155–156

feminist, 16, 109, 160
Ferber, Marianne A., 16
firstness, 33–37, 39, 40, 69–72, 74, 84, 138
Frazer Institute, 130–131
Friedman, Milton, 65, 122

Gates, Bill, 17
Goodrich, Peter, 24
ground, 9, 11, 15–16, 23, 27, 43, 48–49, 64, 70, 73, 76, 98, 104, 149, 153, 163

habit, 2–4, 11, 15, 19, 27, 32–33, 36, 39, 43, 47, 62–64, 76, 78, 87–88, 96,
104, 110, 119, 123, 125, 132, 138, 150, 159, 161
Hadfield, Gillian, 109
Harrison, Jeffery, 62
Hayek, Friedrich A., 27–28, 32
housing, 126–127, 167, 172
humility, 44, 118, 121–125, 133, 160, 165

icon, 45, 46 (n.53), 58, 89
ignorance, 20, 43, 83, 86–87, 121–122, 143, 149, 171
impartial spectator, 19, 20, 64, 66–69, 112, 115, 120
indeterminate, 1–5, 11, 27, 32, 36–37, 41–43, 47–48, 72, 76, 78, 82–85, 87, 89, 119, 124, 126, 132, 134, 137, 147–148, 160, 161
index, 4, 40, 46–47, 58, 65, 72, 84, 88, 138, 152, 159, 163, 165
information, 33, 42, 57, 73–74, 80–81, 83–84, 87, 92, 96, 98–99, 104, 117, 121, 132–133, 156, 171
International Society for the Semiotics of Law, 24
interpersonal utility comparisons, 17, 19–20
interpretant, 34, 70–72
invisible hand, 90

Jackson, Bernard, 24
jurisprudence, 2, 8, 23, 153–154
justice, 2, 7–8, 10, 38, 130, 166

Kaldor–Hicks efficiency: *see* efficiency
Kennedy, Duncan, 24
Kevelson, Roberta, 1, 23, 27–29, 58
Kirzner, Israel, 27–28, 55, 78, 83–84, 86–88
knowledge, 43–44, 81, 83–84, 86, 88, 98, 103–104, 143, 149

Landa, Janet, 136
Law and Society Association, 24
leasing, 81–82, 145
linguistics, 28

McCloskey, D.N., 16
measure, 124, 126, 140–141, 156, 164
methodological individualism, 4, 60–61
money, 30–31, 45–46, 52, 65, 130, 140, 148, 169
moral sentiments, 90, 118
mortgage markets, 1, 14, 51–55, 74, 112, 127, 143–144, 172
    secondary, 50–52, 54, 112, 143, 173
multivalued, 2, 120

Native American (Indian), 53, 162–164
Nelson, Julie A., 16
neoclassical economics, 40, 65, 82, 108
normative, 7, 9, 10–11, 16, 22, 36–37,
   137, 140–141, 165
norms, 3, 26, 48, 68, 72–73, 108, 110,
   113, 114, 119, 123, 136
nuisance, 26

object, 34, 39, 46 (n.53), 48, 70, 110, 122
   dynamical, 43, 71, 73, 82, 122, 156
   perceptible, 5, 84
opportunity costs, 33, 70

Pareto efficiency: *see* efficiency
path dependent, 102
Paul, Ellen Frankel, 160
Paul, Jeremy, 24
Peirce, Charles Sanders, 20, 23, 27–29,
   32–34, 39–40, 55, 58, 60, 62 (n.9),
   67, 70–72, 76, 84, 87, 89, 110, 119,
   125, 132, 138, 143, 158, 160
permutation, 6, 17, 29, 30–31, 71–72, 77,
   79, 106, 118, 125, 150
person, 18, 41
pollution, 90, 157
position, 7, 20–21, 34–35, 38–39, 41, 46,
   48, 62, 64, 69, 71, 80, 99, 104, 112,
   115, 120, 122, 126, 128, 141, 156,
   159, 164
positive (positive economics), 1, 5, 7–8,
   15, 17–18, 20, 27, 38, 46, 49, 54,
   131, 139, 141, 174
Posner, Richard A., 8, 11, 23, 26,
   138–139, 141
power, 16, 31, 41, 109, 159–163
pragmatism, 23, 35
precedent, 76, 146–147
preferences, 18–20, 35, 59, 60, 80, 83,
   101–103, 124, 142 (n.8)
   endogenous, 60–61, 74, 104
   exogenous, 60, 61, 104
prisoner's dilemma, 12–13
profit, 1, 53, 86, 88, 95, 151–152, 172
property, 14, 18, 25, 30, 61, 69, 91, 93,
   112–113, 115–116, 120–123, 129,
   130–131, 142, 164, 168, 172, 174
prostitution, 1, 140–141, 155–156
public choice, 99–101, 103–104, 114

rape, 26, 108, 111
rational, 3, 12, 76
   rationality, 27
real estate, 52, 61, 63, 142–143
   transactions, 50, 112, 171–173
reciprocity (reciprocal), 27, 29, 39, 44, 64,

   69, 73, 118, 121, 125–128, 130, 134,
   160, 163
referent, 30
representamen, 34, 70–73
rhetoric, 16, 27, 139
   rhetorical strategies, 21–22, 41, 48–49,
   104, 137, 153–154, 156–160,
   162–171
Round Table on Law and Semiotics, 24
rules,
   formal, 136
   informal, 136

scale, 123–126, 140–141, 156, 164
scarcity, 37–38, 57
Schumacher, E.F., 45
secondness, 33–37, 39–41, 69–72, 74, 84,
   138, 158
self-interest, 1, 12, 27, 37, 44, 46, 52, 55,
   57, 59, 64–69, 73, 84, 87–88, 90,
   97–100, 107, 110, 115, 117–118,
   120, 123, 125, 142, 158, 160–161,
   174
semiosis, 21, 33–35, 60, 64, 69, 87, 132,
   152
semiotics, 2–6, 8, 11, 15–18, 21–23,
   25–27, 29–31, 33, 34, 36, 39, 43, 45,
   48, 55, 57–58, 63, 68, 70–71, 74–76,
   78, 101, 120–121, 125, 128, 130,
   136–137, 140, 146, 160, 166
Semiotic Society of America, 24
semiotic space, 39, 43–44, 46, 48, 73, 79,
   82, 86–88, 115, 119, 122
sign, 1, 18–19, 28–30, 32–34, 38–43, 45,
   46 (n.53), 48–49, 59–60, 62–64, 70,
   72, 74, 76–77, 82, 84, 96, 103,
   105–106, 114, 120–121, 125, 128,
   134, 143, 146, 158, 160–161
Simpson, O.J., 75
Smith, Adam, 19, 32, 41–42, 47, 55,
   64–69, 89–90, 109, 111–115, 118,
   120
social justice, 1
Sowell, Thomas, 160
split the dollar game, 66
stewardship, 97, 162
substitution, 6, 17, 19, 26, 29–31, 33, 35,
   37, 44–45, 58–59, 63, 70–72, 79, 88,
   106, 118–119, 123, 136, 148–150,
   156
surrogate mother, 1, 108, 156
sustainable wealth formation, 2, 4, 8, 16,
   18, 21–22, 36, 44, 47, 55, 62, 76–77,
   88–89, 98, 104–106, 114, 117–119,
   129, 131, 134, 137, 143, 146, 148,
   153, 166–167

symbol, 18, 19, 39–40, 46, 58, 75, 96, 103

technology, 80, 82, 84, 124, 133, 170,
173
thirdness, 33–37, 40–41, 46 (n.52),
69–72, 74, 84, 138
Thomas, Clarence, 160
token, 18, 30, 45, 47, 70, 89, 148
trade, 1, 96, 128
transaction costs, 91–94, 96, 98–100,
102–104, 108, 118, 121, 155–156
Trebilcock, Michael, 109
triadic, 28, 34, 69–72, 76, 87

urban revitalization, 124, 173–174
utility, 18, 109, 110–111, 113
marginal, 1, 17–19

valuation, 61
contingent, 125
hedonic, 125
market, 125
value, 1, 3–4, 6, 8–11, 15, 18–20, 22, 26,

29, 30–31, 38, 43, 45–49, 54, 58–59,
65, 70–72, 82–84, 88, 94–95, 97,
104, 110, 112, 116, 118, 120, 122,
128, 130, 136, 139–143, 145–146,
148–149, 157, 159, 161, 164–165,
167, 170–171, 174
variance, 4, 88, 110, 138, 150

wealth, 4, 21
effect, 93
sustainable wealth formation: *see*
sustainable wealth formation
transfers, 17
wealth maximization, 1, 5–6, 10–11, 17,
22, 36–37, 44, 47, 58–59, 65–67,
76, 89–91, 97, 107–109, 131, 136,
138–139, 143, 148, 155, 174
proactive, 21, 36, 47, 78, 89, 110,
119–120, 125, 136, 152
reactive, 21, 36, 47, 78, 89, 136, 152
welfare, 61–62, 117, 124
Williams, Walter, 160
workfare, 62